The Problem of Democracy
in Cuba

The Problem of Democracy in Cuba

Between Vision and Reality

Carollee Bengelsdorf

New York   Oxford
OXFORD UNIVERSITY PRESS
1994

Oxford University Press

Oxford New York Toronto
Delhi Bombay Calcutta Madras Karachi
Kuala Lumpur Singapore Hong Kong Tokyo
Nairobi Dar es Salaam Cape Town
Melbourne Auckland Madrid

and associated companies in
Berlin Ibadan

Library of Congress Cataloging-in-Publication Data
Bengelsdorf, Carollee.
The problem of democracy in Cuba :
between vision and reality /
Carollee Bengelsdorf.
p. cm. Includes bibliographical references and index.
ISBN 0-19-505826-7 (cloth)
ISBN 0-19-509014-4 (pbk.)
1. Communism—Cuba—History.
2. Democracy—Cuba—History.
I. Title. HX158.5.B45 1994 335.43′097291—dc20 93-8052

2 4 6 8 9 7 5 3 1

Printed in the United States of America
on acid-free paper

For Sidney Bengelsdorf,
for the visions of his youth,
and the realities of his life

Preface

A substantial portion of this book was written well before the world turned upside down at the end of the 1980s. Because of these tremendous changes, I found myself refusing to let it go, thinking that major revisions were certainly called for. What was perhaps most difficult and most agonizing for me was how little, in the end, I had to change. The chapters that lay out the theoretical framework of my argument remain much as they were in 1987, when the book was first accepted for publication, as do the first two chapters which deal with Cuba. The remaining chapters, which examine the jolting events and evolving trends and countertrends in Cuba since the mid-1980s, are, of course, of more recent vintage. Yet even as I wrote about the current situation on the island, I found it extraordinarily difficult to part with the manuscript: there is, in Cuba today, an overwhelming sense of impending change, and, typically as a North American, I realized I was awaiting *the* event. It took me time to realize the degree to which the transformation is *already* underway.

In sum, I have lived with this book for a very long time, gathering, as I went along, multiple debts. The first of these debts are to the people with whom I work, who have, without fail, provided the atmosphere of intellectual stimulation and personal support in which the book is rooted: I must mention here, in particular, Miriam Slater, Margaret Cerullo, Nina Payne, Jill Lewis, E. Frances White, Kay Johnson, Mitziko Sawada, Frank Holmquist, Michael Ford, Penina Glazer and Lynn Hanley. I am further indebted to the long list of people who have read, commented upon, and thereby helped me rethink drafts of the manuscript in earlier incarnations, among them, Willard Johnson, Josh Cohen, Brian Smith, Marifeli Pérez-Stable, Nelson Valdés, Sam Bowles, Jim Petras, Malena de Montis, Patricia Vidil and Edmundo Desnoes. My fieldwork project in Cuba, at a moment when few foreigners were being allowed to undertake such work, was enormously facilitated by a group of individuals who endlessly discussed my findings and conclusions, argued with me, pointed me in fruitful directions, and whenever they could, helped to make possible my often quite clumsy ventures on these paths: here I want to thank María Rosa Almendros, Rafael Hernández, Carmen González, David González, Juan Valdés Paz, Haroldo Dilla, Alfredo Prieto, Maby González, Armando Entralgo and, most particularly, José Arañaburo. José Fuster, the Cuban painter and ceramicist whose drawing graces the cover of the book, was driven nearly mad trying to capture visually its wildly ranging subject matter: he was a joy to work with. Finally, a small group of unbelievably persistent friends and colleagues never let me forget that there was an unfinished manuscript tucked away in my worktable drawer. They variously read and re-read chapters, thought of new and ingenious methods to alternately badger and encourage me to finish, and, at moments, literally fished the manuscript out of the recesses in which I tried to stash it. Here, I want to mention Eqbal Ahmad, Fred Weaver, Dan Smith, Andy Zimbalist, Susan Eckstein and, above all, Carmen Diana Deere, who finally sat me down at her dining room table, fed me on cue, and persisted until I had put the period mark at the end of the final sentence. Karen Graubart, Mary Hardy, Gloria Weinberg and Yen Chun Mao were heroines in helping me to prepare the manuscript for publication; Catherine Clements was a most sensitive and thoughtful editor in attempting to rein in my prose and eliminate my mixed metaphors; Valery Aubrey and David Roll of Oxford were consistently helpful, calm and patient. Needless to say, none of these individuals bears any responsibility for the final results.

Amherst, Mass.   C.B.
July 1993

Contents

The Problem of Democracy
in Cuba

Introduction

The experience of socialism in the twentieth century has been framed by a series of simultaneously curious and momentous paradoxes; none is more curious in its perversity nor more momentous in its impact than the manner in which socialism—its essence, its meaning, its purpose—somehow became separated from the idea of democracy. Democracy and socialism have come to be viewed virtually across the political spectrum as, if not diametrical opposites, then at least unrelated phenomena.

Yet there is an entirely contrary argument to be made, that at its core, the classical Marxist project of communism is inextricably infused with a profoundly emancipatory vision, based on the dis-alienation of human beings in every arena of their existence and activity. It is an idea intended to extend and expand the formal definition of democracy, in its understanding of the people as subject rather than subjected, as the determining rather than the determined element, as the authors of their own histories. It celebrates democracy as a people empowered, as a society that has reabsorbed into itself the authority that formerly stood above it. Egalitarian popular participation in determining and carrying out public policy and in directly controlling the process of production lies at the center of the Marxist definition of socialist society, although it is only a sketch in the body of Marx's work. Participation informs Marx's differences with the formal definitions of democracy; it becomes both the means by which individuals will develop to the fullest their capacities and the manifestation of those freedoms. Nor did Marx see the actualization of this idea as a distant goal, an abstract ideal made possible only by the "construction" of socialism. Rather, it is the very means by which all other goals—the transformation of both the individual and the society as a whole—are to be achieved.

Marx's vision of the rule "of the immense majority, in the interest of the immense majority"[1] stands in starkest contrast to the historical practice of "actually existing socialism"[2] in this century. The measure of this contrast is nowhere more succinctly captured than by the former Polish Communist Party leader Edward Gierek in his now infamous instructions to Polish workers in 1971: "You work well, we will govern well."[3]

If we are to recover the Marxist notion of democracy, we must first try to understand why it has been lost. The roots of the divorce between socialism and democracy are multiple.

First, there is the critically important fact that, contrary to Marx's assumption, every socialist revolution in this century has occurred in conditions of underdevelopment. Fred Halliday captures the implications of this: "if socialist revolution is an attempt to expand and consolidate the 'realm of freedom' . . . such revolutions [have taken] place overwhelmingly in the 'realm of the necessity.' "[4] The nature and extent of this "realm of necessity" in the Third World is an painful litany familiar to any student of underdevelopment: poverty, the lack of material resources, the absence of a viable infrastructure to begin at least to exploit those resources efficiently, the scarcity of people educated and technically able to carry on such exploitation—these are just a few of its features.

The effect such conditions have had on the possibilities for a socialism structured around democracy has been disastrous. Underdevelopment has tended everywhere in the Third World, at least until the late 1980s, to emphasize the centrality of the state and to cast it as the major actor in resolving the whole range of these problems. Mark Selden, a perceptive analyst of Chinese revolutionary history, speaks for a long line of observers of, or participants in, actually existing socialism by identifying this as the source of the fundamental contradiction between democracy and socialism. "The central problem of the transition [from capitalism to communism]," he writes, "is this: The enlarged and transformed role of the state is both essential for socialist development and the single greatest obstacle to the fulfillment of its liberating promise of fulfilling the material and spiritual needs of individuals and communities."[5] The mechanisms that appear critical in providing the force to overcome scarcity and achieve goals in health and education have become all too frequently the very mechanisms whose other face is the arbitrary use and abuse of power; that is, the eradication of the democratic content of socialism. This alone raises the question of whether the Marxian socialist project is viable for the Third World. Many analysts have argued that for the countries of the Third World what was called socialism represented, at base, an alternative and essentially authoritarian noncapitalist path to industrialization, in which the state played the orchestrating role that the bourgeoisie plays in the classical Marxist capitalist model.[6]

Second, the origins of the divorce between socialism and democracy lie in the actions of those who over the course of its history have opposed the socialist project. No revolution made in the name of socialism has ever occurred in the absence of a crisis created by physical attack, or the threat of it, from outside. These very real external dangers, commonly allied with internal counterrevolutionary threats, created severe problems for democratic practice. What they produced historically has been the opposition of "liberal" freedoms—freedoms of speech, assembly, press, and so forth—to "socialist" freedoms, an opposition that is nowhere inherent in the Marxian concept of socialism. These freedoms, for Marx, were in no case granted from on high; they were struggled for and won from below. But states of emergency, even in those societies calling themselves liberal democracies, have witnessed the suspension of various rights; we have only to think of the internment of Japanese Americans during World War II. Every attempt at socialist revolution has had to confront a seemingly endless series of external threats in the form of military aggression, economic strangulation, or both—in short, a kind of semipermanent state of emergency. Here is surely one of the central paradoxes in the practice of socialism: these "liberal" freedoms *must* be a measure of the content and reality of democracy in a transitional society (indeed, in any society), yet the emergency conditions that have consistently characterized those societies has meant that these very freedoms are the most adversely affected.

It would be hard to underestimate the impact of external antagonisms in limiting the possibilities for a democratic socialism. External threat has consistently compelled socialist revolutions to move in the direction of militarization, internal surveillance, and centralized and secretive decision-making structures, regardless of their initial tendencies. As a consequence, these pressures have contributed to the destruction of organized political autonomy and pluralistic expression within these revolutions.

But underdevelopment and counter revolutionary pressures cannot by themselves explain the divorce of socialism and democracy in the twentieth century: the socialist project itself is implicated. The perversions so characteristic of socialism in this century have been paralleled by perversions of the theoretical construct that gave it form. That the distortion of the socialist project has consistently sought legitimation within a theoretical construct that has proven equally distortable is due at least in part to this construct's unresolved and perhaps unresolvable weaknesses. It is on this underdeveloped theoretical underpinning and its inability to address the issues involved in the historical separation of socialism from democracy that I intend to focus in the first three chapters of my study.

This, then, necessitates an inquiry into the theoretical inheritance itself in an attempt to understand what happened to it. For if the theoretical heritage concerning postcapitalist society has a vital and profoundly emancipatory moment, it is simultaneously plagued by a series of silences, absences, simplifications, and contradictions. These are rooted in part in the tendency inherent in classical Marxist thought to reduce all contradictions to the category of class. This tendency determines in critical aspects the outlines of the Marxist vision of the transition to socialism; indeed, there is perhaps no other aspect of Marxist theory as consistently and deeply infused with and damaged by its profound underestimation of the capacities of states, genders, and races to dominate. Throughout this book, I focus on two silences in the theoretical construct of the transition to socialism that emanate from its class-reductionist framework.

The first (and, in the end, most damaging) of these silences has to do with the absence of consideration of the *need* for effective autonomous institutional forums, which might serve as counterbalances to forces or groups seeking domination and might challenge the entrenchment and durability of such groups' power. There is nothing in the key texts of the Marxist tradition that gives us much of a blueprint for understanding, much less charting, the transition; we can hardly demand from these texts guides to a history that their writers did not themselves live. Rather, it is the absence of virtually any analysis or discussion, not of the manner in which the emancipatory idea would need to be mediated, but of the very need for such mediation, that is critical. This failure to consider even the need for autonomous agencies of political mediation is derived directly from classical Marxism's class-reductionist tendencies. If the political arena is defined as the stage on which one class enforces its will upon another, then the end of class domination means, effectively, the end of politics. The beginning of "real history" in classical Marxism is to be marked by the reabsorption by civil society of political society. Therefore, questions of political society—of the form and nature of political institutions—are no longer relevant. The boundaries between the state and civil society are thereby erased; indeed, the very need for such boundaries goes unrecognized or denied. The result, as subsequent history would show with such terrible clarity, was the confiscation of civil society by the state: statification rather than socialization.[7] Theory itself assisted those who were to unravel the fabric of socialism and democracy.

Silence in the theoretical construct about the need for mediating agencies is matched by a second major silence: the pull between the extraordinarily decentralized vision of political organization in the transition, which emerged from Marx's account of the Paris Commune and was fervently reasserted in Lenin's *State and Revolution,* and the centralizing impulses inherent in much of the rest of the Marxist heritage. This is true particularly, although not exclusively of economic concerns, where a class reductionist analysis effectively avoids confrontation with the entire range of critical issues related to what Rudolf Bahro described as the "vertical division of labor,"[8]—that is, the power and authority inherent in different levels of skills and knowledge. What, for instance, of the contradiction between full democratic participation and the complex and technical content of economic planning?

This dichotomy between centralization and decentralization has important ramifications for political organization. Class reductionism alleviates the need to come to terms with the fundamental problem of reconciling particular and universal interests. Marx, in his description of the Paris Commune, celebrates a series of principles that center on people having direct authority and direct involvement in determining what affects them. These principles emphasize an extreme decentralization of decision making, the dominance of local popular control over decisions, and the direct and constant accountability of those selected to supervise the execution of decisions to those who have selected them.[9] But how can such direct control be applied on a national scale? Where does such an analysis allow for conflicts, and the means to reconcile them, between particular groups of interests when potential bases for such conflicts are not recognized?

There are vast and critical areas dealing with the relationship between state and society in the transition besides the two that I have mentioned, in which the theoretical legacy concerning the transition has shaped in part the problem of its practice. We need only think of what meaning democracy has when even the limited discussion of its application is confined to the public, rather than the domestic, sphere, and when the entirely male imaging of the public sphere is left completely unchallenged. Here again, these limits are derived from an analysis that uses class as the single consequent determinant of domination.

In the first two chapters of this study, I will limit myself to dealing with the two problems to which I have pointed, much as I will focus on the ideas of the two major figures—Marx and Lenin—in whose work they are embedded. There are certainly many other individuals whose view of politics during the transition strikes off in other directions; I focus on Marx and Lenin because historically they defined the basic parameters of the Marxist notion of the transition.

There is, however, a further dimension to the history of the separation of socialism and democracy: we must come to terms, as well, with what has been done to the theoretical legacy. Most centrally, we must look to the impact of official Marxism-Leninism. It has been this body of dogma, the product essentially of the Stalinist years, which served as the major crucible in which the theoretical heritage was processed and refined. And in this processing, the formalities of disentangling socialism from its democratic intent were accomplished. The formulas that emerged, at times little more than a parody of the classical Marxist idea of socialism, would, in the end, spell the death of the socialist project in its twentieth-century incarnation.

We can see this clearly if we return to the paradoxical juxtaposition of civil liberties and socialist democracy. Official Marxist-Leninist rhetoric dismisses civil liberties as "bourgeois freedoms"; as such, they are permanently expendable in the realization and practice of socialism. But, as Rosa Luxemburg once asserted, "there are no bourgeois civil liberties, there are only liberties as such."[10] It was exactly the danger of forgetting this that she warned of (in her 1918 critique of the actions of the Bolsheviks in power) when she wrote from her prison cell of "necessity" made into "virtue" and of "tactics necessitated by fatal circumstances" frozen into a "complete theoretical system."[11]

The destructive impact of this official dogma has been staggering. For some of the countries of actually existing socialism, it provided the theoretical framework for the wholesale imposition of formulas that had no internal logic. For the countries of the periphery that experienced revolutions (or experienced revolutionary wars of liberation and later espoused some form of socialist development), it provided distorted and rigid models, which neither responded to the concrete realities with which they were confronted nor communicated the actuality of a rich historical experience. A generation of Cuban, Angolan, and Tanzanian intellectuals were reared on manuals embodying this dogma, prescribing its formulas as solutions to the problems they faced. This education served only to cut them off from the critical and nourishing roots of a tradition that is, at its best, a flexible and evolving body of theory, inextricably linked to practice and the very antithesis of dogmatism.

It seems, then, incumbent on us to explore how official Marxism-Leninism evolved by briefly examining the Soviet experience; the third chapter of this study concerns itself with exactly such an exploration.

These first three chapters make no pretense at originality. They only serve, first, to reinvoke a historical debate largely drowned in the rejection of socialism; and second, as a necessary, if lengthy, preamble. The remainder of the book deals with the question of democracy and socialism in the context of the thirty-three years of the Cuban revolutionary experience. Each of the socialist revolutions of this century marked its own particular milestone in history or set that history in new direction: so, too, has the Cuban Revolution. It represented in its promise, a critical turning point in the quest to revitalize the socialist project, to reweave the fabric of socialism, to restore and reintegrate its democratic content. It initiated a period that would see a series of revolutions, defining themselves as Marxist and socialist, in small countries located in the Third World. The possibilities as well as the limitations inherent in the Cuban situation had both political and economic relevance to the revolutions that followed, which occurring in countries with nothing like the population or material resource base of the U.S.S.R. or China.

Further, the Cuban Revolution revived for many the vitality of the connection between democracy and socialism. We can surmise, for instance, that the renewal and rethinking of the Marxist heritage with regard to socialism and the state that began among western Marxists in the early 1960s was in part sparked by the Cuban Revolution. Indeed, the sense of popular mobilization and mass participation that the accounts of every sympathetic visitor to Cuba evoked seemed to give substance to the notion that, perhaps particularly in small peripheral economies, it was only through the fullest expression of participatory democracy that the problems of underdevelopment, resource scarcity, and constant external threat could be overcome.

The issue of the bond between socialism and democracy has in some form haunted the Cuban Revolution through all its peregrinations and reversals of course. This study intends to examine the succession of critical moments at which the question of democracy was raised—indeed, by the leadership itself—and the nature of its response (or lack of response). We do this within a very specific framework. The pattern of these responses cannot meaningfully be understood in terms of the imposition of external forms on Cuban reality—the dominant paradigm employed by western and particularly American Cubanologists in some form since 1959. Rather, it must be examined in the light of the actual history and the internal dynamics of the Revolution itself, and the multiple legacies from which it has drawn sustenance. The heritage of José Martí and the Cuban revolutionary tradition has at key points intersected with, tempered, and molded the manner in which Marxist precepts would be understood and applied. Just as the social project of the Cuban revolutionaries was at least as Martían as it was Marxist, so, too, their understanding of the state. For instance, the leadership's refusal to create anything other than transient institutions during the 1960s was evidence of its evaluation of the bureaucratized and ossified political structures in countries which called themselves socialist. But it was, equally, a reaction to the manner in which the Martían ideal had been corrupted in the bankrupt political structures of the Cuban republic and an attempt to realize the Martían strategy of unity. Its adoption and adaptation of Soviet-type political structures in the 1970s was conditioned above all by this same Martían principle of unity. Its critique of these structures in the late 1980s and early 1990s comes in a moment in which the balance of its emphasis in the political sphere is shifting from Marx toward Martí.

Each of the critical turning points we will examine was heralded or initiated by an emancipatory moment. Each involved an expansive critique of what had existed at that point. In effect, each can be understood as an explicit or implicit confrontation with the problematic Marxist legacy concerning socialism and democracy. As such, each held the promise of radical movement in the direction of the idealized, Marxist vision of postcapitalist society. In the end this promise of radical change has been reined in. If Cubans addressed the theoretical legacy, they did not redress it; in large part they recreated in a new setting its silences and contradictions.

The chapters dealing with Cuba, then, will trace the pattern of these moments of crisis and change. We begin with the Revolution's accession to power and its experimentation in the last half of the 1960s with the radical idea of "simultaneously constructing" socialism and communism, a project that came to a crashing halt with the 1970 failure of the sugar harvest. We move on to the initiation of a period of "institutionalization," which occupied much of the 1970s and ended officially in the 1980s in the midst of impending economic crisis and the enunciation of a "rectification campaign," whose purpose was to challenge and "correct" the institutionalization process itself. We conclude with the disintegration of the socialist world and the Cuban reaction to this disintegration.

I must make two further clarifications. The first of these involves the scope of this study. My work on Cuba concerns itself with delimited areas of investigation. It is by no means a detailed investigation of the range of contexts that must be considered in a full evaluation of democracy in Cuba. It does not touch upon the workplace, nor does it deal with the various mass institutions, for instance, the women's federation, or the neighborhood organizations, that the Cuban leadership would understand to be arenas of popular democracy. Rather, it takes as a case study the formal state structures (or lack of them) during the thirty-three years of the Revolution. In particular, it focuses upon the institution of "Popular Power," that is, the state system put into place on a national scale in 1976. Here the material I use draws largely on my field observation, carried out from 1974 to 1983, and most intensively from 1977 to 1979. This field observation, although not comprehensive in the sense of surveying the workings of Popular Power on a systematic basis across the island, did manage to encompass a study of the system at each of its levels of operation and, most intensively, its functioning at the base, neighborhood level. Given the virtual ban upon the social sciences in effect at Cuban universities during the 1970s, and the restrictions upon non-Cuban researchers, it represents, I believe, the only extended external effort to examine the system during those years.

The second clarification I must make speaks to intent. It is not my purpose to reify democracy. One has only to think of the 1990 elections in what was then East Germany, touted in the Western press as that country's first "free" elections since 1932—and we all know who became Chancellor in 1932—to understand the cynicism with which many in the world react to the United States government's solicitude for democracy. Indeed, Latin Americans, playing upon the phrase "low-intensity warfare" that characterized U.S. policy in Central America in the 1970s, have dubbed the American concern for elections and all their trappings as a new strategy of "low-intensity democracy."[12]

Conversely, I do not wish to glorify what was known as "socialist democracy" in the countries of actually existing socialism, where civil liberties came to be portrayed and treated exactly as expendable trappings. One of the many jokes currently circulating in Cuba involves the epigram (or epitaph) with which the leadership ends its speeches: *socialismo o muerte* (socialism or death). On the streets of Havana (and elsewhere), people joke that this is simply a repetition of terms.

Nor will I argue that those who remain Marxists should have illusions that the collapse of what passed for socialism in Eastern Europe and the Soviet Union will begin to pave the way for the realization of a "truer" vision of Marxism. As various observers have pointed out,[13] for the overwhelming majority of those who lived under the system, command socialism *was* socialism, and despite what they face in a "transition to capitalism," they will not rapidly be inclined toward anything that hints of what they experienced for more than forty years—and for good reasons.

Amilcar Cabral once wrote of the "weapon of theory"[14] and, in so doing, sought to recover in a context far removed from the nineteenth-century European world of Karl Marx the relevance of the Marxist concept of praxis for Third World struggles against colonialism. And he underlined once more that the crisis of Marxism is a crisis of theory as well as historical practice. This crisis did not begin with the collapse of the world of actually existing socialism; rather it began with the birth of that world. Nor does this crisis end with its demise. Despite renewed proclamations about "the end of history,"[15] Marxism as a viable way of thinking about the world is hardly dead. As long as world capitalism continues to live down to its critics' expectations, that is, as long as the problems that Marxism addresses continue to plague humankind, it will, in some form, continue to be relevant.

The collapse of command socialism in Eastern Europe and the Soviet Union frees us in a sense to rethink the theory in terms of its social relevance for the world we inhabit at the beginning of the new century.

The question is complex; it involves, among other things, not simply issues of production and the production process, but the very meaning of production itself. I do not pretend to deal with these questions here. But this rethinking must involve as well a reconsideration of the very meaning of democracy itself; the situation in country after country in the Third World alone gives the lie to the idea that capitalism and the market are somehow inherently democratic. And in this reconsideration we would do well to remember what it was that was (and remains) so compelling in the Marxist vision: its promise, in Che Guevara's words, to see human beings free from alienation.[16] Despite its absences and its silences concerning the postcapitalist state, in its conviction that human beings can be the authors of their own lives, Marxist theory gives material substance to a formal concept of democracy. For this reason alone, it points us toward a radical process of rethinking and recovery.

1

Marx and the State in the First Phase of Communism

The controversy concerning the relationship between the Marxist vision of socialism and democracy originates with Karl Marx himself. What we intend to do in this chapter is locate this controversy and attempt to move beyond it by examining Marx's widely scattered and unsystematized reflections on the relationship between state and society in the transition from class to classless society. Our argument will be that the legacy Marx left concerning the socialist project contains within it multiple faces. Its central message is the conviction that democracy, in the sense of the people as subject, is the very content of socialism; the two concepts are not only inseparable, for Marx, they had no meaning individually. At the same moment, the very manner in which Marx conceived of and articulated this union provided the basis for its subversion. This, then, is the other face of the Marxist legacy to socialism.

We will reexamine, in this light, the fundamental concepts and texts that comprise Marx's thinking about the postcapitalist state—in particular, the concepts of the dictatorship of the proletariat and the withering away of the state—and his interpretation of the Paris Commune. Our task will be to understand these writings in historical context and textual detail in an effort to begin to get at their potential meanings; for the heritage, taken as a whole, had the most profoundly contradictory implications for the future socialist project.

Marx's scattered reflections concerning the nature of postcapitalist state and society cannot be understood outside the traditions within which he worked. Karl Marx's singular originality was contained above all in his ability to synthesize. The essence of his theories was derived from three distinct and mature sources: his methodology was rooted in German philosophy; his economic model, in English thought; and his social vision, in French social theory.[1] This synthesis was filtered through a framework constructed from Marx's understanding of the scientific method and of the Darwinian theory of evolution. He attempted to apply both in a societal context. He saw himself as the originator of a "scientific" brand of socialism, scientific exactly in its use of a dialectical analysis in applying, as Lenin has said, "the theory of evolution—in its most consistent, complete, well considered and fruitful form—to modern capitalism."[2]

Yet if the strength of Marx's work is derived from these roots, they are, as well, responsible for crucial aspects of its weaknesses; the Marxist heritage is comprised of both.

These weaknesses are consistently clear in Marx's effort to rationally and scientifically situate every phenomenon. The logic of this very typically nineteenth-century rationalism, and his belief in movement from one stage to a higher stage in human society, led him, for instance, to be blind about the persistence—indeed, the heightening—of nationalist sentiment at the very moment he predicted its demise.

His belief—again following Darwin's understanding that individual species develop to their fullest possibility before evolving into a higher form—that communism was imminent in the most highly developed societies has been disproven by history. For it is, as we know, not the advanced industrial countries that have experienced socialist revolutions; consistently, this century has seen revolutions that have identified themselves as socialist in the underdeveloped world.

Darwinism served as well to rationalize Marx's belief in class as the determining category in societal organization and division. In correspondence with both Engels and the French socialist Lasalle during the months following the 1859 publication of Darwin's *Origin of the Species,* Marx wrote, "Darwin's book is very important, and serves me as a basis in natural science for the class struggle in history."[3] Darwin's identification of different families of plants and animals related to each other in their structure and their needs provided Marx with "proof" for what many see as the major weakness in Marx's thought: his class reductionism. His idea that the category of class subsumes all other categories explains, in part, his blindness to such fundamental societal divisions as race or gender. There is no room in Marx's thought, for instance, for an exploration of the possibility that women—even working-class women— might have demands and interests different from, and even contrary to, those of proletarian men who were able to represent *their* interests as class interests.[4]

If the Marxist heritage as a whole is stamped with the imprint of what appears at its worst moments as a mechanical rationality, nowhere was this tendency toward mechanical interpretation more permanent and more debilitating than in the former societies of actually existing socialism. There it was used as the justification, if not the cause, for rigidly controlling discussion just when discussion should have been unreined.

All this is particularly ironic given the brevity of Marx's treatment of postcapitalist society. Indeed, almost all our knowledge about Marx's concept of future society is contained in any significant detail in only a few texts. As Shlomo Avineri points out, his vision remains constant in these texts, despite the fact that "Private Property and Communism" is among the earliest of Marx's writings (*The 1844 Manuscripts*) and *The Critique of the Gotha Program* is among the last.[5] But neither of these two documents provides a thorough picture; neither are polished pieces of work—entirely understandable, as neither was intended for publication. A third text, *The Civil War in France,* is a finished document, but was written, as Avineri notes, very much in response to, and as a political eulogy for, the 1871 Paris Commune; therefore, it must at least in part be understood in those terms.

Why was it that Marx had so little to say about the future shape of human society? It is by now a platitude to argue that Marx was entirely concerned with existing capitalist societies and their impending demise; thus his simplistic vision of future, postcapitalist society. A platitude, however, usually expresses the kernel of a truth: Marx's refusal to "compose the music of the future"[6] was consistent with both his theoretical premises and with his specific political objectives.

Its outlines and source can be traced to the work of Hegel, whose influence on the young Marx was so profound. In the *Philosophy of Right,* Hegel wrote, "since philosophy is the exploration of the rational, it is for that very reason the apprehension of the present and the actual, not the erection of a beyond, supposed to exist, God knows where."[7] Marx echoed this sentiment throughout his writings. Any discussion of the future, by definition, had to conflict with the basic premises of historical materialism, which inherently denied the validity of notions rooted in the minds of men rather than in actual historical circumstances. For Marx, Avineri points out, "communist society [would] be determined by the specific conditions under which it is established."[8] Thus, for instance, in his famous 1881 letter to Domila-Nieuwenhuis—a letter we shall have cause to return to later—Marx replied to an inquiry about what measures should be taken by a socialist government in power by asserting that the question itself is a mistake. He went on: "One thing you can at any rate be sure of: a socialist government does not come into power in a country unless conditions are so developed that it can above all take the necessary measures for intimidating the mass of the bourgeoisie sufficiently to gain time—the first desideratum—for lasting action."[9]

There was, as well, further reason for Marx's reticence on the subject of the future society. Marx wrote and was politically active at the end of a period that had produced all sorts of schemes for socialist utopias. He was anxious, in both theoretical terms and in terms of his activities in the Workingmen's International, not to be confused with or seen in the same stream as these other socialist thinkers; remember that Marx sought to distinguish his socialism as scientific prescription rather than a dreamer's vision. Moreover, the few images that Marx *did* give us concerning the final stage of communist society provide perhaps an additional clue to his reluctance to go into any detail: no French utopian socialist enunciated a more romantically bucolic and idealistic picture of the future than the famous image set forth by Marx in *The German Ideology:*

> [I]n communist society, where nobody has one exclusive sphere of activity but each can become accomplished in any branch he wishes, society regulates the general production and thus makes it possible for me to do one thing today and another tomorrow, to hunt in the morning, fish in the afternoon, rear cattle in the evening, criticize after dinner, just as I have a mind, without ever becoming hunter, fisherman, shepherd or critic.[10]

We should note here that the concept of communism and communist society hardly originated with Marx. As Hobsbawm has pointed out, "Marx and Engels were relative late-comers" to the revival of communism as an active movement in the first half of the nineteenth century.[11] And indeed, the body of their writing on the form and substance of communist society as such reflects this; it is almost entirely derived, and at some points taken literally, from the schemes set forth by the major utopian socialists. This fact lends a certain irony to Marx's rejection of utopianism; for instance, Marx's distinctly and peculiarly unindustrial image cited above of the communist person as "hunter, fisher, shepherd, and critic" is taken directly from Fourier, much as his related assertion that communism would see the elimination of the differentiation between town and country is derived from both Fourier and Owen. And the famous ruling principle of the first stage of communist society, "from each according to his ability; to each according to his work," a phrase so connected to Marx and Marxism, is borrowed virtually intact from Saint Simon.[12]

Although it became common to articulate the transition from capitalism to communism as proceeding in stages, Marx neither conceived nor labeled them as such. Rather, he spoke of the "first phase of communist society" (in *The Critique of the Gotha Program*)[13] or of "crude communism" (in *The 1844 Manuscripts*).[14] The description of this first phase remains basically constant:

> What we have to deal with here is a communist society, not as it has *developed* on its own foundations, but, on the contrary, as it *emerges* from capitalist society; which is thus in every respect, economically, morally and intellectually still stamped with the birth marks of the old society from whose womb it emerges.... But these defects are inevitable in the first phase of communist society.... Right can never be higher than the economic structure of society and the cultural development thereby determined. [Marx's emphasis.][15]

So, therefore, is the state structure determined: Marx spoke about it in the first phase of communist society as the rule, or dictatorship, of the proletariat.

This phrase, "the dictatorship of the proletariat," evokes images that are both repugnant and, particularly in the aftermath of 1989, so outdated as to be ludicrous. In our context, it marks the point in popular understanding at which the separation of the Marxist concept of socialism and the concept of democracy originates. For this reason alone, it demands of us a thorough investigation. The phrase itself must be examined in the context of Marx's larger understanding of the state as a historical entity. It is yet another surprise that, despite his continuous references to it throughout the body of his work, nowhere in his writings does he subject the state to a systematic and thorough analysis. According to a note by him, circa the late 1850s, it was indeed his intention to carry out exactly such an analysis as part of the project from which *Das Kapital* eventually emerged.[16] As we know, no such study was in fact undertaken. Rather, as Miliband notes, what we have of Marx's views on the state are elaborated first in his early writings, then in scattered statements throughout his work and, in greatest detail, from three pieces written very much in the context of actual politics, as historical polemics. These three pieces are *Class Struggles in France, The Eighteenth Brumaire of Louis Napoleon,* and *The Civil War in France.*[17] The clearest, most explicit, and best-known summary of the dominant formulation by Marx of his concept of the state is contained in *The Communist Manifesto;* there he wrote that "the executive of the modern (capitalist) State is but a committee for managing the common affairs of the whole bourgeoisie" and political power is, in essence, "merely the organized power of one class for oppressing another."[18]

If then, as Engels argued, capitalism is the dictatorship of the bourgeoisie, by easy transposition, the dominance of the working class in postcapitalist society means that state power devolves on them to exercise against those forces that oppose them. As we shall see, the ease of this transposition highlights one major conceptual weakness surrounding the dictatorship of the proletariat.

The importance Marx attached to the concept of the dictatorship of the proletariat is debatable. We have, on the one hand, Marx's 1852 letter to Weydemeyer. In his attempt to summarize the historical significance of his work, Marx first clarified that he deserved no credit for the "discovery" of classes and class struggle in modern society. Rather, he wrote:

> what I did that was new was to prove (1) that the *existence of classes* is only bound up with *particular historical phases in the development of production;* (2) that the class struggle necessarily leads to the *dictatorship of the proletariat;* (3) that this dictatorship itself only constitutes the transition to *abolition of all classes and to a classless society.* [Marx's emphasis.][19]

Here then, what Marx called the dictatorship of the proletariat seems to be at the heart of his understanding of the evolution of history.

On the other hand, the absence of a full discussion anywhere in Marx's work of the dictatorship of the proletariat undermines any belief in its centrality. His fullest effort to define it is at best sketchy. In *The Critique of the Gotha Program,* Marx wrote: "Between capitalist and communist society lies the period of the revolutionary transformation of one into the other. There corresponds to this also a political transition period in which the state can be nothing but *the revolutionary dictatorship of the proletariat.*" [Marx's emphasis.][20]

The phrase used by Marx and, far more frequently, by Engels to describe the state in the period of the transition has, from the first, given rise to controversy. "Dictatorship," even when followed by the word "proletariat," is, as Lenin once said, "a harsh, heavy and even bloody word"[21] to our ears (and to the ears of many socialists since the mid–nineteenth century). The disagreements, of course, center on what precisely Marx meant by "dictatorship" in this context. It is critical that we situate historically both the word dictatorship and Marx's use of it if we are to gain any understanding of his meaning in using the phrase dictatorship of the proletariat. Most of the efforts to do this derive their substance from Hal Draper's exhaustive exploration of Marx's use of the term.[22]

Draper proceeds in two directions. First, he explores the connotation of the word dictatorship in Marx's time. It becomes clear that the current connotation of dictatorship—drawn largely from the experience of Hitler and Stalin—varies in fundamental ways from the connotation prevalent in the 1850s. If the notion of dictatorship today evokes images of rule by a single person, possessing unmediated and unlimited power for an indefinite period of time, dictatorship in Marx's day, according to Draper, differed significantly on each of these points.

Draper and other sympathetic scholars following him argue that Marx's and his contemporaries' use of the word was drawn directly from its meaning in ancient Rome. For some three centuries, the Republic's constitution allowed—in times of emergency—the election for a period of six months of a dictator with limited powers and, explicitly, no power to make new laws or change the constitution, nor any right of access to the treasury. Moreover, once the six-month period ended, the dictator was held fully accountable for any injustice he may have committed. In the ninety times in which the Roman Senate employed this provision for the election of a dictator, these rules remained in place: Julius Caesar's self-appointment as dictator for life came only with the decay of the Republic. For the Romans then, as Richard Hunt, following Draper, argues, the institution of dictator was not the "antithesis to the republican rule of law [but]...its ultimate defense."[23]

The French Revolution, in its constant harking back to Roman political terms and parallels, if anything, must have served to renew this understanding of the term dictator. French dictionaries published following the Revolution defined the term solely in terms of its Roman meaning. Thus Draper argues that Marx used the term as an equivalent, at most, of what he might label martial law, or state of siege, that is, to indicate the need for a crisis or emergency government.[24] This allows Draper and, following Draper, Miliband, Johnstone, and Ollman[25] to assert that, in

Marx's mind, dictatorship never meant either extralegal or violent rule by a single individual or a small group of men and that, "[i]f Marx is to be faulted, it is not for any authoritarian bias, but for greatly understating the difficulties of the libertarian position."[26]

The controversy swirls as well around what has become an etymological argument: Marx's use of the German word *herrschaft*, meaning "rule," at certain points and his use at other points of the word *diktatur*, meaning, of course, "dictator." Kautsky, on this basis (and conveniently in line with the currents of his own political turnings) argues that *diktatur* was "an unimportant little word that Marx let slip once or twice,"[27] while Lenin, from an opposite political perspective (and also conveniently) argues that *diktatur* was intended all along.

Hal Draper analyzes occurrence by occurrence of the use of the word *diktatur* in the work of both Marx and Engels[28] and convincingly argues that the term appears within three delimited time periods: the period from 1850 to 1852 (i.e., after the revolutions of 1848); the period from 1871 to 1875 (i.e., the aftermath of the Paris Commune); and after Marx's death, in the work published by Engels from 1890 to 1893. His point is that the use of "dictatorship of the proletariat," in place of "rule of the proletariat" had direct political connotations. Draper argues more specifically that Marx's use of dictatorship of the proletariat was conditioned by attempts in the first two periods cited to form, in times of great popular upsurge, political alliances with the Blanquists—the followers of August Blanqui. The Blanquists were indeed the inheritors of a tradition of beliefs that found its most concrete expression in the Jacobin phase of the French Revolution—belief in the necessity of dictatorship during periods of revolutionary transition. For the Blanquists, dictatorship *always* meant the dictatorship of a small group of people in the know, a ruling committee of the educated elite. It was in the wake of Marx's and Engels's efforts in 1850, in the aftermath of the revolutions of 1848 and in full expectation of the imminent revival of revolutionary upsurge, to forge a united front with the French Blanquists exiled in London by creating the Universal Society of Revolutionary Communists that the phrase dictatorship of the proletariat first appeared in Marx's work. Draper argues, essentially, that the phrase was the result of a compromise with the Blanquists, a compromise that facilitated the temporary "united front," altering the Blanquist concept of dictatorship while leaving Marx's prior formulation of the rule of the proletariat substantively unchanged.[29]

And this is key: remember that, for Marx, the rule of the proletariat, as he stated in *The Communist Manifesto*, was synonymous with the rule "of the immense majority, in the interest of the immense majority."[30] Indeed, Marx's very formulation of "dictatorship of the proletariat" was intended by him exactly to clarify the fundamental difference between his conception of dictatorship and this other conception held by the Blanquists (and by the majority of mid-nineteenth-century socialists). Blanqui himself, perhaps recognizing this, *never* used the term dictatorship of the proletariat, contrary to popular belief.[31] It is interesting to note in this regard that, in his initial use of the phrase "dictatorship of the proletariat," Marx was careful to place before it the word "class"; that is, he spoke of a "class dictatorship of the proletariat." Thus, in the first appearance of the phrase in *Class Struggles in France,* Marx wrote:

> *the class dictatorship of the proletariat* [—the emphasis is Marx's—is] the necessary transit point to the abolition of class distinctions generally, to the abolition of all the relations of production on which they rest, to the abolition of all the social relations that correspond to these relations of production, to the revolutionizing of all the ideas that result from these social relations.[32]

This phrasing should itself dispel any lingering doubts one might have concerning Marx's meaning in the use of "dictatorship"; in its coupling with "class," Marx is asserting, or reasserting in altered form, the necessity for the political rule not of an (educated) elite, but of the entire proletariat in the aftermath of the revolution that would displace capitalism.

An examination of the second period in Marx's work in which the term dictatorship of the proletariat resurfaces supports these arguments. In the aftermath of the destruction of the Paris Commune, the possibility and need for an alliance with the Blanquists, who again flooded into London as refugees, arose particularly around the urgency of opposing the anarchist followers of Proudhon and Bakunin in the First International. And in fact, from 1871 to 1872, the Blanquists joined Marx in opposing the anarchists. The dictatorship of the proletariat was, as Richard Hunt has argued, the "ideal slogan"[33] for this alliance and the battle it waged and won. This second united front between Blanquists and Marxists broke apart only in the aftermath of the expulsion of Bakunin from the International.

This, then, would seem to cast doubt on the argument of all those who point to Marx's employment of the phrase dictatorship of the proletariat to prove his adherence to a conspiratorial, elitist revolutionary concept. Indeed, Marx and Engels, over the entire period of their active lives, repeatedly critiqued such beliefs and strategies. In 1850, at the very moment of their first strategic alliance with the Blanquists, they chastised the members of the secret societies (among them, the followers of Blanqui) so prevalent in France as the "alchemists of revolution . . . characterized by exactly the same chaotic thinking and blinkered obsessions as the alchemists of old."[34] And nearly twenty-five years later, in 1874, in the aftermath of their second, short-lived alliance with the Blanquists, Engels, in his "Program of the Blanquist Commune Refugees," spelled out in the most explicit terms the fundamental difference between Marxist and Blanquist in the use of the concept of dictatorship:

> Since Blanqui regards every revolution as a coup de main by a small revolutionary minority, it automatically follows that its victory must inevitably be succeeded by the establishment of a dictatorship—not, it should be noted, of

the entire revolutionary class, the proletariat, but of a small number of those who accomplished the coup and who themselves are, at first, organized under the dictatorship of one or several individuals.[35]

On the basis of this investigation, Draper concludes that, in his use of "class dictatorship of the proletariat," much as in his use of "class rule of the proletariat," Marx sought to underline the composition of the ruling body in the transition from class to classless society, rather than the actual structure of such a body. Marx's accent, writes Draper, "is on the social basis of the power, rather than on the political forms or methods of a regime."[36]

One could, however, from the same evidence draw a different conclusion. The use of "dictatorship of the proletariat" by Marx came in periods when he was mobilized as an active revolutionist: hence the explanation of its appearance as strategic. Moreover, it was in periods when revolutionary upsurge as well as political necessity forced him to think *concretely* about not only the substance, but the *form* of transitional state and society. This, then, would at least imply that in speaking of the dictatorship of the proletariat, Marx was speaking not simply about the social basis of the transitional state, but, as well, its specific political form. Although he does not base his assertion on such arguments, Ralph Miliband reaches much the same conclusion when he argues that "for Marx, the dictatorship of the proletariat is *both* a statement of the class character of the political power *and* a description of the political power itself; and that it is in fact the nature of the political power which it describes which guarantees its class character." [Miliband's emphasis.][37]

Yet in either form—the "rule" or the (class) "dictatorship of the proletariat"—the concept points to difficult and unresolvable problems in Marx's idea of the postcapitalist state. Although it was Lenin who would stamp Marxist theory indelibly with the idea that the dictatorship of the proletariat parallels the dictatorship of the bourgeoisie, the parallel was articulated by both Engels and Marx at various points. In this parallel we begin to see the extent of the problem. As many critics have pointed out, if it is simple and symmetrical, the phrase dictatorship of the bourgeoisie exactly in its simplicity does real violence to our ability to comprehend the range of political forms that can evolve in capitalist societies. Marx clearly indicated in his writings (for instance, on the United States or England and most prominently in his development of the theme of relative autonomy in *The Eighteenth Brumaire*) his understanding of the differentiated patterns of capitalist political development and of the importance of understanding these differentiations. Why should we not assume that if the notion of the dictatorship of the bourgeoisie flattens out and makes incomprehensible the varieties of capitalist political structures, then the phrase the dictatorship of the proletariat equally destroys for us any ability to expect or understand complexity and variation in postcapitalist political structures?

Beyond this, there remains a seemingly inescapable problem inherent in the use of the word dictatorship, even in its most benign interpretation. It is a problem that Marx, in his vision of the seamlessness of the process by which the postcapitalist state is reabsorbed by civil society, managed not to confront. Yet the concept of dictatorship unavoidably raises the issue of what Leo Panitch has labeled the conflict between coercion (or discipline) and consent (or democracy).[38] It is clear, particularly in the writing of Engels, that the content of the state for some indefinite period of time after the revolution has to do with repression. In an 1875 letter to Bebel, he echoed and amplified Marx's words concerning the necessity to "appeal for a time to force" when he wrote:

> As, therefore, the "state" is only a traditional institution, which is used in the struggle, in the revolution, in order to hold down one's adversaries by force, it is pure nonsense to talk of a "free people's state"; so long as the proletariat still *uses* the state, it does not use it in the interests of freedom, but in order to hold down its adversaries, and as soon as it becomes possible to speak of freedom the state as such ceases to exist. [Engels's emphasis.][39]

What was to follow in the twentieth century gives particular urgency to the questions arising out of these assertions, questions unanswered by Marx and Engels. What is the balance between coercion and consent? How is it possible to wed the authoritarianism inherent in this image with the nonauthoritarian structures Marx evoked elsewhere, most vividly, as we shall see, in his description of the Paris Commune? And even for those who can accept an initial emphasis on coercion,[40] how and when and by whose authority does consent become the dominant, even the exclusive, defining element in society?

This leads us to a question we posed earlier: What are the actual images and outlines in Marx's writing about the postcapitalist state?

There is only one document in Marx's work that gives concrete form to these images, and it must be used with great care in this context. We refer, of course, to Marx's account of the 1871 Paris Commune in *The Civil War in France*.

Marx's portrayal of the Paris Commune has led to yet another argument among Marx scholars. This one disputes whether the Paris Commune did indeed represent for Marx the dictatorship of the proletariat. Analysts such as Shlomo Avineri tend to downplay the literal significance of the Commune in this regard,[41] while others, such as Hal Draper, Ralph Miliband, Monty Johnstone, and Robin Blackburn,[42] argue that Marx's portrayal of the Commune in *The Civil War in France* "irrevocably and publicly define(d) the Marxist conception of the dictatorship of the proletariat."[43] Strangely enough, the picture is clarified by drawing on both of these lines of analysis. The Paris Commune did not (as we shall argue), and by its very premises *could* not, represent for Marx the dictatorship of the proletariat. At the same time, the "tendencies" Marx saw in its actions and in its self-organization clarified for him the terrain on which to begin to explore the principles that must anchor the dictatorship of the proletariat.

His examination and interpretation of the Commune led to basic alterations in how Marx envisioned the postcapitalist state. Thus, if the Commune were not the dictatorship of the proletariat, it did indelibly stamp
its imprint on how Marx, and after him, all Marxists, thought about the
essential meaning of the state in the transition from class to classless society.

It seems important to note at the outset of this discussion that nowhere
in anything he wrote did Marx *ever* refer to the Paris Commune as the
dictatorship of the proletariat come to life. It was, in fact, Engels who
made the direct connection. In his 1891 introduction to the third edition
of *The Civil War in France*, Engels's conclusion—an attack on the German
Social Democratic Party—asked "do you want to know what this dictatorship looks like? Look at the Paris Commune. That was the Dictatorship
of the Proletariat."[44] Engels then repeated this three months later, in June
of 1891, in his *Critique of the Erfurt Program*.[45]

Marx clearly was far more reticent in this regard. It is ironic, given
this reticence, that the Commune and his misrepresented connection to
it made Marx, overnight, world famous.[46] His reluctance had several
sources and can be derived from both his general view of history and his
understanding of the Commune. It must be remembered that his major
and enduring statement on the Commune, *The Civil War in France*, was
presented to the I.W.M.A.* just days after the bloody defeat of the Commune—as Avineri has said, a eulogy is hardly the place to undertake an
autopsy.[47] It becomes apparent, however, through his own writings and
statements that Marx's relationship to the Commune was much at variance
with the popular image.

Marx's evaluation of the Paris Commune as a historical event in and
of itself is perhaps the clearest example of this disparity: from its inception,
Marx viewed the Commune as doomed. His correspondence reveals that
prior to its establishment, he was hostile to the idea of the Commune; he
thought it, and its eventual demise, would be disastrous for the cause of
socialism in France. In a letter to Engels written at the beginning of
September 1870 in the context of the imminent defeat of France at the
hands of Germany, Marx noted that he had sent a French supporter (Ser-
ailler) to attempt to prevent the Blanquists and the Jacobins from "do[ing]
all kinds of follies in the name of the International...[and] bring[ing]
down the Provisional Government, to establish a Commune of Paris."[48]

Once the Commune had been established, he believed it inevitable
that it would collapse. He foresaw that collapse at every turn; already by
April 6, 1871, a few days after the Commune was set up, Marx wrote to
Wilhelm Liebknecht, "It appears that the defeat of the Parisians was their
own fault."[49] In response to an April 27 plea for advice on appropriate
projects by Leo Franckel, a German who had been appointed Minister of
Public Works in the Commune, Marx replied some two and one-half weeks

---

*International Working Men's Association.

later (an enormous amount of time in the context of the seventy-one day duration of the Commune) with a letter that gave no such advice.[50] That is, in no way did Marx respond with an outline of the future society; rather he was full of cautions and warnings for Franckel and the Communards. "The Commune," he wrote, "seems to me to be wasting too much time on trivialities and personal quarrels." He added, in a line telling of his interpretation of the matter: "One can see that there are other influences besides the workers."[51]

Marx's critical attitude toward the Commune was shaped by several factors. As Avineri understands it, Marx's analysis of the social composition of the Commune was the basis for this attitude;[52] according to estimates, only one-third of the members of the Commune were working class.[53] Indeed, there is clear support for this assertion in the early drafts of *The Civil War in France*. In the first draft, written during the Commune itself, Marx, commenting on the social enactments of the Commune, declared that "[t]he principle measures taken by the Commune are taken for the salvation of the middle class... there is nothing socialist in [these measures] except their tendency."[54]

But the explanation of why Marx could not see the Commune as the incarnation of the dictatorship of the proletariat must be understood in a far more basic context. The dictatorship of the proletariat, as Marx said in the *Gotha Program* critique, is the form the state takes in the period between capitalism and communism. There had been, neither in Paris nor in France during 1871, a social revolution which had overthrown the capitalist order and altered completely its mode of production. Given this, the Commune logically *could not be* the dictatorship of the proletariat. Thus in the famous 1881 letter to Domila-Nieuwenhuis referred to earlier, Marx wrote, in response to the inquiry about the appropriate actions for a new socialist government, "Perhaps you will point me to the Paris Commune; but apart from the fact that this was merely the rising of a town under exceptional conditions, the majority of the Commune was in no sense socialist, nor could it be."[55]

Why, given all this, did Marx in the final draft of *The Civil War in France* call the Commune "the political form at last discovered under which to work out the economic emancipation of labour"?[56] The most succinct answer is given throughout the various drafts of *The Civil War in France:* "Whatever the merits of the single measures of the Commune, its greatest measure was its own organization,"[57] or "[t]he greatest measure of the Commune is its own existence";[58] such phrases echo through each of Marx's three drafts. Indeed, the major import for Marx of the Commune is contained in these phrases; by its very existence and its rejection of the entire apparatus of preceding governments, the Commune set itself off from all previous social uprisings.

> [T]he working class cannot simply lay hold on the ready-made state-machinery and wield it for their own purpose. The political instrument of their enslave-

ment cannot serve as the political instrument of their emancipation. . . . The first condition for the hold[ing] of political power is to transform [the] working machinery and destroy it.[59]

The greatest achievement of the Commune for Marx was then its destruction of what he excoriated in the *Civil War* drafts (and earlier, in much the same words, in *The Eighteenth Brumaire*) as "[t]he huge governmental parasite, entoiling the social body like a boa constrictor in the ubiquitous meshes of its bureaucracy, police, standing army, clergy and magistrature, [which] dates its birth from the days of absolute monarchy."[60]

What Marx understood as the significance of the Commune was its reversal of the pattern of aggrandizement of the state that he had so vividly traced in his historical essays. If the Commune spoke to the future for Marx, it was because it moved in the direction of the "reabsorption of the State power by society as its own living forces instead of as forces controlling and subduing it, by the popular masses themselves, forming their own force instead of the organized force of their suppression."[61] It is for this reason that Marx, at the same moment he spoke of the inevitable fall of the Commune, wrote to his friend Kugelmann, "The struggle of the working class against the capitalist class and its state has entered upon a new phase with the struggle in Paris. Whatever the immediate results may be, a new point of departure, of world historic importance has been gained."[62]

When Marx began to speak in more concrete terms about what this "new point of departure," this "reabsorption of the State by society" would look like, the phrase "moved in the direction of" that we used earlier becomes useful. Engels, in a letter to Edward Bernstein, written some thirteen years later, commented (approvingly) that what Marx did in *The Civil War in France* was to set forth "the *unconscious* tendencies of the Commune . . . to its credit as more or less conscious plans [Engels's emphasis.]"[63] Engels thus underscored not simply the political context in which the address was given but that the directions the Commune seemed almost instinctively to move were what was critical for Marx. Indeed, the specific language of the drafts of *The Civil War in France* speaks to this contention; as Avineri rightly points out, Marx employed consistently the conditional future tense in his discussion of the structure of the Commune. Thus, "[t]he Commune *was to be* a working, not a parliamentary, body, executive and legislative at the same time. . . . Police agents . . . *were to be* the servants of the Commune. The judicial functionaries *were to be* divested of that sham independence. . . . Like the rest of public servants, magistrates and judges *were to be* elective, responsible and revocable. . . . The Commune *was,* of course, *to serve* as a model to all the great industrial centers of France."[64]

Avineri contends on this basis that Marx's comments refer not to the Commune as it actually was, but to Marx's projections based on what the Commune suggested. He concludes, "It is not the Paris Commune of

1871 that provides the model for future society, but the immanent reason Marx saw in it *had* it survived."[65]

In this regard it is true that Marx elaborated on actions the Commune initiated, not from generally espoused ideological convictions, but on the basis of pragmatic necessity, in what was not a script, but straight improvisation. Lenin, as we shall see in *State and Revolution*, puts heavy weight on the "principle" of abolition of standing armies and looks to the Commune for support of this principle.[66] Actually, the Commune abolished the permanent army and conscription in favor of a National Guard made up of armed citizens because the army had been repeatedly used in France to crush movements such as the Commune. Thus, too, the Commune's espousal of municipal autonomy, seen particularly by anarchists as fundamental to the Commune's purposes, came from the Communards' recognition of their need to win sympathy from other French cities and the French countryside and their awareness that provincial France had long harbored resentment against the Parisian-based post-Napoleonic centralized authoritarian structure. Again, the acts that assured popular control of government figures (through recall), the merging of legislative and administrative functions, and the salary limitations on those chosen were not the result of previous ideological principles, but rather a reaction to the high level of political careerism that had arisen in the wake of past revolutions in France. Indeed, it is doubtful, given the short lifetime of the Commune and the constant and urgent problem of physical survival in the face of military threats, that it could have put forth a set of principles and attempted to enact them. Nor were the members of the Commune in any kind of agreement on such a set of principles; socialism, as Schulkind points out, was as yet a vague notion to the majority of the Communards.[67]

Even given all this, Avineri's conclusions, at least in their implications, are too strong. For what Marx learned from the Commune was far more than his own elaboration, presumably in directions he had already charted out. This is the only way we can understand his assertion in the new foreword he wrote in 1872 to *The Communist Manifesto* that "the Paris Commune, where the proletariat for the first time held political power for two whole months," had rendered the program originally set forth in the *Manifesto* "in some details . . . antiquated."[68] What were these "details"?

From Marx's writings about the experience of the Commune, a set of "principles" giving form to the state in the period of the transition were extracted and, through the medium of Lenin, these principles found a permanent niche in the catechism of the societies of actually existing socialism. These principles celebrate, above all, antiauthoritarianism and the decentralization and deinstitutionalization of political power; they speak of "the people acting for itself, by itself."[69] They include:

1. The abolition of permanent armies, and their replacement by the armed people.

2. The abolition of the separation of legislative and executive functions, and with this,
3. The end of state functionarism, that is, the elimination of bureaucracy. All officials, including judges, to be elected by universal
   suffrage.
4. Constant and direct electoral control over the entire government
   apparatus, through the continuous right of recall.
5. The limitation of wages of government workers to those of workers
   as a whole in society.
6. The end of "parson power," with the complete separation of
   church and state.[70]

The set of principles Marx derived from the experience of the Paris
Commune draws on both the primary and the secondary strains in his
interpretation of the state. If his sketch gives a sense of the content of the
class dictatorship of the proletariat, each principle also embodies the need
to prevent the reemergence and usurpation of power by a centralized state
"apparently soaring high above society"[71] and seemingly autonomous from
it, " . . . [W]here it had legitimate functions to fulfill, these functions were
not to be exercised by a body superior to the society, but by the responsible
agents of the society itself."[72]

All this together represents a conception of the political power to be
exercised by the proletariat entirely distinct from the political power that
preceded it. The Paris Commune state, for Marx, was not simply a state
in which the rule of one class has been supplanted by the rule of another;
it was a new type of state altogether. In this sense the Paris Commune
did indelibly stamp its imprint on how Marx, and after him, all Marxists,
thought about the essential meaning and the elements of the relationship
between state and society in the transition from class to classless society.

Having said this, it seems fair to add that Marx's concept of the
Commune state raises more problems than it resolves and has historically
evoked deep confusion among those seeking to identify the meaning of
democracy in socialism. The first of these problems involves the issue of
centralization versus decentralization. While Marx emphasized the devo-
lution of political power to the base, he asserted, almost as an afterthought,
that the "unity of the nation was not to be broken."[73] This was not a
retreat to the past nor the realization of the dreams of Montesquieu or
the Girondins, he wrote; those who saw in the Commune an "exaggerated
form of the ancient struggle against over-centralization"[74] were entirely
mistaken. And yet, Marx's description of the Commune overwhelmingly
seems to argue that if the "legitimate functions" of government were to
be "wrested from an authority usurping preeminence over society itself,
and restored to the responsible agents of society,"[75] this meant an enormous breakup of concentrated centralized power and a dispersal of that
power to the Communes themselves. Indeed, he speaks of the "few but

important functions"[76] that would still remain in the hands of a centralized authority. If *The Civil War in France* seems to tip the scales in the direction of decentralization, it clearly contrasts starkly with Marx's writings elsewhere, which give far more weight to the role of centralization in the economy.

Marxian socialism is, of course, grounded in the assumption of a developed capitalist economy. For Marx, the revolutionary nature of capitalism expressed itself in its enormous effectiveness in organizing the economic structure for the production of surplus. This meant movement in the direction of both increased rationality and increased scale. Marx argued that it was exactly capitalism's inability to be rational beyond a certain point that would spell its doom. In part, socialism represented the end to the remaining irrationality in its introduction of economic planning for the production of a surplus that would satisfy the needs of the entire population.

But planning and large-scale production, to say nothing of equitable distribution, imply centralized functions. As Alec Nove logically argues, they clearly indicate some body, or bodies, at the center, planning, and such a requirement inevitably calls into existence some form of bureaucracy. Nove asserts that "[t]he functional logic of a centrally planned economy . . . requires hierarchy to ensure constancy and to resolve conflicting claims on resources by administrative decision."[77]

Moreover, the technological development that paralleled the growth of capitalism after Marx's death places further constraints on the possibilities of decentralized administration by making it ever more unlikely that the general public will, in fact, have command of the skills they need to play their part in state administration. All this leads Tom Wohlforth, writing about the Bolsheviks, to conclude that the failure to make of the soviets a governing structure "exposed the impossibility of directly combining the decentralized Soviet system with the needs of a modern centralized state."[78]

A second and in the end perhaps far more critical problem in Marx's imaging of the Commune involves the obvious, stark inadequacy of the political structures it posits as a model for state and society. We can understand better the meaning and implications of what Gregor McLennan terms Marxism's "failure of theoretical and political nerve"[79] if we consider Marx's celebration of the Commune together with the one notion vis-à-vis the future that preoccupied Marx and Engels both before and after the Commune: the inevitable "disappearance" or dying out of the state. Their continual return to it provides, as Hobsbawm argues, "powerful evidence of their hopes for and conception of the future communist society; all the more so because their forecasts on the matter contrast with their reluctance to speculate about an unpredictable future."[80]

The phrase so connected to Marx in this regard—the withering away of the state—was actually never used by Marx himself.[81] Rather, it was

Engels who, in his *Anti-Duhring* and in *Socialism: Utopian and Scientific*, gave currency to the specific wording "withering" away or "dying out."[82] Marx himself spoke rather of the "transcendence" of the bourgeois state.[83]

Marx's vision of the abolition of the state is yet another example of the extent to which his conception of the future borrowed specifically from the teachings and projections of the utopian socialists. Actually, as Hal Draper points out, the notion of doing away with the state has its origins in the very beginnings of the history of protest and dissent. It is embedded in the philosophy of ancient Greece and China and is certainly, Draper notes, "older and more primitive than either socialism or anarchy as ideology or movement."[84] The early utopian socialists drew upon this tradition in their assertion of opposition to the state. But it was Saint Simon's words, spelling out what the abolition of the state would entail, that Marx specifically borrowed; the phrase "administration of things replacing the government of men" was taken virtually whole from Saint Simon.[85] (Actually, given Saint Simon's generally hierarchical vision, Draper asserts that he no doubt had an entirely different intent in his use of the phrase than did Marx: "the administration of men as if they were things."[86])

It is, as well—particularly in the form, "withering away," that Engels gave it—one of the clearest examples of the overlay of Darwin's biological images on Marxist social images. Like an organ no longer needed for any bodily function, the state would seemingly shrivel up and disappear. Listen to Engels's description of the procession of events:

> As soon as there is no longer any social class to be held in subjection; as soon as class rule and the individual struggle for existence based upon our present anarchy of production, with the collisions and excesses arising from these, are removed, nothing more remains to be repressed, and a special repressive force, a state, is no longer necessary. The first act by virtue of which the state really constitutes itself as the representative of the whole of society — the taking possession of the means of production in the name of society — this is, at the same time its last independent act as a state. State interference in social relations becomes, in one domain after another, superfluous and then dies out of itself; the government of persons is replaced by the administration of things and by the conduct of the processes of production. The state is not abolished. It dies out.[87]

Draper traces out three stages in Marx's and Engels's employment of the concept of the abolition or withering away of the state. Engels' exposition of it above in the *Anti-Duhring* (whose writing was carefully supervised by Marx)[88] represents only the final and most mature of these stages. Curiously, the second and third stages, as Draper sets them forth, to some degree parallel the use by Marx and Engels of that other phrase, dictatorship of the proletariat. The first of these stages represents the years directly after the two became communists; here their use of the concept, which was at the time "the veriest commonplace of radicalism, even of pink radicalism,"[89] came as part of the territory (or as Engels later wrote, "we were making use [of the phrase] when we were simple youngsters"[90].)

It was only in the second stage distinguished by Draper—the period from 1847 to 1851—that they began to define their use of the concept as distinct from other socialists, particularly, in this case, as distinct from the anarchists, represented at this point above all by Proudhon. In his *Poverty of Philosophy,* an attack upon Proudhon, Marx developed, with all the sharpness of tongue so characteristic of his critiques, the idea he had set forth the year before in *The German Ideology* that "(the) State collapses of itself as soon as all its members leave it. . . . (T)his proposition reveals all the fantasy and impotence of pious desire."[91] In *The Poverty of Philosophy,* Marx set forth in essence what would be his fundamental and unbroachable disagreement with anarchism in general, whether Proudhon's or Bakunin's: the state is not the originator, but rather the expression of antagonisms in civil society, antagonisms resulting from the economic organization of that society. Eliminate those antagonisms through a social revolution that fundamentally alters this economic organization, and you eliminate the need for the state. Whereas for Proudhon, and after him, Bakunin, the elimination of the state was the first order of things, for Marx and his followers, as *The Communist Manifesto* makes clear, it became the ultimate aim of social revolution.[92]

This basic articulation is simply more fully developed in what Draper identifies as the third stage in Marx's and Engels's use of the term, the period of the Paris Commune and its aftermath. Marx's and Engels' reinvocation and elaboration of the abolition or withering away of the state was the result, first, of the Commune itself and the concrete questions it raised about the postrevolutionary state, and second, of the surge of Bakunin and his followers and what Marx and Engels saw as the renewed threat anarchism posed to the organized revolutionary movement. Bakunin gave new currency to the old slogan, "the abolition of the state," and in what E. H. Carr labeled the infamous 1870 "Fiasco at Lyons,"[93] tried unsuccessfully to put it into action. In the brief September 1870 Lyons uprising, Bakunin and his followers took City Hall and literally *decreed* the abolition of the state (an action authoritarian in form, even if "liberatory" in content, as Engels correctly pointed out).[94]

Marx and Engels made clear their differences on this point with Bakunin and the resurgent anarchist movement over and over again. For instance, Engels wrote in his 1872 letter to Theodor Cuno:

> Bakunin maintains that it is the *state* which has created capital, that the capitalist has his capital *only by favor of the state.* As therefore, the state is the chief evil, it is above all the state which must be done away with and then capitalism will go to hell of itself. We, on the contrary, say: do away with capital, the appropriation of the whole means of production in the hands of the few, and the state will fall away of itself. The difference is an essential one. Without a previous social revolution the abolition of the state is nonsense. [Engels's emphasis.][95]

Engels elaborated on this same essential idea in his *Anti-Duhring* of 1878. His later explication of the withering away of the state in *Socialism: Utopian and Scientific* was simply a further refinement of his basic concept.

But, more concretely, what does it mean to consign the state to the "scrapheap" or to the "Museum of Antiquities, by the side of the spinning wheel and the bronze axe,"[96] as Engels was later so picturesquely to write? Does everything we now connect with the state make the journey to the museum? Do none of its functions remain in place, even in new form?

Marx himself posed this very question in his *Critique of the Gotha Program:* "The question then arises," he wrote, "what transformation will the state undergo in communist society? In other words, what social functions will remain in existence there that are analogous to present day functions of the state?"[97] Unfortunately, and for all the reasons we have already cited, if he posed the question, he had not the slightest intention of answering it. But there are some suggestions in his writing that lend color to the black-and-white image of state–no state suggested by the idea of abolition, or withering away, of the state.

In *The Communist Manifesto,* Marx wrote that "when, in the course of development, class distinctions have disappeared and all production has been concentrated in the hands of a vast association of the whole nation, the public power will lose its *political* character."[98] The implication of this, here and elsewhere, is that by "political character" Marx meant the repressive functions of the state, its powers of coercion. If we examine the principles he drew from the experience of the Commune, his meaning is clarified: the organized bodies of coercion—the army, the police—were to be immediately abolished and all capacity for force turned back over to the people as a whole. But if, as he wrote in *The Civil War in France,* there would remain "a few . . . legitimate functions" that were to be "restored to the responsible agents of society,"[99] then he did recognize that there were legitimate, nonpolitical functions that were now to be exercised by the people as a whole.

There is little in the body of Marx's work that makes this any more specific, except perhaps the wonderfully cutting, but no more clarifying, comments scribbled in the margins of Bakunin's *Statism and Anarchy,* which is itself in part a diatribe against what Bakunin terms Marx's "statist socialism."[100] "What does it mean: 'the proletariat raised into the ruling class?' " asks Bakunin. "Can it really be that the proletariat as a whole would be at the head of the government?" Marx, in his marginal scribbles, replied:

> Can it really be that in a trade union, for example, the entire union constitutes the executive committee? Will all division of labor in a factory disappear and also the various functions arising from it? And in Bakunin's construction "from the bottom up" will everybody be at the top? Then there would be no "bottom." Will all the members of the Commune likewise administer the common interests of the Region? In this case, no difference between Commune and Region.

And in response to Bakunin's querulous query that "[t]here are about forty million Germans. Will all forty million be members of the government?" Marx wrote: "Certainly! Since the thing begins with the self-government of the Commune." Bakunin goes on, and so does Marx. To Bakunin's charge that "by popular administration they understand administration of the people by means of a small number of representatives elected by the people," Marx replies:

> The ass! This is democratic nonsense, political windbaggery! The character of elections depends not on these designations but on the economic foundations, on the economic ties of the voters amongst one another and from the moment these functions cease being political (1) no governmental functions any longer exist; (2) the distribution of general functions takes on a business character and involves no domination; (3) elections completely lose their present political character.[101]

We begin to move beyond the dictatorship of the proletariat, the lower phase of communism, into the "realm of freedom," full communist society. Indeed, in doing so we underscore the fact that for Marx there was no demarcation that separated the two phases or froze them into discernable stages. Marx spoke only of the transition from capitalism to communism, from class to classless society.

While Marx's belief in the transcendence or withering away of the state represents one of the clearest indicators of the emancipatory vision that informs his work, for all its attractiveness it exemplifies perhaps the most important inadequacies and contradictions in his thinking concerning postcapitalist state and society. Domination for Marx and Engels, has a homogeneous source; all domination is equatable with class domination; therefore (in somewhat simplified form), no classes equals no domination equals no state. This conceptualization of the source and the content of power and authority illustrates and compounds what we noted earlier as their tremendous simplification of postcapitalist state and society.

The withering away or abolition of the state and its reabsorption by civil society represents for Marx the final station on the road to the end of the division between political and civil society, itself an expression of the alienation of human beings. Dis-alienation—true human emancipation—would be achieved only with the fusion of political and civil society. What this means in effect is a total devaluation of the political realm along with the very *need* to consider the types of institutions, or agencies of mediation, that might comprise it. "True democracy," in Marx's terms, means the end of the state and, with it, of all such institutions. By direct implication, questions concerning the state in postcapitalist society are clearly of minor importance, with the result that, as Christopher Pierson has summarized it, Marxism "furnish[es] a drastically impoverished account of both the effectiveness of, and the internal divisions within, political power."[102] Consideration of the boundaries between civil society and the state becomes an irrelevant exercise, and with it, the need, for instance, to think about the institutions that might guarantee to the individual continuation of the procedural rights—freedom of speech, freedom of assembly—won during earlier periods. State intrusion upon, or elimination of, these rights is, after all, by definition impossible.

In the end, although in Marx's bucolic idyll, humans wander from fishing to hunting to debating, we know nothing of the framework in which they undertake these activities. Gregor McLennan in an understated manner, comments that Marx "was strong on diversity but weak on institutional pluralism. He, and the tradition which bears his name, tend to assume a quasi-natural, spontaneous medium for the realization of human projects, needs and exchange."[103] This failure to conceive of the very need for institutional pluralism as the basis for allowing humans to develop fully their diversity (and therefore their differences), would in the end permit not the absorption of the state into civil society but the collapse of civil society itself.

What can we say about the legacy Marx and Engels left concerning the postcapitalist state? It would be simply ridiculous to ask of them or their work specific formulas for a history they could not know. Indeed, the attempts by certain countries that labeled themselves socialist to justify actions taken on the basis of specific words of Marx or Engels (or Lenin) regarding the dictatorship of the proletariat were often little more than ludicrous. Nonetheless, Marx did leave a legacy concerning the postcapitalist state, and it is a legacy rife with absences, inconsistencies, and unresolvable dilemmas. It carries with it a central and irreducible belief. Marx's notion of the relationship of the postcapitalist state and society is, we have attempted to argue, infused throughout by a deep-reaching emancipatory vision, a vision encompassing, above all, a people empowered to retake control of their own lives, a society that has reabsorbed the authority that formerly stood above it. It is a vision dominated by antiauthoritarian and antibureaucratic concerns, as Ralph Miliband has written, "not only in relation to a distant Communist society, but also to the period of transition which is to procede it. True, the state is necessary during this period. But the only thing which, for Marx, makes it tolerable is popular participation and popular rule."[104]

Even as we recognize that there is much that seems inapplicable or inadequate in Marx's sketchy picture of postcapitalist society, his belief in popular participation and popular rule must retain a profound relevance for all those who wrestle concretely with the issue of democracy in the late twentieth century. Yet it is exactly this primary message that has proven so often dispensable or forgettable. Its own formulation would, in the end, set the terms that twentieth-century practitioners would use, in tragic irony, to obscure, perhaps irrevocably, this message.

2

Lenin and the Dictatorship of the Proletariat

It was Lenin who, more than any other person, put into operation, and thereby enshrined, the notion of the dictatorship of the proletariat inherited from Marx and filtered through Engels. And for so doing, it is Lenin who has become for many people across the political spectrum the key agent in giving form to a socialism bereft of its democratic content. It is our intention in this chapter to examine in detail *State and Revolution*, Lenin's principle contribution to the theoretical formulation of the nature and content of the postcapitalist state, in order to peel back the layers of intentional or unintentional distortion that have come to surround it. In so doing, we will argue that Lenin essentially extended and made more extreme both streams of the Marxist legacy concerning the socialist project.

On the one hand, Lenin's elaboration of the general emancipatory essence of socialism becomes almost libertarian. He draws not simply from the legacy left by Marx, but as Marcel Liebman has so effectively demonstrated, from the spectacle of constant and spontaneous popular organization that was Russia of 1917. On the other hand, in recapturing the emancipatory content of the theory, Lenin recapitulates and greatly exacerbates its inherent weaknesses. That is, he further reduces the complexity of concepts that in Marx's formulation were already reduced (we speak here of his interpretations of the dictatorship of the proletariat, or the withering away of the state). Moreover, the power and attractiveness of his image of "every cook an administrator" essentially allows him, following Marx, to avoid any substantive discussion of the need for forms or agencies of mediation that would be required to guide the transitional

33

process and encapsulate and insure that this democratic dynamic remain at its core. And this is critical exactly because the scheme Lenin sets out was put forth as if it *were* a viable design for the transition.

Lenin's *State and Revolution* was, and remains, the most complete elaboration of his understanding of the postcapitalist state. As such, the pamphlet (which Marcel Liebman has aptly dubbed the hastily drawn up "doctrinal birth certificate of the Soviet state"[1]) has taken its place since 1917 among the "sacred texts"[2] of Marxism. Yet it is in actuality a recompilation and simplification of the ambiguous and sketchy Marxist vision of the workers' state. It shares this tendency toward simplification with most of Lenin's writing. As Althusser points out, Lenin was hardly a philosopher in the traditional sense of the word. As he wrote to Maxim Gorky in 1908:

> I am not a philosopher, I am badly prepared in that domain. I know that my formulations and definitions are vague, unpolished; I know that philosophers are going to accuse my materialism of being 'metaphysical'... that is not the question. Not only do I not 'philosophize' with their philosophy, I do not 'philosophize' like them at all. Their way of 'philosophizing' is to expend fortunes of intelligence and subtlety for no other purpose than to *ruminate in* philosophy. Whereas I treat philosophy differently, I *practice* it, as Marx intended, in obedience to what it is.[3]

If Marx was obsessed with understanding the world in order to change it, Lenin's obsession focused above all on power and how to seize it. Marx was a man of ideas whose ideas impelled him to action; Lenin was a man of action who looked to ideas both as justification and as a guide for action. James Billington is entirely correct when he points out that Lenin "adopted Marxism not as an open body of criticism for understanding society, but as a finished blueprint for changing it."[4] Yet despite the pamphlet's simplified conceptual structure, it is to *State and Revolution* that Marxists have been obliged, in some form, to look to delineate the shape of socialist society; that is, to answer the crucial question, What will the workers' state actually look like? Lenin's answer to that question echoes the most humanistic and utopian strains of the Marxist tradition, the strains that speak to human liberation, to the end of bonds on human capacity. His major points pick up the themes that Marx put forth in his description of the Paris Commune and that Engels amplified and simplified in his writings on the Commune after the death of Marx. Lenin tends to circle back to these points without significant additional evaluation. We want here simply to lay out these themes. We will return to a more critical examination of them later in this chapter.

Lenin's argument rests on his definition of the state. He draws on only selected strands of what we have seen to be Marx's ambiguous and incomplete legacy. He takes from Marxism the notion of the state put forward in *The Communist Manifesto:* the state is a weapon through which the ruling class enforces its will. The state, Lenin writes, is a "special apparatus for compulsion,"[5] a "special organization of force; . . . the organization of violence for the suppression of some class."[6] There is here no ambiguity, no indication of circumstances that might lead to a relatively autonomous state, no mention of other functions that state institutions might perform. Lenin categorically asserts, closely following Engels, that "every state is a 'special repressive force' for the suppression of the oppressed class."[7] Indeed, he uses his previously developed elaboration of the concept of imperialism[8] to underscore this point: Monopoly capitalism has evolved into a more advanced form of expression, imperialism, which has in its wake brought international conflict, increased militarism, and war. Thus the repressive and violent nature of the state had become ever more clear, ever more apparent in the course of European history in the late nineteenth and early twentieth centuries.

Having established the definitional foundation of his argument, Lenin proceeds to his second theme and his most central concern in *State and Revolution:* to prove to his followers the absolute necessity that the proletariat, in carrying out its revolution, destroy completely the entire structure of the bourgeois state, rather than simply take over its machinery. This, Lenin asserts, is *the* main lesson drawn by Marx from the experience of the Paris Commune, a lesson, he argues, that had been lost in the Social Democrats' willingness to compromise and cooperate with established governmental structures. Lenin's "Letter from Afar" and his "April Theses" had desperately presented this understanding; it was for this reason, at least in part, that he demanded on his return to Russia an end to all Bolshevik cooperation with the post-February order. "All revolutions which have taken place up to the present," he asserts in *State and Revolution,* "have helped to perfect the state machinery, whereas it must be shattered, broken to pieces. This conclusion is the chief and fundamental thesis in the Marxist theory of the state."[9]

Lenin goes back repeatedly to this point. It is, as Lucio Colletti has pointed out, the basic theme of *State and Revolution.*[10] In page after page he argues that "the bourgeois state does not 'wither away' . . . it is 'put an end to' by the proletariat in the course of the revolution."[11] Moreover—again following closely Marx's evaluation of the Commune—this proletarian revolution is unlike all previous revolutions, which far from having destroyed state institutions have reinforced them. The revolution, he writes, must *"concentrate all its forces of destruction* against the state power, and . . . regard the problem as one, not of perfecting the machinery of the state, but of *breaking up and annihilating it."* [Lenin's emphasis.][12] *State and Revolution* is frequently taken to be Lenin's panegyric to the necessity of violent revolution. While it would be foolish to deny Lenin's belief in the necessity of violence (although it should be noted that from February 1917 until the onset of repression during the July days, he actually believed that Russia's passage to socialism could be enacted peaceably), it is crucial to understand the real focus of his violent rhetoric in *State and Revolution.* As Colletti and Miliband have stressed, for Lenin, "the essential point of the revolution, the destruction it cannot forego (and of which violence is not in itself a sufficient guarantee) is rather the destruction of the bourgeois state as a power separated from and counterposed to the masses, and its replacement by a power of a new type."[13]

The nature of this "power of a new type" is Lenin's third major theme in *State and Revolution*. He asserts, again faithfully following Marx and Engels, that it is the dictatorship of the proletariat that emerges as the state with the triumph of the proletarian revolution. He presses the centrality of this concept in the Marxist tradition; leaning heavily here on Marx's 1852 letter to Wedemeyer, he writes, "He who recognizes *only* the class struggle is not yet a Marxist. . . . To limit Marxism to the teaching of the class struggle means to curtail Marxism—to distort it, to reduce it to something which is acceptable to the bourgeoisie. A Marxist is one who *extends* the acceptance of the class struggle to the acceptance of the *dictatorship of the proletariat*." [Lenin's emphasis.][14] Lenin, as Marx before him, leaves open the question of exactly how long this dictatorship might endure; he writes only that it will last "for the entire historical period which separates capitalism from 'classless society,' from Communism."[15] If Marx gives the impression that this historical period will be brief, Lenin thinks otherwise—it will, he writes, "obviously be a rather lengthy process."[16]

Lenin's understanding of the dictatorship of the proletariat is rooted in an interpretation that stresses as has been said, the dominant Marxist definition of the state as an instrument of force, although that vision is far more tempered in *State and Revolution* than elsewhere. Therefore, it follows that the dictatorship of the proletariat, "the organization of the vanguard of the oppressed as the ruling class for the purpose of crushing the oppressors" will entail "*an immense extension of democracy* which for the first time becomes democracy for the poor, for the people, and not democracy for the rich folk."[17] It will mean "democracy for the vast majority of the people, and suppression by force, i.e., exclusion from democracy, of the exploiters and oppressors of the people."[18]

Moreover—and this is the fourth major theme of *State and Revolution*—the state that emerges with the victory of the proletarian revolution is a state that immediately begins to wither away. It is, as Lenin variously refers to it in the pamphlets, a "dying state," or a "nonpolitical state,"[19] or "something which is no longer really the state in the accepted sense of the word."[20] The phrase "withering away," as we have seen, was first employed by Engels. But if Engels puts forth only a vague and generalized image of what is meant by the withering away of the state, Lenin goes far beyond this: he attempts to give a sense of the proportions of the process of withering away. What becomes most clear in Lenin's discussion of the process of withering away is not the continued repressive functions of the state—much to the contrary. What is most clear—and most startling, given the traditional understanding of Leninism—is the exact degree to which the state in *State and Revolution* has already withered. It is a state, as Ralph Miliband has observed, already in an "advanced stage of decomposition."[21] This is, of course, not to say that it is a weak, powerless body: Lenin spends some time in the text of *State and Revolution* saying nasty things about the anarchists in this connection. And although he argues firmly and repeatedly (further differentiating himself from the anarchists) that "only communism renders the state absolutely unnecessary, for there is no one to be suppressed,"[22] nonetheless for the Lenin of *State and Revolution,* the process of the state's withering away begins immediately and intensely with the proletarian accession to power.

What is left is a state that "signifies a gigantic replacement of one type of institution by others of a fundamentally different order,"[23] in short, a state transformed and unlike anything that has existed in the past. It is, above all, devoid of the principle mechanisms through which all states had traditionally maintained their repressive functions: a standing army and a complex bureaucratic network, those "parasite(s) on the body of bourgeois society."[24] The proletarian state is transformed from a "state of bureaucrats" into a "state of armed workers,"[25] which then replaces the traditional standing army. The bureaucratic apparatus, although not altogether eliminated, is reduced to its proper position as "servants" rather than "masters of society,"[26] and its functions, once simplified to their proper dimensions, are taken over as well by the workers themselves—immediately. "If there be subordination," writes Lenin, "it must be to the armed vanguard of all the exploited and the laboring—to the proletariat. The specific 'commanding' methods of the state officials can and must begin to be replaced—immediately, within twenty-four hours—by the simple functions of 'managers' and bookkeepers, functions which are now already within the capacity of the average city dweller and can well be performed for 'workingmen's wages.' "[27] (It should be noted that Lenin differentiates between professional and administrative skills. He writes in a parenthesis, "The question of control and accounting must not be confused with the question of the scientifically educated staff of engineers, agronomists and so on. These gentlemen work today, obeying the capitalists; they will work even better tomorrow, obeying the armed workers."[28]) Or: "[T]he mass of the population rises to independent participation . . . in the everyday administration of affairs. Under Socialism all will take a turn in management, and will become accustomed to the idea of no managers at all."[29]

Lenin is speaking here not simply in normative terms. For him, all this is not simply something that is desirable, but something that can be demonstrated in Marxist terms to be scientifically possible. He transposes to the political and administrative realm the Marxist analysis that it is capitalism itself that makes communism materially possible by its development of the means of production to the point at which abundance becomes realizable. Capitalist culture and methods of organizing work have conglomerated and simplified "the accounting and control necessary

...to the utmost, till they have become the extraordinarily simple operations of watching, recording, and issuing receipts, within the reach of anybody who can read and write and knows the first four rules of arithmetic."[30] Lenin puts forth the postal service as a perfect incorporation of large-scale capitalist organizational imperatives into the administrative structures of the state:

> A witty German Social Democrat of the 'seventies of the last century called the post-office an example of the socialist system. This is very true. At present the post-office is a business organized on the lines of a state capitalist monopoly ...But the mechanism of social management is here already at hand. Overthrow the capitalists, crush with the iron hand of the armed workers the resistance of these exploiters, break the bureaucratic machine of the modern state—and you have before you a mechanism of the highest technical equipment, freed of "parasites," capable of being set into motion by the united workers themselves who hire their own technicians, managers, bookkeepers and pay them all, as indeed, every "state" official, with the usual workers' wage.[31]

And once more Lenin looks to the Commune as the historical proof of the practicality of the idea and the possibility that it can be invoked *immediately* upon the proletarian seizure of power:

> To *break up* at once the old bureaucratic machine, and to start immediately the construction of a new one which will enable us gradually to reduce all officialdom to naught—this is *no* Utopia, it is the experience of the Commune, it is the direct and urgent task of the revolutionary proletariat [Lenin's emphasis.][32]

This then brings us to the final underlying thread weaving through *State and Revolution:* the notion of unmediated class rule, an idea which, as Miliband points out, is far more commonly associated with anarchism than with Marxism[33] or certainly with Leninism. Yet for all Lenin does in *State and Revolution* to separate himself from the anarchists, insisting at the same moment that he talks of "reduc[ing] officialdom to naught," that "we are not Utopians, we do not indulge in 'dreams' of how best to do away *immediately* with all administration, with all subordination,"[34] nonetheless, what emerges from the pamphlet is an overwhelming image of the people themselves, organized by themselves, without any intermediaries, assuming their own rule and their own defense of that rule. If this is not stated explicitly, it is *almost* so stated—and it is returned to repeatedly. For all its vague sketchiness, it is a powerful democratic image.

Lenin's radical vision and interpretation in *State and Revolution* (and in other writings and talks directly before and after November 1917[35]) has stirred controversy on numerous planes since its day of publication. This controversy extends to the very question of why it was written in the first place. Indeed, this is hardly a peripheral matter: it raises issues absolutely central to an understanding of Leninism and of the Russian Revolution as a whole.

At its heart the argument centers around a view of Lenin as primarily the subject or primarily the object of the specific history through which he lived. Most unsympathetic historians tend to see *State and Revolution* as the ultimate proof of Lenin's unprincipled opportunism. Lenin, they argue, wrote *State and Revolution* not because he believed what he wrote; much to the contrary. The real Lenin was the Lenin of *What is to be Done?*—a Lenin who had no faith in the masses nor in the results of any mass spontaneity, who believed in the absolute leadership of a rigid hierarchical party made up of only the most conscious members of the working class and informed by déclassé intellectuals. This Lenin was to emerge again, they argue, in full force following the Bolshevik victory; this itself is taken as final proof of the disingenuousness of the Lenin of *State and Revolution.* That Lenin was actually an unscrupulous Machiavellian, interested only in the Bolshevik seizure of power and capable of pretending to adhere to the most radical democratic, even anarchistic, creed to facilitate this seizure. Adam Ulam stresses what he sees as typically Marxist opportunism in Lenin in one of the major themes of his classic, *The Bolsheviks:*

> [Lenin] was a genuine Marxist. . . . It was part of his greatness that he could argue with conviction and passion for the very thing he was to combat and destroy during his remaining years, revolutionary anarchy. And his conviction was all the stronger because the Russia of 1917 was for him only the means.[36]

This view of Lenin in general, and the Lenin of *State and Revolution* in particular, has been in turn challenged by historians basically sympathetic to Lenin and the Bolsheviks. These historians—most prominently the Belgian, Marcel Liebman, have suggested a wholly different conception of Leninism. Liebman, in his book *Leninism Under Lenin,* argues that Lenin's understanding of the issues of the relationship between leadership and led, between the party and the working class, was never constant, that it changed not simply in 1917 but continuously, determined in accordance with Marxist methodology by the changing historical moment in Russia. Liebman identifies five different stages of "Leninism" from the period of Lenin's earliest political activity and observation to his death.[37] *What Is To Be Done?* in this context represents only one—specifically the second—of these five stages and responds to the particular historical situation in Russia. In like manner, Lenin in *State and Revolution* is, in Liebman's analysis, reacting to and reflecting the reality of the historical moment: it is the situation in Russia from February 1917 on that leads Lenin once again to examine the basic relationship between leadership and the masses. Liebman contends that from the moment of his return to Russia, the direction this reexamination would take was clear: " 'The country' of the workers and poor peasants," Lenin wrote in May of 1917, in a caustic response to the declarations of an obscure Duma member, "is a thousand times more leftward than the Chernovs and Tseretelis, and a hundred times more leftward than we are."[38]

State and Revolution was probably drafted before the February Revolution. Lenin had given over the last months of 1916 to it, and just before the February uprising, he wrote in a letter to Kollontai, "I am preparing... an article on the question of the relationship of Marxism to the state."[39]

There seem to be at least three sources of inspiration that led him to tackle the question of the state and socialist society at the particular moment he did. The first, according to Robert Daniels, was a series of articles on the same subject by Bukharin, which were published or at least seen by Lenin during 1916.[40] That these were a direct impetus to Lenin becomes clear in the same letter to Kollontai, in which Levin evidenced a need to underscore and, in his terms, take further the arguments Bukharin was making. He wrote, "I have already come to conclusions more sharply against Kautsky than against Bukharin."[41]

The second source, of course, was Lenin's constant and continuing attack upon German Social Democracy, which in his thinking had shown its true colors by supporting the German war effort. His dialogue—or rather diatribe—against German social democracy and, in *State and Revolution*, particularly against Karl Kautsky, is clear, bitter, and without mercy.

But it was the third source that was perhaps more profound and more immediate: Lenin, from all indications, believed in 1916 that revolution, not only in Russia but throughout Europe, would follow inevitably in the wake of World War I. Despite his oft-quoted comment to young Swiss workers in January of 1917 that "we of the older generation may not live to see the decisive battles of this coming revolution,"[42] Krupskaya made it clear in her memoirs that Lenin was quite certain that the revolution was close at hand. She wrote, "Never before had Vladimir Ilyich been in such an uncompromising mood as he was during the last months of 1916 and the early months of 1917"—exactly the period in which a preliminary sketch of *State and Revolution* was produced. "He was," she continued, "positively certain that the revolution was imminent."[43] That coming revolution put the question of what socialist society would look like on the agenda. Moreover, the very question of the shape and structure of socialist society spoke, in Lenin's mind, directly to the question of what he saw as key strategies for achieving it. Thus, as we have mentioned, the absolute necessity to build socialist society on the ruins of the old state apparatus had immediate implications for any tendency the Bolsheviks may have had toward cooperation or coalition with other parties in the post-February 1917 period.

A letter to Kamenev in July of 1917 gives some indication of what work Lenin had already done on the pamphlet during those months prior to his return in April 1917. Lenin wrote:

> Entre nous: if they do me in, I ask you to publish my notebook: "Marxism on the State" (it got left behind in Stockholm). It's bound in a blue cover.

It contains a collection of all the quotations from Marx and Engels, likewise from Kautsky against Pannekoek. There are a number of remarks and notes and formulations. I think it is to be important.... The condition: all this is absolutely entre nous.[44]

The final draft, however, was written by Lenin while in hiding in Finland during July and August of 1917. As such, it reaffirms much of what Lenin had written and said since February 1917 and what he was to write and say in the months directly after November. Most basically, Lenin here completely inverted the relationship between leadership and masses, between party and class, that he had put forward in an earlier period—the *What is to be Done?* period. Liebman contends, quite convincingly, that the source of Lenin's "libertarian vision" was in fact the Russia of 1917 and the enormous revolutionary upheaval in process during the months *State and Revolution* was taking final shape.[45]

Indeed, times were such that Liebman is led to assert that the model for direct democracy of which *State and Revolution* speaks was to be found exactly in the "spectacle" of Russia from February 1917 forward. He points to eyewitness accounts of both observers and participants in molding this interpretation. The sense of popular "permanent mobilization"[46] is captured by the seemingly constant debates and demonstrations in which literally millions participated. Russia, according to Albert Rhys Williams, "had become a nation of one hundred million orators."[47] Endless dialogue—to the degree that John Reed reports, "[a]t every meeting attempts to limit the time of speakers were voted down"[48]—was matched by the unlimited, and again, spontaneous, formation of committees, or soviets, in every conceivable context—in workplaces, in the countryside, in houses, among housewives. Liebman cites the experience of Jules Destree, a Belgian socialist, who reported that by the end of a slow train ride from Petersburg to Moscow, those who shared his compartment on the train had formed themselves into a "traveling committee"![49] All this gives support to Marc Ferro's assertion that no established political grouping had control, that "any delegation of power was excoriated, any authority unbearable."[50]

The same self-directed impetus that marked the formation of the soviets and the attempts at workers' control echoed through every situation. Liebman points out that even the counterrevolution's major effort between February and November 1917, Kornilov's attempted coup, was met by a spontaneously generated defense network. The formation of militias; the efforts of the telegraph and railroad workers to disrupt communications and transportation; the leaflets put out by printing workers—all on their own initiative[51]—gives sure evidence that the radicalism of the masses, from the February Revolution on, far outran that of any of the political parties, the Bolsheviks included. What had occurred in actuality was the very inversion of leadership and the people as a whole to which Lenin was to give voice in *State and Revolution*.

This inversion was invoked by him as the very reason and justification for the Bolshevik seizure of power. In the course of trying to convince the Bolshevik Central Committee to undertake a second revolution (and specifically in response to the charge that such an insurrection would prove the Bolsheviks were Blanquists, rather than Marxists), Lenin laid out the necessary conditions for such an uprising: "To be successful, insurrection must rely not upon conspiracy, and not upon a party but upon the advanced class. That is the first point. Insurrection must rely upon *a revolutionary upsurge of the people*. That is the second." [Lenin's emphasis.][52]

State and Revolution brings up another basic—perhaps more critical—controversy for the Marxist tradition. For the fact is that although it remained for seventy years a reference point for all those seeking to understand the nature of postcapitalist society, it did not, in any way, speak to the enormous and critical problems with which it was concerned. All this led Miliband, writing in 1970, to assert that it was the very practice of socialism itself that proved again and again to be the Achilles' heel of Marxism.[53] The events of the last half of the 1980s underline starkly this conclusion. This then requires of us a critical reexamination of the pamphlet and an evaluation of its weaknesses, of what it does and does *not* say about these problems. We do this understanding that *State and Revolution* is unfinished: as Lenin wrote in its afterword, his work on the piece was "interfered with" by the October Revolution itself.[54]

Let us, therefore, return to the major themes of *State and Revolution*, beginning with the structure on which the work rests: Lenin's definition of the state. Lenin might have looked with the benefit of historical hindsight to the full range of Marx's ambiguous understandings of the state. He might, in particular, have considered the applicability of the idea Marx developed in *The Eighteenth Brumaire of Louis Bonaparte* that, given a certain weakness in the capacities of a ruling class, the state can achieve a position of autonomy from the class whose interests it actually represents. Instead, he chose to concentrate exclusively on only one strand—the simplest one—within the complex of Marx's thought and, as a result, was caught in the deepest waters of the Marxist reductive trap. For Lenin, the state is always an organ of repressive force used by one class against another. His definition allows absolutely no direct reference or even allusion to the wide range of functions and mediations that a state must perform. The extreme narrowness of his conceptualization of the state provided the means by which the leading actors in the drama of actually existing socialism could use *State and Revolution* to legitimate everything the pamphlet, taken as a whole, seems to oppose. We include here his own actions after the Bolsheviks seized power: the logic of his definition of the state provided the justification for both the 1918 dissolution of the Constituent Assembly and the periodic banning of competing parties, climaxing in 1921 with their permanent abolition. Given that parties represented classes, then, as Gregor McLennan observes, allowing them to exist and compete for power within the political arena would be, in effect, "postponing the advent of a classless society. By definition, the existence of multiple organized groupings has no basis in [a classless society]."[55] It is an easy, if troubling, leap from this to banning organized factions within the party itself.

Lenin's exclusive use of the class-domination model, moreover, has irretrievable implications for what we have called the central theme of *State and Revolution:* the necessity to destroy the existing state apparatus. Lenin, says Robert Daniels, "failed to grasp the basic rationale of the smashing dictum—protection of society against the dangerous independence of the state machinery—and as a result he allowed the entire program of mass control over the exercise of political power to be vitiated after his party came to power."[56]

Perhaps exactly because of Lenin's limited definitional base—his understanding of the state as the ruling class's organ of repression—there is in *State and Revolution* none of the ambiguity that characterized Marx's use of the term "dictatorship." To Lenin it is clearly an instrument for suppressing opposing classes, and despite the notion put forth in *State and Revolution* that the dictatorship of the proletariat is the most democratic of all states since it is a dictatorship for the first time of the majority, there are no doubts about nor limits on the repression (or as Lenin puts it, the "exclusion from democracy"[57]) of classes other than the workers and their allies. Hal Draper, in his efforts to distinguish Marx's concept of the dictatorship of the proletariat from Lenin's, focuses precisely on this definitional issue. Draper argues that Lenin "worked out for himself, or invented, a unique definition" that drew principally on the very antidemocratic conceptualization of dictatorship by Georgi Plekhanov, the founder of the Russian Social-Democratic movement.[58]

Moreover, although Lenin speaks of a "gigantic replacement of one type of institution by others of a fundamentally different order," there is little in *State and Revolution* to indicate precisely what these new institutions will look like or how they will be formed. There is, to be sure, a brief reference to the soviets. Certainly, Lenin returned to Russia in April 1917 declaring that the Bolshevik slogan must be "all power to the soviets." And elsewhere around the same period in which *State and Revolution* was written he was more explicit about the centrality of the soviets as the basis upon which the new state would be constructed. Indeed, everything he said or wrote from the moment of his return to Russia is littered with references to the soviets as the incarnation of the Paris Commune and the ready made base for the Bolshevik state.[59] Thus, in his essay, "Can the Bolsheviks Retain State Power?" (written, with some confidence, before they had actually seized state power), he argues:

> The fourth plea of the councils for the bourgeoisie is that the proletariat will not be able "to set the state apparatus in motion". . . . We could not, of course, either lay hold or or set in motion the old state apparatus. The new apparatus, the Soviets *has already* been set in motion by "a mighty burst of creative enthusiasm that stems from the people themselves."[60]

But *State and Revolution* itself spends far more time denouncing parliamentarism than discussing its alternative—logical, on one level, given the fact that parliamentarism was his immediate enemy in the Russia of 1917.

> To decide once every few years which member of the ruling class is to repress and oppress the people through parliament—this is the real essence of bourgeois parliamentarism, not only in parliamentary constitutional monarchies, but also in the most democratic republics. . . . The way out of parliamentarism is to be found, of course, not in the abolition of the representative institutions and the elective principle, but in the conversion of representative institutions from mere "talking shops" into working bodies.[61]

He continues at a later point to suggest that these "working bodies" will in fact be the soviets. "In a Socialist society," he writes, "this 'something in the nature of a parliament' [using Kautsky's words in an ironical attack on him] will consist of workers' deputies."[62] These workers will "break up the old bureaucratic apparatus, . . . shatter it to its very foundations until not one stone is left upon another"[63] and insure against any reemergence of bureaucratic form by remembering and acting upon the lessons of the Commune: "(1) not only electiveness but instant recall; (2) payment no higher than that of ordinary workers; (3) immediate transition to a state of things when *all* fulfill the functions of control and superintendence, so that *all* become 'bureaucrats' for a time, and *no one,* therefore, can become a 'bureaucrat.' " [Lenin's emphasis.][64]

The problem is that the formula has never proven sufficient. By 1921, shortly before the introduction of the New Economic Policy (the NEP), E. H. Carr notes the degree to which Lenin had reversed himself on this issue: "Can every worker know how to administer the state? Practical people know that this is a fairy tale."[65] The vast bureaucratic apparatus that came to characterize the states of actually existing socialism was already apparent in the Soviet Union during the brief years between the Bolshevik accession to power and Lenin's death in 1924. And, in truth, this was as inexplicable to Lenin as to any of his followers. By 1920, Lenin was forced to admit that Russia was a "socialist state with bureaucratic distortions." Indeed, historians like Moshe Lewin have painstakingly documented the struggle—his famous "last struggle"—which Lenin carried on, literally from his deathbed, against these bureaucratic distortions.[66] But the truth is that, given his formulas, Lenin was unable to grasp the nature and sources of the mushrooming Soviet bureaucracy. He tended to see it as a leftover from the past—the affliction of the old Russian state come to haunt the new one[67]—and as a consequence of the Bolsheviks' inability to shatter the old state structures to their "very foundations, until not one stone is left upon another."[68] We will have cause to return to this point when we discuss more fully *State and Revolution* in the light of the aftermath of the Bolshevik seizure of power.

The enduring bureaucracy directly challenges the fourth major theme of *State and Revolution:* the withering away of the state. Lenin argues in *State and Revolution* that the state begins to wither *immediately* upon the workers' accession to power, yet we hear him, as early as the Seventh Party Congress, in March of 1918, asserting that "for the present, we stand unconditionally for the state."[69] It is true that, in one sense, this statement does not contradict *State and Revolution;* Lenin saw the need for a strong postrevolutionary state power to carry on the task of repression of opponents. But this state, as it is envisioned in *State and Revolution,* has been transformed. It is no longer a state in its usual sense, but a state in which the workers—armed—are themselves the power. And it becomes only too clear in the aftermath of the October Revolution that this state of armed workers, directly empowered, is not the state that came into existence.

The final theme of *State and Revolution,* unmediated class rule, is clouded both before, and particularly after the Bolshevik seizure of power by an element Lenin refers to only obliquely and in passing in the pamphlet: the Party.

The omission in *State and Revolution* of any discussion of the Party—an element so central to Lenin's thought and work—ranks as probably the most startling aspect of the pamphlet. There are by generous count only three possible references to the Party[70] in the text and only one of these, as Miliband notes, even ambiguously speaks to its relationship to, or role in, the dictatorship of the proletariat. Lenin writes, at one point, "By educating a workers' party, Marxism educates the vanguard of the proletariat, capable of assuming power and of leading the whole people to Socialism, of directing and organizing the new order, of being the teacher, guide, and leader of all the toiling and exploited...."[71] But, Miliband points out, even this assertion is open to two interpretations. It is not clear, given the phrasing, whether it is the proletariat as a whole or whether it is the vanguard workers, that is, the Party, that is "capable of assuming power." Miliband effectively demonstrates that both interpretations are possible.[72] It is true that discussion of the role of Party is present elsewhere in Lenin's work during the same months that saw the final draft of *State and Revolution.* Thus, for instance, in *Can the Bolsheviks Retain State Power?,* written in September 1917, Lenin does speak of the role of the Party. But even here the role envisioned is a limited one. The essay, in a discussion of the machinery of the new socialist state, alludes to the formative role of the rapidly growing Party and those who vote for it, but Lenin's discussion of who will mold the state includes not only these; rather, it will be the task of the whole people:

> The chief thing [he writes] is to imbue the oppressed and the working people with confidence in their own strength, to prove to them in practice that they can and must themselves ensure the *proper,* most strictly regulated and organized distribution of bread, all kinds of food, milk, clothing, housing, etc. *in the interests of the poor.* Unless this is done, Russia *cannot* be saved from collapse and ruin. The conscientious, bold, universal move to hand over administrative work to the proletarians and semi-proletarians, will, however,

rouse such unprecedented revolutionary enthusiasm among the people, will so multiply the people's forces in combatting distress, that much that seemed impossible to our narrow, old bureaucratic forces will become possible for the millions, who will *begin to work for themselves* and not for the capitalists, the gentry, the bureaucrats, and not out of fear of punishment. [Lenin's emphasis.][73]

The question of exactly *why* Lenin so totally ignores the Party in *State and Revolution,* and basically in all his work of this period, is a difficult one to answer. It evokes the controversy concerning Lenin's opportunism discussed earlier. But there is another possible explanation—again emerging from the actual historical moment in Russia during which *State and Revolution* was written. It was Lenin's historical genius to recognize that it was not any party calling the shots in Russia in 1917. It was the people who were the most radical force in Russia, and 1917 was their triumph. The Bolsheviks gained power only because, under enormous prodding from their leader, they recognized this and went along with it. As we shall see, this "symbiotic relationship" between party and people,[74] this confidence in the spontaneity of the masses might have been true in 1917; the moment, however, was to change rather drastically. Even given this, it remains nonetheless a fact that the entire question of political leadership—of the existence of leadership, of its role, of its relationship to the population as a whole—is not dealt with in *State and Revolution.* And this, in the light of history, was to prove a crucial silence.

There is a related, perhaps even more critical conceptual deficit in the pamphlet: its failure to come to any kind of terms at all with the question of political mediation. In this, as in other aspects of his argument in *State and Revolution,* Lenin is merely embroidering on and extending, in a simplified manner, implications directly traceable to Marx himself. The logic of Lenin's vision of unmediated class rule, unfettered by a state in the advanced stages of disintegration, allows him to sidestep entirely any discussion of the need in any but perhaps the simplest of human interactions for autonomous agencies of political mediation, which would provide the loci in which diverse people could express, mobilize around, and militate for diverse interests and points of view. If, for instance, this need is reduced to a rule by a single party—and this, of course, is exactly what happened in post-October Russia—then, as Ralph Miliband points out, the assumption must be that there is a single, commonly shared, uniform popular will. Such an assumption, Miliband argues, is simply unreasonable: "In no society, however constituted, is there an undivided, single, popular will. This is precisely why the problem of political mediation arises in the first place." The radical democratic vision of *State and Revolution* may be just "so much hot air . . . unless adequate provision is made for *alternative* channels of expression and political articulation."[75]

The absence of discussion of the critical need for diverse and autonomous agencies of political mediation, as we shall see in the next chapter, would fortify the theoretical vacuum that permitted, or justified, the 1921 ban in the Soviet Union of all parties except the Communist (Bolshevik) Party and, with it, the ban on organized factions within that single party. That is, it allowed the conclusive elimination of the key element in the kind of "socialist pluralism"[76] embedded, for instance, in Rosa Luxemburg's understanding of the dictatorship of the proletariat.[77] Lenin's literal interpretation of Marx's reductionist logic obscured or helped to blind the old Bolshevik leadership to the consequences of their actions, consequences captured at least in part by Trotsky (who ironically had, with Lenin, proposed the inner-party ban) some eighteen years later:

> Whoever prohibits factions thereby liquidates party democracy and takes the first step toward a totalitarian regime.... It is true that the Bolshevik Party forbade factions at the Tenth Party Congress in March 1921, a time of mortal danger. One can argue whether or not this was correct. The subsequent course of development has in any case proved that this prohibition served as one of the starting points of the party's degeneration. The bureaucracy presently made a bogey of the concept of "faction," so as not to permit the Party either to think or breathe. Thus was formed the totalitarian regime which killed Bolshevism.[78]

We are faced, finally, with two interwoven questions. The first of these questions concerns reasons: why did Lenin's radical vision in *State and Revolution* fade and vanish? We will spend a good part of the next chapter exploring a range of answers to this question. The second question concerns consequences: to what degree is *State and Revolution* itself implicated in what was to happen? Did it actually shape or even influence the course of history? To what extent did its central concepts, riddled as they are with unresolved dilemmas, leave a fateful imprint on what was to follow?

The question of consequences serves to focus, more sharply, arguments we have already presented. Remarkably, the controversy concerning the legacy of *State and Revolution* has continued to reverberate into the present: two recent studies draw on elements of Ralph Miliband's assessment to put forth diametrically opposed arguments. Samuel Farber, in his book, *Before Stalinism*, echoes Miliband in declaring *State and Revolution* a "distant... socio-political vision" that was not in any way a "programmatic policy statement let alone a guide to action for the period immediately after the successful seizure of power."[79] The Bolsheviks themselves, he asserts, made crystal clear their limited and strategic faith in developing a soviet form of government in any number of ways, beginning with their immediate empowerment of a centralized Council of People's Commissars (the Sovnarkom) as distinguished from the Central Executive Committee of the Soviets, thereby dividing the executive from the legislative in the very manner deplored by Marx in *The Civil War in France*. Farber argues that Bolshevik advocacy of the Soviets in 1917 faded after the repression of the "July days" when they came to be seen by Lenin and the Bolshevik leadership as "obstacles in a life and death struggle against the Provisional

Government," or, in Lenin's words, "mere fig leaves of the counterrevolution."[80] Once the Bolsheviks took power, Farber writes,

> [G]overnmental euphoria with War Communism... implicitly revealed the political and ideological priorities of mainstream Bolshevism. Thus, while this set of policies greatly expanded the powers of the central state and vigorously attempted to reduce the role of the market, at the same time it not only consolidated the Red Terror but for all intents and purposes eliminated workers' control of industry and democracy in the soviets. Again, there is no evidence indicating that Lenin or any of the mainstream Bolshevik leaders lamented [these losses] as a retreat.... In fact... the very opposite is the case.[81]

In essence then, although Farber (following Miliband) grants *State and Revolution* "doubtless sincerity," he is not far from Ulam in his conclusions about the pamphlet, even if he follows a different path in reaching these conclusions.

On the other hand, A. J. Polan, in his *Lenin and the End of Politics* indicts *State and Revolution* as a "dangerous document"[82] that was directly responsible for what was to follow: "[T]he crime of Lenin's text," he argues, "is not that it did not work; it is that it did." Thus Polan identifies the shadow of *State and Revolution* darkening the post-1917 Soviet state in all its incarnations: "before *and* after the Bolsheviks secured the monopoly of power, before *and* after the decline of the Soviets as significant institutions, before *and* after the rise of Stalin's power."[83] Polan's reading of Lenin's text underlines harshly many of the dilemmas identified earlier in this chapter: he focuses particularly upon its severe simplification of the functions of the state and its resultant failure to consider the need for a diversity of political institutions to represent diverse interests and points of view. In its conflation of all institutions into a single entity, Polan argues, Lenin's state form is severely one-dimensional: "It allows for no distances, no appeals, no checks, no balances, no processes, no delays, no interrogations, and above all, no distribution of power.... The new state form will be transparent, monological and unilinear."[84] Such a state, he asserts, is a denial of the inevitable differences among any group of human beings. "Because the government and the bureaucracy were already the expression of that one genuine politics and by definition a more coherent and profound expression than could be found among the people themselves, the politics of the people were rendered redundant. Politically, the people were abolished."[85]

Polan's critique of *State and Revolution* is powerful. It ignores, however, several important issues. The first of these issues involves the tradition on which *State and Revolution* draws: Lenin borrows the greater part of his argument concerning the socialist state directly from Marx. The central aspects of his vision are extended (if simplified) discussions of the themes Marx wrote of in *The Civil War in France* and in all of his discussions of postcapitalist society. The problem then is not simply embedded in the Leninist political tradition, it grows from the very roots of the Marxist tradition. Polan's reading of Lenin's text, by dismissing its antecedents as irrelevant, fails to see this. This same relegation lets him reject out of hand the other half of the classical Marxist tradition (recapitulated by Lenin) concerning the socialist state: its deeply emancipatory vision. Polan's assertion that "the 'libertarian' Lenin bears a responsibility for the Gulag with the 'authoritarian' Lenin"[86] is not wholly wrong, but it does simplify the contradictory heritage on which Lenin draws. In so doing, Polan takes away value from this tradition and, more importantly, denies the necessity of reexamining it from its roots.

In the end, as Harding so correctly concludes, Lenin fails to "square the circle" that Engels had created by declaring the Paris Commune the incarnation of the dictatorship of the proletariat.[87] He succeeds only in further impoverishing an already severely impoverished model for the state in the transition from capitalism to socialism. The problem is that generations of political leadership in the countries of actually existing socialism consistently looked to, or rather, cited *State and Revolution* as the theoretical basis for and justification of the shape of their particular states. And it is, at least in part, in this context that the import of *State and Revolution* must be understood and evaluated. (Indeed, if one examines the constitutions or official documents written to explain and situate the form and nature of the state in those societies, these documents sought theoretical justifications for the structures they created in the pages of *State and Revolution* and, perhaps with less specificity, in Marx's writings on the postcapitalist state. Thus, the *Constitution of the Organs of Popular Power*, which serves as the theoretical explanation as well as the initial description of the Cuban state system established experimentally in 1974, explicitly draws on *State and Revolution* not simply as part of the heritage in which it is rooted, but as a guideline to the actual construction of the socialist state.[88])

But perhaps more important than this, *State and Revolution* was forced, as it were, to play a key role in the language of official Marxism-Leninism. The freezing and distortion of the theoretical dialogue that official Marxism-Leninism represented meant that the document—in terms not of its core message but of its image of the form of the socialist state (or the lack thereof)—remained the "sacred text" on the subject, although the historical experience that followed in this century, and reflections on that experience, should long ago have challenged, honed, contradicted, and superseded it.

3

The "Dictatorship of the Proletariat" in Practice: Actually Existing Socialism in the Soviet Union

This chapter picks up the discussion with which we concluded the prior chapter: the decay of revolutionary democracy in the early years of the Soviet Union, the period that set the terms for the consolidation of the antidemocratic image of the "dictatorship of the proletariat." This discussion seems critical for at least two interrelated reasons. First, it is with the Russian Revolution that the world, in Rosa Luxemburg's words, takes its first steps onto "new territory." It is the Russians who must first face her "thousand problems"[1] in trying to translate theory into actual practice. For this reason alone, this first revolution made in the name of socialism, and its application of theory, would inevitably have a profound effect on all that were to follow.

And second, the effect was a distorted and distorting one. What was passed down was not so much the history of the Soviet Union, but rather, a rewritten and dogmatized version of this history, complete with a set of "laws" about the transition from capitalism to socialism. These laws, validated by a theoretical heritage that could easily be interpreted or twisted to approve them, crystallized the separation of the concepts of socialism and democracy. Paul Bellis has written, using a fairly elaborate image, that this crystallization "formed the cryogen whose glacial contact immobilized socialism and the theory and practice of Marxism in the U.S.S.R. indefinitely."[2] In actuality its effects went far beyond the borders of the Soviet Union. This distorted version of history determined and defined the shape and the boundaries of the societies of actually existing socialism. This held true in those societies whose supposedly socialist structures were imposed from above and, ironically, in those that experienced real revolution; it held true for those societies that were relatively developed in economic terms, as well as for those that were underdeveloped. Clearly, there was diversity; in certain cases, the dogmatized Soviet structure of politics and economics was adopted wholesale, while in others, there were interludes during which a conscious attempt was made to seek an alternative and unique path to socialism and communism. Nonetheless, even in the second case the "official" model of Soviet society, functioning as a reactive element, structured debate concerning the transition and helped to frame its outcome. In short, it defined and obscured at critical points the common understanding of the very meaning of socialism and communism.

Given this, it would seem imperative for us to examine the Soviet experience to clarify the elements at work in unraveling the fabric of revolutionary democracy. We will attempt to do this by first very briefly sketching the proportions of this unraveling of democracy and socialism in the pre-1985 Soviet Union, with specific reference to the story of what became of the soviets.

We will then turn to the major question in this chapter: why? Was the form the "dictatorship of the proletariat" took in the Soviet Union the result of historical constraints particular to the Russian experience? Was it the inevitable result of the isolation and extreme civil strife that gripped the Soviet Union almost from the moment the Bolsheviks seized power? Was it the peculiar creation of Stalin, a distortion imposed by him to serve his own purposes? Or is there something inherent in the actual theory of the dictatorship of the proletariat that permitted, or indeed led, to its form in the Soviet Union? In undertaking this examination, we will underline the manner in which this history itself became embedded in theory as the axiomatic bases of actually existing socialism.

Even the most cursory survey of the relationship between state and society in the pre-Gorbachev Soviet Union confronts us with a stark reality: while Engels had predicted a withering away of the state in the transition from capitalism to communism and the early Bolsheviks a state essentially absorbed by society, in the Soviet Union it was unmistakable that the opposite had occurred. A system had been molded in which no institution or entity existed separate from, or independent of, the party-state, capable of developing and expressing its own point of view. A monostructural, tied set of institutions allowed no legally sanctioned loci of discussion, nor autonomous sites of social organization. The state had absorbed civil society and, as a consequence, enlarged itself in a manner that would have been anathema to the founders of socialism. Rudolf Bahro, the East German critic who coined the term "actually existing socialism" captured well the situation when he contrasted the process of "statification" to the "socialization"—society absorbing the state—that Marx had envisioned.[3] Control from below, which Marx had underscored as a defining element in the process of socialization, was substituted by a system run in almost every aspect from above. Structures that had given direct voice to the citizens and workers of 1917 Russia gave way, or at most became hollow reminders of what, for so short a moment, they once were. Thus, the soviets, the institutions that were to be the bulwark of the new socialist state, remained on paper, into the late 1980s, the heart of the Soviet system. Yet they were stripped of all the features that had given them revolutionary definition.

From the opening salvo—the November victory of the Bolsheviks— the soviets at every level, particularly at their base, began a tailspin. The form of the soviets had evolved spontaneously from the strike committees that arose during the 1905 convulsions in Russia. Their reemergence and the crucial role they played in 1917 was logical. But it was Lenin, having already accomplished the task of identifying the soviets as the heirs of the Paris Commune (and therefore, following Engels, the incarnation of the dictatorship of the proletariat), who put them forth as the skeleton of the new state. On the very night of his return to Russia, in Kheshinskaya's reception room, he declared, to the shock of everyone present, "We don't need a parliamentary republic, we don't need any Government except the Soviet of Workers', Soldiers' and Farm-labourers' deputies." As Sukhanov relates, "Lenin's constitutional system was a bolt from the blue not only for me . . . [o]f course every listener with any experience in political theory took Lenin's formula, fired off without any commentaries, for a purely anarchist schema."[4] Yet shortly, the Bolsheviks would adopt this schema and make as their own the slogan "all power to the soviets." Their banner, however, did not remain intact for long. Bertrand Russell, after a visit to the Soviet Union a few years later, gives us some measure of this:

> Before I went to Russia I imagined that I was going to see an interesting experiment in this new form of representative government. I did see an in- teresting experiment, but not in representative government. Everyone who is interested in Bolshevism knows the series of elections, from the village meeting to All-Russian Soviet, by which the people's commissaries are sup- posed to derive their power. We were told that, by the recall, the occupational constituencies, and so on, a new and far more perfect machinery had been devised for ascertaining and registering the popular will. One of the things we hoped to study was the question whether the Soviet system is really superior to Parlementarism in this respect. We were not able to make any such a study, because the Soviet system is moribund.[5]

The official records make it clear, for instance, that prior to 1989, elections themselves never had more than one candidate running for any given post and never seemed to record less than 98 percent of the pop- ulation voting. Perhaps the ultimate comment upon the nature of these elections came in a 1947 *Pravda* article Joseph Stalin received 2,122 votes in a local Soviet district comprised of only 1,617 voters. *Pravda* explained that "the extra ballots were put into the urns by citizens in neighboring constituencies anxious to seize the opportunity to express their gratitude to their leaders."

As for the soviets at the higher levels of government, they became little more than rubber-stamping committees. This was nowhere more evident than at the very highest of levels. Whereas in the early years of the revolution each meeting of the Supreme Soviet was, as Roy Medvedev characterizes it, an "outstanding historical event,"[6] a pattern of less and less frequent meetings gradually took shape. In 1918 the Supreme Soviet met five times; by 1922 it was meeting once a year. And under Stalin, this pattern was accelerated. Indeed, during the period from 1931 to 1935, there were *no* recorded meetings of the Supreme Soviet. Moreover, from 1937 until 1988, every decision taken at the fifteen hundred member Congress of the Supreme Soviet was unanimous.[7] Under Stalin, this powerlessness took on ludicrous proportions. Stalin's disdain for the Supreme Soviet was such that he only bothered to submit national budgets for approval after they had been in effect for considerable periods of time.[8] When Stalin broke with his alliance with England and France to join Hitler in the 1939 invasion of Poland, the Supreme Soviet concluded that the matter did not merit discussion, given the "clarity and consistency of the foreign policy of the Soviet government."

If the Stalinist period must be seen as the height of a crescendo, nevertheless, the basic tune remained the same. Medvedev writes in the mid-1970s that, despite the fact that it had the constitutional right to introduce new legislation, the Supreme Soviet had never made use of this right, nor had it ever rejected or returned for amendment a bill introduced by the Council of Ministers.[9] Note, moreover, Medvedev's recital of the agenda for a single day during the July 1970 plenary session of the Supreme Soviet: the election of a new Presidium; the formation, without discussion, of a Council of Ministers; a new national labor policy, the first since 1922, introduced, debated, and approved in a matter of one-and-one-half hours.[10] And Barrington Moore's 1950 description of the nature of these sessions remained appropriate thirty-five years after he wrote it:

> The sessions of the Supreme Soviet have given observers the impression of a well-rehearsed play. A study of the stenographic reports of the sessions confirms this impression. It seems that each person who speaks has a set part to play. There are "bit" parts for making procedural motions, and longer parts with formal speeches. Everything proceeds smoothly without objections or interruptions from the floor or the chair until unanimous decisions are adopted.[11]

It was the Communist Party itself that came to fill the vacuum within the state structure. Indeed, at every level of this structure, key positions were uniformly held by members of the Communist Party. At the uppermost levels, every official, without exception, was a Party member. Thus, in effect, the Party and the state collapsed into one structure. At the very top, this meant that the ruling organs of the Party were the ruling organs of the state. The lines of power were made explicit in the Constitution of 1936. All laws now required ratification by the Central Committee of the Communist Party before they were presented in the Supreme Soviet. The

Presidium of the Supreme Soviet, the agency that was supposed to act as the directing organ of the state between meetings of the Supreme Soviet, was itself subordinated to and controlled by the Central Committee.[12] And in a situation in which the Party itself had degenerated, this meant that power in a practical sense rested with the small group of men who occupied the highest positions in the Party and consequently in the state.

Thus the paradox: in a society that proclaimed its state as the dictatorship of the proletariat, the proletariat, as Paul Bellis observed, had been "institutionally excluded from the administration of its own state, a monopoly of which [was] ensured for the Soviet bureaucracy."[13] The level of bureaucratic morass that developed was literally stupefying. If Marx and the Lenin of *State and Revolution* had envisioned a system in which bureaucracy would, at last, disintegrate and lose forever its hold upon society, the opposite seemed to occur. The bureaucracy wound itself around every structure of state and society: never had Marx's boa constrictor been more omnipresent or more stultifying. Its effect—and perhaps as the Budapest School theorists argue, its purpose—was to block anything that represented change or the resolution of problems. Agnes Heller, Ferenc Fehér and György Márkus in their scathing 1983 examination of Soviet-type societies, *The Dictatorship Over Needs,* argue cogently that bureaucrats in the societies of actually existing socialism did not fail in their roles; rather, they were eminently successful:

> The Soviet bureaucracy has to be inefficient in order to accomplish its true aim: to stem the tide, to defer the satisfaction of the population's needs. In the case of a food shortage, the bureaucracy has to be inefficient in distribution; in the case of an accommodation shortage, the bureaucracy has to adopt a tactic of deliberately disheartening the applicants; in the case of a machinery shortage, the bureaucracy must constantly delay in issuing machinery to factories that cannot function without it. Hence, paradoxical as it may sound, Soviet bureaucracy executes at least one of its sovereign's wishes by being inefficient. Its function is primarily to practice a dictatorship over needs, and this is being done thoroughly.[14]

The result, then, as Fehér, Heller and Márkus phrase it, was a "spectacular world-historical fiasco," which was not socialist, but rather, "the culmination of de-enlightenment."[15]

> If, according to Kant, enlightenment is humankind's release from its self-incurred tutelage, de-enlightenment means the relapse into that same tutelage. If enlightenment requires the use of one's own reason, de-enlightenment requires that one should never use it but should rely upon the collective intellect of the Party, which does the thinking.... If enlightenment requires that one should reflect before acting, and find out whether one's option is good, de-enlightenment requires that one should never reflect but unhesitatingly obey the Party. Enlightenment emphasizes personal responsibility; de-enlightenment substitutes sheer obedience for personal responsibility. De-enlightenment "liberates" humankind from moral, intellectual and political freedom. Nothing is more characteristic of the norm of de-enlightenment

than the slogan of the Komsomol, the Communist youth organization and "primary school" for future Party members: "The Party is our reason, honor and conscience." The slogan holds the secret of de-enlightenment: self-alienation becomes a publicly professed creed.[16]

We are faced then, with the question of why. What was it that brought about this situation? What was it that permitted the enshrinement of a static, vertical, and closed party-state as the "correct" form of "socialist democracy." Leaving to one side explanations that stress the malevolent goals of the Bolsheviks, the most common reading emanates from the notion of inevitability, or the "force of circumstance": given the context and the course of events, it was bound to be so. Among those who consider (or considered) themselves Marxists, the notion of inevitability covers a wide spectrum of focuses. Its principle advocates stress the idea that responsibility rests with the force of historical circumstances: scarcity, isolation, severe internal conflict. Others emphasize the influence of the heritage of tsarist Russia, both in a specific and in a general way. These theories range from analyses of the staying power of the tsarist bureaucracy to Rudolf Bahro's 1979 reassertion of Wittfogel's notion of the Asiatic mode of production in his analysis of the "noncapitalist road" to development.[17]

The main version of the force of circumstance argument focuses particularly on the period leading up to 1921, the climactic year of the Kronstadt Revolt, the Tenth Party Congress, and the introduction of the New Economic Policy. It traces a chain of events that led to the dissolution of the soviets—particularly local soviets—as effective participatory bodies and the gradual—at first erratic, then systematic—elimination of dissent, first outside the Party in society as a whole, and then, in 1921, within the Party structure itself. The argument roots itself in the Civil War, which engulfed Russia from 1918 to 1921, producing the grimmest imaginable results.

Perhaps most pointedly for the future of the world's first workers' state, the Civil War decimated the working-class population; the most loyal, most class-conscious working-class supporters of the Bolsheviks were surely among those who perished on the front lines of the struggle. The level of decimation, either through battle, starvation, or the dissolution of industry, was marked by the evaporation of people from the major cities and corresponding decline in the total number of industrial workers, by more than half.[18] Thus, according to the force of circumstance argument, the very constituency on which the future was to be built no longer existed.

Moreover, the Civil War had put an end, for all intents and purposes, to the autonomy of the major institutions through which Lenin, in 1917, had envisioned the dictatorship of the proletariat would be expressed. The militarization of public life in the course of the Civil War inevitably spelled the doom of the soviets as they had functioned after the February Revolution. By the Eighth Party Congress in 1919, Lenin had, in essence, written their obituary. He phrased it this way: "[T]he Soviets, which by virtue of their programme are organs of the government by the working people, are, in fact, organs of the government for the working people by the advanced section of the proletariat, but not by the working people as a whole."[19]

And, perhaps most critically, the Bolsheviks took power with a belief that their actions would only speed up the process of socialist revolution in neighboring countries in Eastern Europe, and particularly, in Germany. Indeed—at least before November 1917—the Bolsheviks understood implicitly that without these revolutions, their own could not survive. It was on this basis that Trotsky, when appointed Peoples Commissar for Foreign Affairs, declared (perhaps with some exaggeration), "I shall publish a few revolutionary proclamations and then close shop"[20]—no ministries of foreign affairs would be necessary in a world dominated by socialism.

But by 1921 it was obvious that there was to be no immediate world socialist revolution: the failure of efforts in Germany made this particularly clear. This isolation, compounded by the active hostility of the West, left the Bolshevik leaders either to accept their tragic fate as revolutionaries who had "come before their time"[21] or to exercise power without the support they had believed in November 1917 would be available to them. They chose, of course, the latter road. And, indeed, the challenges to their rule were overwhelming and not simply from the forces actively opposed to them in the Civil War.

By 1920 after several years of this war, starvation and the forced food requisitioning of War Communism had generated widescale opposition to the Communists (the name the Bolsheviks took in 1919). The peasantry, identifying with the party that had given them their land in 1917, rejected the party that imposed requisitions in the following years and took up the cry, "We are Bolsheviks, not Communists."[22] Waves of unrest swept the countryside with the conclusion of the Civil War. By 1921, for the first time since 1917, the largest part of what remained of the working class joined with the peasantry in unmistakable opposition to the Communists. Every indication was that if free elections had been held in the soviets in 1921, the Communists would have been handily defeated.

All this was hardly lost upon opposition groups: here the matter of any postwar attempt to revive the soviets becomes pertinent. In the months following the Civil War, each opposition group focused anew upon the soviets as the avenue of change. Medvedev relates that in 1921 the Menshevik Central Committee made it mandatory for members to "become actively involved in elections to the workers Soviets and in the work of the Soviets themselves."[23] As the Menshevik leader Dan later stated, "Free elections to the Soviets as a first step towards replacing the dictatorship by democratic rule—that was our everyday political slogan."[24] The Right Social Revolutionary resolution concerning elections passed on February 15, 1920, told its people: "Do participate in the election. Where it is possible to display the party roll, display prominently a list of those in prison."[25] The motto of the Left Socialist Revolutionaries became "Soviets without Communists."[26] Even exiled monarchists suddenly became staunch supporters of the soviet form of government. Medvedev cites an article that appeared in an emigre journal put out by the "All-Russian Monarchist Council": "Our émigré community must appreciate that the local Soviets, purged of Communists and scum working against the people, now contain a genuinely creative force capable of reconstructing Russia. This faith in the creativity of the truly Russian, popular and profoundly Christian Soviets must become property of our émigré community."[27]

So goes the force of circumstance argument: the Communists were faced with a dilemma. If they ceded power—let us say, in free elections— the result, in their view, would have been unending years of civil war and chaos. Since no party was likely to gain a majority, the Communists saw only "utter confusion followed by open counterrevolution" as their successors.[28] If they maintained themselves in power, it meant inevitably an irresolvable conflict between dictatorship and democracy, as Isaac Deutscher so eloquently puts it. Until this point, Deutscher wrote, it had been assumed by the Communists that Soviet democracy and proletarian dictatorship signified the same thing. Now the formula came apart:

> If the working classes were to be allowed to speak and vote freely, they would destroy the dictatorship. If the dictatorship, on the other hand . . . abolished proletarian democracy it would deprive itself of historic legitimacy, even in its own eyes. It would cease to be a proletarian dictatorship in the strict sense. Its use of the title would henceforth be based on a claim that it pursued a policy with which the working class, in its own interest, ought and eventually must identify itself, but with which it did not as yet identify itself.[29]

It was, characteristically, Trotsky who most clearly captured the horrible convolution in beliefs and logic that all this indicated in his reply to the Workers' Opposition demands for trade union and local factory committee control of industry, at the climactic 1921 Tenth Party Congress: "It is necessary to create among us the awareness of the revolutionary historical birthright of the party. The party is obliged to maintain its dictatorship, regardless of temporary wavering in the spontaneous moods of the masses, regardless of the temporary vacillations even in the working class."[30] The circle swings full around: the dictatorship of the proletariat has become the dictatorship of the Party, even against the will of the proletariat itself. It is at this point that eleven other parties (whose operations had been suspended for varying periods of time during the Civil War) are formally abolished and opposition leaders jailed or exiled. The Communist Party becomes the sole organized political force.

This abolition, in the Party leaders' minds, paradoxically was made even more essential by the liberalization in economic policy expressed in the New Economic Policy (NEP) introduced in 1921 at the moment of the ban. A regression—according to the force of circumstances argument, an unavoidable regression, given the disastrous state of the economy—

to an economic structure that allowed a degree of freer commodity relations required—again unavoidably—a tightening of the political reins. The
Communists lived in fear of a new coalition of forces that might spring
up, nurtured by the NEP, if a ban were not declared. The effect on the
soviets was direct. By the end of 1922, Medvedev relates:

> The Soviets had lost all claim to be described as multi-party organizations.
> Within them, the Bolsheviks had now become not the dominant party, but
> the only one. . . . Where earlier the various parties had had to fight it out in
> the Soviets in order to gain influence and leadership, now these organs were
> limited to conducting the decisions of the Party leadership to the working
> masses.[31]

Lenin's bold cry of "all power to the Soviets" was forever altered; the
soviets had become what Stalin later termed "levers" or "drive belts"[32]
between the Party leadership and the masses.

And the logic of the ban on other parties led inevitably to a ban on
organized factions taking opposing views within the Party itself. This
inner-Party ban was put into effect as well at the 1921 Tenth Party Congress. It was accompanied by a secret resolution giving the Central Committee the right to expel all offenders, no matter what their rank in the
Party structure. Trotsky has argued that he and Lenin saw both the ban
on organized opposition outside the party and the inner-Party ban as
temporary expedients, required by the moment and clearly dangerous if
made permanent, as in fact they became. The moment of the inner-Party
ban marks yet a further station on the path to unabashed dictatorship: it
is the moment at which the dictatorship of the party—which has replaced
the dictatorship of the proletariat—becomes reduced once more, distilled
now into the dictatorship of the Party's ruling faction. We have moved a
long distance from the idealized Paris Commune.

The contradiction between dictatorship and democracy was illuminated sharply in 1921, first in the Kronstadt Rebellion, Lenin's "flash
which lit up reality better than anything else,"[33] and almost simultaneously
in the defeat of the Workers' Opposition. Both Kronstadt and the Workers'
Opposition represented in certain respects a return to the fundamental
values that had won Bolsheviks their support in the course of 1917. Yet
both, as the force of circumstance argument goes, had to be defeated if
the revolution were to survive; in the case of Kronstadt, this defeat would
be grimly bloody. In the Kronstadt rebels' somewhat confused call for
restoration of liberties, end to a Bolshevik monopoly of power, freedom
of speech and press for the anarchists and other left socialist parties, and
restoration of power to reinvigorated local soviets, the Communists faced
the first direct challenge to the newly articulated equation of the dictatorship of the Party and the dictatorship of the proletariat.

The replacement of the dictatorship of the proletariat with the dictatorship of the Party, and finally with the Party select, was reinforced by
the bureaucratic veneer that quite rapidly clouded every aspect of state

institutions. Here we have another distinct line of argument within the notion of inevitability; indeed, the force of circumstance argument comes heavily into play in a variety of explanations for the evolution in the Soviet Union of what Barrington Moore described as "the bureaucratic state par excellence of modern times."[34]

It was Lenin himself who first sought to explain what he described as a "bureaucratic distortion" with recourse to the force of circumstance argument. The state, he discovered after the Bolshevik seizure of power, could after all not be run by cooks; and the scarcity of personnel, compounded by the destruction of the Civil War years, required the employment of the old tsarist personnel, he argued. Until at least 1932, according to a Soviet account, up to 50 percent of the personnel in some sections of the administrative structure were left over from tsarist times.[35] The result of this, Lenin stated, was disastrous at the same time that it was unavoidable. Lenin's understanding of the problem is revealed in his 1922 report to the Fourth Congress of the Comintern:

> We took over the old machinery of state, and that was our misfortune. Very often this machinery operates against us. In 1917, after we seized power, the government officials sabotaged us. This frightened us very much, and we pleaded: "Please come back." They all came back, but that was our misfortune. We now have a vast army of government employees, but lack sufficient educated forces to exercise real control over them. In practice it often happens that here at the top, where we exercise political power, the machine functions somehow; but down below government employees have arbitrary control and they often exercise it in such a way as to counteract our measures. At the top, we have, I don't know how many, but at all events, I think, no more than a few thousand, at the outside several tens of thousands of our own people. Down below, however, there are hundreds of thousands of old officials whom we got from the tsar and from bourgeois society and who, partly deliberately and partly unwittingly, work against us.[36]

That this situation was, in Lenin's view, unavoidable comes through clearly in a message he sent in 1923 from his sickbed to the Central Committee, a message made public only in 1956:

> Conscience decrees that we describe as "our own" an apparatus which is alien to us throughout. It is a bourgeois and tsarist shambles which, in five years lacking any outside help and "preoccupied" as we have been with military affairs and the war against famine, we have had no opportunity to reform. ... Under these conditions, the derisory proportion of Soviet and Sovietized workers are going to drown in that sea of chauvinist Greater Russian swill, like flies in milk.[37]

To the end of his life, Lenin never abandoned this view of the origins of the Soviet bureaucracy.[38] Despite what Liebman describes as Lenin's "anguished awareness ... that the problem was real and growing," Lenin's answers, in the end, provided no solution. Rather, the creation, at his urging, of a People's Commissariat of Inspection to monitor the bureaucratic structure added yet another stratum to that structure.[39]

Trotsky picked up Lenin's argument and carried it on, trying thus to explain the seemingly endless generation of a privileged bureaucratic structure. In *The Revolution Betrayed,* he described the circumstances that inevitably perpetuated this structure. Trotsky located the "breeding ground" of bureaucracy in the continued, and to some extent deepened, scarcity that was to characterize Russia for decades after 1917. The Marxist ideal of the

> reduction of the state to functions of "accounting and control," with a continual narrowing of the function of compulsion . . . assumed at least a relative condition of general contentment. Just this necessary condition was lacking. No help came from the West. The power of the democratic Soviets proved cramping, even unendurable, when the task of the day was to accommodate those privileged groups whose existence was necessary for defense, for industry, for technique and science. In this decidedly not "socialistic" operation, taking from ten and giving to one, there crystallized out and developed a powerful caste of specialists in distribution.[40]

Since the problem was defined as the conscious or unconscious actions of functionaries at the local level, the solution was ever-increasing control by the center, an ever more intense absorption of local authority by central authority, which served in practice to strengthen the monopoly of power by the central party. Only the Communist Party itself was capable of insuring reliable control over the various sectors of the state apparatus. Key positions, then, had to be occupied or supervised by trusted Party members. Thus, Medvedev, employing a force of circumstance argument, explains how the upper strata of the state organization came to coincide ever more exactly with the upper strata of the Party. Given a one-party state, this inevitably meant the blending, until nearly indistinguishable, of the "supreme institutions" of the Communist Party and the "supreme institutions" of the state.[41]

There is a wide range of variants of the force of circumstance explanation of what happened in the Soviet Union, just as there are, of course, critiques of each of them. Lenin's views on the source of Soviet bureaucracy seem, for instance, definitively disproven by the continuing domination of these bureaucratic structures within the Soviet Union, as well as by the omnipresence of a "bureaucratic distortion" in other actually existing socialist societies with no tsarist heritage.

But taken as a whole, the inevitability or force of circumstance argument in its most common formulation carries with it enormous weight and logic. The story becomes virtually a Greek tragedy: the telling of it in this fashion is exactly what makes it so compelling. And it has other advantages: it allows us to locate, chronologically, the stations of the route along which any possibility of democracy in the first socialist revolution evaporated. It identifies and labels these climatic moments: the treaty of Brest-Litovsk, the horrible strife of the Civil War, the failure of revolution in the west, the 1920 trade union debate, the Kronstadt Rebellion and its suppression, the 1921 Tenth Party Congress. It basically takes the first two points raised at the beginning of this book as the fundamental sources of the problem of socialist democracy—the realities of dire emergency created by external and internal threat, and the realities of underdevelopment—and subsumes within their boundaries the explanation for the course of events in the U.S.S.R. And it is undeniable that these realities played a critical role in the mix that was to emerge. Certainly, it would be difficult to make a case that any revolution made in the name of socialism has *ever* faced more overwhelming circumstances, and faced them, moreover, without even the possibility of help from any other socialist country. But the force of circumstance cannot by itself account for what followed. Indeed, by itself it becomes almost a tautology.

This is the conclusion of the Hungarian theorist Istvan Mészáros, who forcefully points out that the arguments of inevitability intentionally cloud the issue in order to freeze the discussion and thus not allow for a critique that might lead future communist development in a different, more truly Marxist, direction:

> [S]ince the prevailing form of political rule must be maintained and therefore everything must remain as it is, the problematical notion of the 'force of circumstance' is used in the argument in order to assert categorically that it could not have been otherwise, and thus it is right that everything should be as it is. In other words, Marx's ideal is turned into a highly problematized reality, which in its turn is reconverted into a totally untenable model and ideal, through a most torturous use of the 'force of circumstance' as both inevitable cause and normative justification, while in fact, it should be critically examined and challenged on both accounts.[42]

Furthermore, the basic structure and thrust of the force of circumstance argument can readily be used to explain, and explain away, what has happened in every socialist revolution in this century. But the question—a key question for the whole of the socialist project—lingers stubbornly: could it have been otherwise? Could other choices have been made? If so, what were those choices and why were they not made?

In fact, as Tom Wohlforth and others have argued, the Bolsheviks constantly made choices throughout the period from November 1917 to 1921. The choices they made, that is, the actions they settled upon, built the structure of the single party state. Wohlforth notes a series of such choices: Lenin's opposition, in the immediate aftermath of the October Revolution, to government by a coalition of socialist parties; the collapse of the one coalition the Bolsheviks did enter into (with the Left Socialist Revolutionaries in the wake of the Brest-Litovsk Treaty); the policy of war communism itself and the imposition of the "Red Terror" in order to enforce it; the establishment of the Cheka and the pattern of its persecution of whole groups in response to individual actions. "Objective conditions," Wohlforth argues, "are not always so immutable as they are described. Human voluntary action interacts at every point with structure . . . the decisions at one point in time create the structure at the next point in time."[43]

But perhaps the most telling voice within this tradition of critique remains that of Rosa Luxemburg, the Polish Marxist and activist assassinated in Germany in 1919. The power of Luxemburg's argument is all the more tangible, given that Luxemburg fully accepted the notion of the dictatorship of the proletariat, seeing in it the vision of its liberating aspects emphasized by Marx. Luxemburg's commentary, at the very moment at which events were taking place, spoke most clearly of what that moment meant for the future. In her critique of the Russian Revolution, Luxemburg measured the reality of Bolshevik Russia against her understanding of the fundamental principles of Marxism. The comparison is revealing in a number of arenas; it is particularly sharp with relation to the questions of state institutions.

Luxemburg acknowledged the enormous difficulties the Bolsheviks faced, difficulties never envisioned by Marx, difficulties she said, forced them to take a "bushel of false steps. . . . It would be demanding something superhuman from Lenin and his comrades," she wrote, "if we should expect of them that under such circumstances they should conjure forth the finest democracy, the most exemplary dictatorship of the proletariat."[44] At the same time, she sounded a note of warning:

> Socialism, by its very nature cannot be decreed by ukase. . . . The negative, the tearing down, can be decreed; the building up, the positive, cannot. New territory. A thousand problems. Only experience is capable of correcting and opening new ways. Only unobstructed, effervescing life falls into a thousand new forms and improvisations, brings to light creative force, itself corrects all mistaken attempts.[45] . . . [T]he remedy which Trotsky and Lenin have found, the elimination of democracy as such, is worse than the disease it is supposed to cure; for it stops up the very living source from which alone can come the correction of all the innate shortcomings of social institutions."[46]

For Luxemburg, then, the Bolsheviks, within the constraints of their possibilities, had to unleash through broad participation the creativity of the populace if they were to give form to the "new territory." This, she argued, was exactly what they had not done. Her comments strike at the heart of the problem:

> In place of the representative bodies created by general popular elections, Lenin and Trotsky have laid down the Soviets as the only true representation of the laboring masses. But with the repression of political life in the land as a whole, life in the Soviets must also become more and more crippled. Without general elections, without unrestricted freedom of press and assembly, without a free struggle of opinion, life dies out in every public institution, becomes a mere semblance of life, in which only the bureaucracy remains as an active element. Public life gradually falls asleep, a few dozen party leaders of inexhaustible energy and boundless experience direct and rule. Among them, in reality, only a dozen outstanding heads do the leading and an elite of the working class is invited from time to time to meetings where they are to applaud the speeches of the leaders and to approve proposed resolutions

unanimously—at bottom, then, a clique affair—a dictatorship, to be sure—not the dictatorship of the proletariat, but only the dictatorship of a handful of politicians.[47]

And Luxemburg went farther; she noted the beginnings of crystallization, of enshrinement, of a method of procedure and of institutions fraught with problems. Indeed—and this was perhaps her most prescient moment—she understood that the legacy of the Russian Revolution might be its greatest tragedy:

> The danger begins ... when they make a virtue of necessity and want to freeze into a complete theoretical systems all the tactics forced upon them by ... fatal circumstances, and want to recommend them to the international proletariat as a model for socialist tactics.... They render a poor service to international socialism for the sake of which they have fought and suffered; for they want to place in its storehouse as new discoveries all the distortions prescribed in Russia by necessity and compulsion.[48]

The tradition to which Luxemburg gave shape has few voices to equal hers.

The Russian Revolution's bequest to twentieth century socialism was exactly "to make virtue out of necessity," to formalize into the "laws" of socialist transition the tragedy of its own demise. It was left to Joseph Stalin to use and abuse this contradictory and simplistic theoretical heritage, and the contradictory and complex history it helped to generate; in short, to finish this task. Here, in Stalin's incredible aphorisms alone, we can see the way in which official Marxism-Leninism managed to draw sustenance from one face of the Marxist legacy concerning the state in the transition, using it to justify killing off the other face—the emancipatory vision that informed it. And indeed, it was Stalin who did the butchering, literally and figuratively. Perry Anderson captures his accomplishment well in this regard when he writes:

> Marxism was largely reduced to a meaningless momento in Russia, as Stalin's rule reached its apogee. The most advanced country in the world in the development of historical materialism, which had outdone all Europe by the variety and vigor of its theorists, was turned within a decade into a semiliterate backwater, formidable only by the weight of its censorship and the crudity of its propaganda.[49]

In achieving this, Stalin drew undeniably from the elements of historical turmoil that had preceded him and from the particular formulations of the theoretical heritage that participants in this historical turmoil had made. Thus, Roy Medvedev points out that Lenin's assertion to Kautsky that dictatorship [is] power unlimited by law and "absolutely unconstrained by rules" found a ready popularizer in Stalin. This definition of unlimited power, says Medvedev, was a particular favorite of Stalin's: he quoted it perhaps more than any other single utterance by Lenin.[50] While Medvedev (and others) portray Lenin as a man who frequently admitted his own errors and who sought, with the termination of the Civil War, to limit the institutions of the state that had been employing power "bound by no laws," he points to what he understands to be Lenin's responsibility in what was to follow in the Soviet Union:

> By blurring the distinctions between concepts such as "the state," "political power" and "dictatorship", he made it much easier for his successors to extend their extraordinary and unlimited power indefinitely. In our country, as long as thirty years after the October Revolution, the government headed by Stalin went about its business unconstrained by any rule of law and in defiance of all constitutional guarantees and Soviet civil rights. Lenin's mistake was to keep on strengthening, needlessly, the already clearly defined meaning of dictatorship.[51]

But it was undoubtedly during the reign of Joseph Stalin that the system crystallized and hardened, and that the frozen dogmatism of official Marxism-Leninism took hold. The ideological baggage that Stalin added to the notion of the "laws" of the transition to socialism—doctrines such as "socialism in one country" and "capitalist encirclement"—provided him with further justification for strengthening and mummifying the imperfect structures he inherited from Lenin. These doctrines gave new form to the concept of socialism. No longer was it to be simply a "way state" in the path of the transition to communism: now it was defined as a stage in its own right, marked forever in a universal way by the particular form it took in the Soviet Union. Think, for example, of the implications of Stalin's axiom that as socialism is "achieved" (an idea, in itself, inconceivable for Marx, although at moments quite conceivable for Lenin), class conflict increases. The meaning of this reversal of Marxist theory is obvious: with the transition to socialism, state structures do not disappear; to the contrary, they must be strengthened, so that they have the capacity to deal effectively with increasing conflict and strife in society. And more than this: by employing the term dictatorship in its most coercive implications, such a theory justified the bloody reign of terror Stalin unleashed on the "enemies" of socialism, a terror conducted by state institutions created and invested with unlimited power. The tendencies that were indicated through the early 1920s now took absolute form: the 1930s saw the institutionalization of the bureaucratic structure and of the stunted form of participation that continued to function in the Soviet Union into the 1980s. Despite the repudiation of aspects of Stalinism by Khrushchev in the famous 1956 declaration and the campaign of "destalinization" that followed, it was clear, as Roy Medvedev and so many others argued well prior to the 1980s transitions, that socialism as it was practiced in this century was in key aspects defined by Stalin in the 1930s and 1940s in the Soviet Union.[52] And it was a definition that had been stripped bare of all but the rhetoric of its essential democratic kernel. The point here, of course, is not to assert that Stalin's ability to manipulate and distort a deeply flawed theoretical legacy led to the abuses that so characterized the system he effected. Certainly Stalin, like Lenin before him, molded that inheritance in response to needs he felt—whether ambition, self-aggrandizement, brutality, survival, external threats, and so on. But it remained true that the classical theoretical heritage concerning the transition provided only the most slippery footing for other socialists, then or later, to fully evaluate, situate, or identify the Soviet experience. That is, the very theoretical heritage that gave the socialist project its impulse permitted, or at least provided grounds for its gross distortion in the first country that sought to actualize it. It may be true that what happened in the Soviet Union was inevitable from whatever point of view that inevitability is traced. It may be true, as Luxemburg so persuasively argued, that the leaders of the Russian Revolution made virtue out of necessity. And it may as well be true that Stalin then enshrined that necessity and called it the dictatorship of the proletariat in its "finest form." Indeed, even if all this holds, Marxist theory as it dealt with the transition period played a congruent role in justifying its own transformation in the first society in which it took hold.

4

Cuba—The First Decade: Paternalist Centralization and Anarchic Decentralization

Bursting upon the world scene in 1959, the Cuban Revolution seemed to turn back the clock on the rhetoric and the pervasiveness of official Marxism-Leninism. The image of a straggly band of young men trooping out of the mountains[1] triumphantly across the island, mobbed everywhere they went by an entire population; the remarkable success of a young David in organizing this population to stand up to a formerly unbeatable Goliath; the informality of the Revolution[2] and the sense the Cubans gave of "inventing" it as they went along,[3] that is, rejecting any prescribed formulas of how they should proceed as well as the official language of these formulas—all this had an enormous impact. It renewed belief in the socialist project, in the *possibility* of a socialism framed around and upon the fullest democratic participation. The enormous mobilizations of the population—not only in military defense of the Revolution but in campaigns like the 1961 effort to put an end to illiteracy in Cuba—gave the strongest impulse to this belief, both inside and outside Cuba. It suggested that a people, through their own efforts, could accomplish anything. Here it seemed, were the beginnings of the realization of the vision of the people as subject, the people empowered. The Revolution, as Che Guevara said, was the "skeleton of total liberty," which now had to be given flesh and blood.[4]

Nor was the meaning and impact of the Cuban Revolution—both the manner of its occurrence and its subsequent career and occasionally astonishing achievements—lost upon the countries of the Third World. Here for the first time was a socialist revolution made in a small, peripheral country, lacking an adequate resource base, right under the nose of the great imperial power whose neocolony it had seemed doomed to remain. Indeed, the Cuban Revolution initiated a period of explicitly socialist (if nationalist as well) revolutionary struggles in countries throughout the Third World (particularly in Latin America and Africa), all of which looked to it or drew from it in some way. It is for these reasons that we turn at this point to an examination of the Cuban Revolution, for it seemed to pick up that abandoned emancipatory thread of the Marxist theoretical legacy and begin again to weave with it a new social fabric.

But if the Cubans wove anew, they were confronted with the other, dominant thread in their fabric, a thread that made no distinct patterns, a thread that was clearly twisted and that transmitted only vague and contradictory messages. And they were confronted as well with the formulas and prescriptions worked out over decades in the dogma of official Marxism Leninism to fill this void and mask its inadequacies. The chapters that follow trace the manner or rather manners in which the Cubans attempted to deal with, or ignore, this heritage. We argue that in the 1960s they took it at face value, and chose simply to ignore it, in effect, by not attempting to structure anything but transitory political forms. Certainly part of the reluctance to create structures had to do with constant external threat and the need for flexibility. Certainly part of it had to do with underdevelopment and scarcity, of resources as well as skills. But certainly, as well, another key ingredient was the Cuban leadership's reflection on the legacy they had inherited, in theory as well as practice. Their avoidance of structure represented a rejection of the rhetorical formulas of Marxism-Leninism, whose adoption, as Che Guevara said, might well destroy the very content and purpose of their Revolution.[5]

In this chapter we will trace the ever more extreme pattern of their efforts in the 1960s to avoid giving more than transitory structure to the participatory impulse that so infused the Revolution and will attempt to elucidate the traps into which these efforts eventually led them. The following chapters will examine the nature and degree of the Cuban effort in the period from 1970 to the present to reevaluate that engagement.

The first defining feature of the Cuban Revolution, and the state structures it set up on taking power, was the absence of much that any Marxist would consider essential. The Cuban Revolution, unlike any socialist revolution the world had to that point experienced, came to power without a party, without a coherently articulated ideology, and with a rather ragtag army, which numbered 3,000 people at its very height in the last weeks before seizing power. Moreover, it achieved power in a startlingly brief space of time. Fidel Castro and eighty-one men reached the shores of Cuba on a broken-down yacht in November 1956. By January 1959, they had overthrown the Batista dictatorship and had set up, by all accounts with the overwhelming support of the population, a revolutionary government.

That this was possible was largely due to the nature of state and society in Cuba preceding the Revolution.[6] Essentially, Castro and his adherents moved into what Nelson Valdés has labeled an institutional vacuum.[7] As Robin Blackburn so cogently argues in his 1963 article, "Cuba: Prologue to Revolution," it was the character of the enemy that "determined the condition of its overthrow."[8] The most striking feature of "the enemy," he asserts, was its fundamental weakness. From the time of Cuban independence, various factors conspired to undermine any coherent national ruling class from establishing itself and a state structure to serve it. Blackburn discerns that the Revolution could take power essentially without a party structure, without an army, without an articulated ideology, in an extremely brief time period exactly because there was no party structure, no strongly held ideology, no loyal army, and no powerful institutions that had to be countered or overthrown. He argues that the very absence of party and ideological structures among the revolutionaries was the "logical product of a prerevolutionary society which itself lacked any decisive institutions or ideological structures."[9] Let us then examine these factors in turn.

The pre-1958 Cuban state, distorted and corrupted, simply reflected in its form a class structure that had been equally distorted and corrupted by a history first of colonial and then of neocolonial domination. Nowhere were these distortions more apparent than within the bourgeoisie, the very class that gives form to the capitalist state in the Marxist model. The Cuban bourgeoisie was characterized above all by what Blackburn notes as its lack of coherence as a class. Its weakness was rooted fundamentally in its dependent nature, in particular its domination by U.S. capital, a domination reflected not only in the economy and, as we shall see, in increasingly corrupted political institutions, but in every aspect of the life of the people of Cuba.[10]

Blackburn refers to the numerical indications of this domination. By 1956, U.S. interests held 40 percent of the production of Cuba's major export product, sugar; 23 percent of all nonsugar interests; and 90 percent of telephone and electrical services.[11] But, as he points out, simple figures do not give a clear indication of the extent of control. There had been what he calls a virtual "confiscation" of the economy by the United States.[12] It was the interests and needs of an extraterritorial agent that determined the functioning of the economy, rather than the interests and needs of any stratum within Cuba itself. Thus, Blackburn reports, in 1956, sugar companies, which owned or controlled 188,000 *caballerías* of Cuban land, cultivated less than half of their land, in response to a U.S.-determined sugar quota. Yet at the same time that fertile land lay fallow, Cuba had to import nearly one-half of the beans and all the rice—in fact, a total of 25 percent of the food[13]—its population consumed (imported, of course, from the United States). In the area of minerals, Cuba had vast nickel reserves that went largely unexploited, given that they were owned and controlled by the U.S. government whose needs were such that nickel was kept in reserve.[14]

The range of actual operation for any national bourgeoisie was clearly and carefully circumscribed. Investment was, in practice, limited to areas in which such investment complemented, rather than competed, with U.S. investment. In effect, then, the bourgeoisie was a class that, in Blackburn's phrase, was structurally integrated within the economy of an alien power,[15] a class almost completely compromised by its collaboration with U.S. capital. The popular film, *The Godfather II*, captures at its most extreme the essence of this Cuban bourgeoisie in a scene of a Havana birthday celebration for a leading U.S. business/Mafia figure. United States and Cuban investors cut into slices a cake baked in the shape of the island itself, which they proceed to consume. But perhaps nothing captures the alienation of the Cuban bourgeoisie from their own national interests quite as well as their refusal, or inability, to react to the Castro threat. Their dependence upon the United States had reached such an extreme that they naturally turned to the United States to bail them out. They put up no self-defense; rather, they left en masse, expecting the United States to enter the fray momentarily, clear out the rebels, and permit them to return without any risk to their own lives. In this they were unlike their counterparts anywhere else in Latin America, all of who tended first to put up some form of fight and later call upon the United States in desperation.

The Cuban bourgeoisie was, then, neither a class "in itself" nor "for itself" in the Marxist sense of these terms. It was a class lacking any sense of cohesion and continuity.

And the state representing this class reflected well this fact. It was in many senses a parody of a state. For the first thirty-two years of Cuba's existence as an independent country, the structure and the major actors in the state apparatus were largely determined directly by the United States. A succession of presidents, from Estrada Palma to Menocal to Machado, were woven together and compromised by their economic ties to the United States and their political reliance on it. The Platt Amendment, which the United States had forced down the throats of the Cubans as a condition of their independence, gave the United States the right to intervene at any moment it was deemed necessary to protect the property and lives of its citizens, a right acted on no less than five times in the first twenty years of Cuba's independence.

In the years following the 1934 abrogation of the Platt Amendment, the pattern of corruption in regimes became ever more deeply ingrained. By the time Grau San Martín, who had been president for six months during the short-lived 1933 "Revolution," returned to power in 1944, this corruption had reached almost comical proportions. Officials in the Grau administration were responsible, according to all reports, for theft of the ceremonial emerald from the Chamber of the Cuban Capitolio, or Senate building.[15] During his rule, the reserve of nongovernmental pension and social security funds lodged within the Cuban Treasury disappeared. As a World Bank report delicately phrased it, "It is evident that the Cuban government had levied a forced loan on nongovernmental pension funds lodged with them, without the formal acknowledgement of the debt and without paying interest."[16] Blackburn cites *Time* magazine's account of the departure from Cuba of Minister of Education, Miguel Aleman:

> On the afternoon of October 10, 1948, he (Aleman) and some henchmen drove four Ministry of Education trucks into the Treasury building. All climbed out carrying suitcases. "What are you going to do, rob the Treasury?" joshed a guard. *"Quién sabe?* Who knows?" replied baby faced José Aleman. Forthwith his men scooped pesos, francs, escudos, lire, rubles, pounds sterling and about 19 million dollars in U.S. currency into the suitcases. The trucks made straight for the airfield where a chartered DC-3 stood waiting.[17]

The brother of Carlos Prio Socarrás, who followed Grau into office, was inextricably and openly involved in the thriving drug trade; his activities were "overlooked" by Prio's friend, the chief of police, Eufemio Fernandez. Thus, even before Batista's 1952 coup, Maurice Zeitlin concludes that "[p]arties and politicians associated with Cuba's 'Congress' were all but universally held in contempt. Parliamentary democracy as the legitimate mode of representative government and the bounds within which major conflicts ought to be resolved and government policy determined had lost its legitimacy, if indeed it ever existed."[18] This begins to provide an explanation for the ease with which Fulgencio Batista seized power in 1952, obviating the need for the election to be held that year. Batista was no slouch in keeping up political traditions: he personally received some three million dollars for permitting the U.S. Mafia to run casinos in Havana, at that time the Mafia's only operation outside U.S. boundaries.[19] And the Batista regime compounded this corruption with a level of illegality and brutality that gave the deathblow to whatever legitimacy and authority the governing structure had retained. The violence—a response to the persistence and popularity of Fidel's rebels—marked the transition of Batista's rule, in Cuban parlance, from a *dictablanda* to a *dictadura.**

In this transition, the regime spelled its own doom. In Blackburn's caricature, Batista's rule is perhaps best symbolized by the national and international criminals who staffed the power apparatus during its last years of existence.[20] They included for instance, Rolando Masferrer, a "senator" who ruled Santiago as his private domain, maintaining a personal army of 2,000 men known as *los tigres de Masferrer. Los tigres* were supervised by gangsters who split the province of Oriente into districts, collecting spoils from gambling, prostitution, and extortion. By the end of his rule, Batista had effectively destroyed whatever remained of Cuban political institutions. Nothing—not the Congress, not the constitution, not electoral politics, not the judiciary, not any political party or trade union—remained undenigrated and respected. The state, in Lenin's terms, did not have to be smashed; it had in essence disintegrated.

---

*From a "soft" to a "hard" dictatorship.

If the institutional vacuum explains the speed with which Castro and his rebel band could take power, it defines, at least in part, the perimeters of the situation facing the rebel leaders on seizing power. Without the problem of inherited structures from the former regime, they were, in theory at least, free to mold state structures to meet their needs and their vision. Yet essentially they created nothing, or at least nothing intended to have any permanence. The process of giving institutional shape to the revolution began only a full decade after its accession to power. The question we must ask ourselves is why?

The Cuban leadership itself gave the official answer to this question when they initiated the process of institutionalization more than ten years later. Raúl Castro, at the 1974 closing session of the training course for delegates newly elected to serve in the then-experimental state structure, "Popular Power," explained the absence of serious efforts to institutionalize in structural terms. He argued, first, that such institutionalization was neither "urgent" nor "vital" nor "decisive" given the early needs of the Revolution. Indeed, he asserted, any institutionalization might have hindered efforts to respond to these needs. Given the constant internal and external challenges to the system,[21] it was essential, Raúl reasoned, to have a single structure in which all power, legislative, executive and administrative, was concentrated, a structure that would have the flexibility to make decisions without any delay.

In addition, he asserted, the material conditions for institutionalization were absent, at least until the late sixties. He was talking here not only about the material scarcity, which would doom any popular structure to failure, but about the scarcity of experienced cadre and of organizations that had the strength and durability to sustain such a structure. He argued that when, by the end of the sixties, such scarcity (at least in terms of human resources) had eased, the 1969–70 drive to harvest ten million tons of sugar (to which we shall return in detail) absorbed all energies, to the extent that institutionalization would have been impossible. Raúl went one step further: he argued, in essence, that as long as the struggle between classes continued, as long as the old socioeconomic forces were not thoroughly eradicated and new relations of production operative, new political structures would fail. For the majority of the Cuban leadership, then, according to Raúl, overwhelming external threat, scarcity, and their ramifications largely dictated the decisions they made—or left in abeyance—with regard to state structure in the 1960s. Raúl mentioned, finally, and somewhat as an aside, the fact that some of those in leadership positions erred in not understanding the need for an institutional framework to give substance to a new brand of revolutionary democracy.[22]

K. S. Karol, five years before Raúl Castro laid out this explanation, focused a great deal of attention on the absence of this institutional framework.[23] And his assessment of its roots centered firmly around this lack of understanding of those in leadership positions of the *need* for institutionalized revolutionary democracy.[24] It is true that at least one member of the leadership, Che Guevara, spoke frequently from the beginning of this need. For instance, in a 1961 interview with Maurice Zeitlin, he noted: "Our task is to enlarge democracy within the revolution as much as possible ... We feel that the government's chief function is to assure channels for the expression of the popular will."[25] And again, in his sketchy and suggestive essay, "Man and Socialism in Cuba," which stands as probably the single most important ideological statement of the Cuban Revolution, Che wrote that it is true that "the institutionalization of the revolution has still not been achieved. We are seeking something new that will allow a perfect identification between the government and the community as a whole."[26]

In a sense, Che Guevara, above all others—at least in the degree of his attention to the matter—seemed aware of the need for democratic participation in decision making and for the institutions or arenas that would guarantee this participation. It was widely reported that during the famous all-night meetings of the Ministry of Industry, Che frequently pointed out, critically, the failure of the industries to engage their workers' active participation in the functioning of their various enterprises.[27] Despite such assertions, Karol points over and over again to the fact that, by and large the entire leadership, including Che, left all questions concerning popular participation in abeyance. He points to the crucial 1961 National Convention on Production, called by Che in his capacity as Minister of Industry, which Karol sees as a natural arena for the discussion of these issues: "during the three days of the Convention ... no one so much as raised the question of popular democracy or workers' control."[28] He cites the fact that during the entirety of the "great economic debate" concerning moral versus material incentives—again a likely context—the issue of popular democracy never surfaced: "Neither Che nor his opponents had come to grips with the problem of political power in, and the political organization of, all those societies where centralized or reformist experiments in planning and economic management were taking place."[29] Karol is, then, arguing that the Cubans, by skirting the crucial issue of participation in decision making, had accepted what Karol labels certain "myths" imported from the U.S.S.R. having to do with the nature of popular representation in a socialist state, myths built upon the notion that workers' interests were identical with those of the state and that a vanguard could, with justice, interpret these interests best. It was as if, Karol reasons, " 'Soviet power' had become a reality and the whole problem no longer concerned them."[30]

Karol's perceptions hit close to the mark, at one level (the leadership's view of itself as the guiding force). He fails, however, to understand the other sources of the Cuban leadership's refusal to set up anything other than temporary institutions. Nor do the "cubanologists"—those mainstream academics whose work has dominated the study of Cuba in the West—get any closer to the mark when they argue, picking up on Karol's conclusions, that the Cubans' understanding of the issue was indeed shaped by their Soviet "mentors."[31] Rather, the leadership's refusal to institutionalize was derived from two interlinked considerations. The first of these centers on a conscious, and at moments articulated, rejection of Soviet-style state structures. This rejection is implicit in Che Guevara's explanation, in *Man and Socialism in Cuba,* that while some experiments "gradually creating institutionalization" have been undertaken, the Revolution was not in a "hurry." His next statement that "we have been greatly restrained by the fear that any formal aspect might make us lose sight of the ultimate and most important revolutionary aspiration: to see man freed from alienation,"[32] reflects clearly his belief that elsewhere in the socialist world, just this aspiration *had* been lost.

The second consideration involves the single most primary factor influencing the Cuban revolutionary leadership from its earliest moments: the central importance of unity.[33] For Fidel Castro, unity stood above *everything* else. It was the major lesson he derived from the experience a century earlier of José Martí. Martí, with patience and persistence, managed to merge historically divided entities into a Cuban revolutionary force that eventually ended Cuba's colonial status. At the same time, it was Martí's failure to end civilian/military separation and to unify this dual jurisdiction that allowed the entry point for subsequent U.S. domination. None of this was lost on Fidel Castro (and indeed, one can see the impact of this lesson on Che Guevara's demand in Bolivia for military and political control, against the wishes of the Bolivian Communist Party,[34] and on the Nicaraguan Sandinista junta, which sought to combine both military and political authority). Unity was also the lesson Fidel learned from the 1933 revolt and its aftermath, when revolutionary groups splintered into terrorist action organizations.

In Castro's mind, unity was the indispensible element in forging a new Cuba able to withstand the enormous internal and external threats that would face the country in the aftermath of the victory of the Revolution. The revolt against Batista, much like the more recent revolt that overthrew the long-standing dictatorship of Anastasio Somoza in Nicaragua, was a nationalist effort that deposed a decadent and crumbling state structure that had maintained itself by corruption and brute force. In Cuba, however, class war broke out in full intensity immediately with the revolutionaries' accession to power. And the opposing classes could find strong and active support in the United States; at the time of the Revolution's triumph, only five years had passed since the CIA openly sponsored and organized the overthrow of the legitimately elected reformist Arbenz government in nearby Guatemala.[35]

It was this requirement for unity that kept Fidel from calling a national plebescite or national election in the first years of the Revolution. Karol tells us how delegates from Eastern Europe ceaselessly urged Fidel to do so during his 1960 visit to the United Nations and were baffled at his reluctance. Indeed, by every estimate—even those of the CIA and the State Department—Fidel would have won an overwhelming victory in any such election.[36] Why then did he not hold elections? It is true that in 1959 Cuba, elections did not have the finest reputation; for years Cubans, with good reason, had connected elections with corruption. "Batista was elected, no?" responded one worker to Maurice Zeitlin in the course of his 1962 interviews with workers in different factories.[37] In the same vein, it was reported that when Fidel marched into Santiago, in eastern Cuba, in the aftermath of Batista's hurried departure from the island, he was booed only once, when he spoke of the resuscitation of a regime centered around a representative assembly.[38] Clearly, these anecdotes confirm the disillusionment and cynicism toward governing structures that Cubans had acquired in the years preceding the Revolution. But the most fundamental reason no such elections were held had to do precisely with this question of unity. Jean Paul Sartre asked Fidel about the question of elections in 1960: "It (a referendum) would be such a triumph and it would nail shut so many hostile mouths that I don't understand why you should deprive yourselves of it." Castro's answer was clear and revealing: "For one single reason. We don't want to pay for the triumph of the revolutionaries by wiping out the revolution. What is the meaning of our group? The unity of views, practical union. At present, what would an elected assembly be? The mirror of our discord."[39]

It was this drive for unity above all else that was largely to determine Castro's decisions vis-à-vis the structuring of institutions at least until the late 1960s. It was a drive moulded by both immediate needs and dangers and by reflection upon the lessons of a century of revolutionary struggle in Cuba. In the manner in which it was defined by the leadership and the way in which it was to determine subsequent events, the overriding necessity for unity largely obscured whatever impetus existed among sections of the leadership to begin to come to terms with the conundrum of Marxism: institutionalized democratic forms.

There is another factor, a trait not often thought of in relation to Castro, that played a central role in his strategy during the first few years of the Revolution: patience. Haydée Santamaría argued that had the United States not forced Fidel's hand, he would have lived with the bourgeoisie for twenty years. He was not a man in a hurry. Rather, his strategy was to let things mature, to control their timing, and to channel their course. If Marx's genius was in synthesizing ideas and Lenin's in action, Fidel is nothing if not a brilliant strategist. Thus, for instance, Fidel chose the moment of the Bay of Pigs attack to announce that the Cuban Revolution was a socialist revolution. History, Fidel once declared, "is a subproduct of action."[40]

The importance of the factor of unity and the strategy of patience can be seen in the destruction, or at least the dismantling, of the potential forces competing for power in the years immediately following Batista's ignominious departure. In essence, what Fidel did was to let each possible contending group play itself out and vanquish itself. Thus he himself did not immediately take a formal place in the new government. Rather, the major positions passed to those leading members of the Cuban bourgeoisie who had worked against Batista and who retained a great deal of respect, that is, who were seen as "clean" and "honest." Manuel Urrutia, the judge at Fidel's 1953 trial who had found him innocent, became president; José Miró Cardona took the post of prime minister;* and Felipe Pazos, an economist of international repute and good credentials in Western financial circles, took command of the economy. These people, who carried prestige from the past, represented the first threat to a unified Fidelista rule; thus they were the first who had to be eliminated. Fidel set the stage for them to eliminate themselves. Frightened by the new import laws, their own class interests threatened by the drastic measures the Revolution quickly had to take—land reform, Soviet petroleum processing, they placed themselves increasingly against Castro. The showdown came when Castro resigned as prime minister in protest against the government he permitted to take power, and the people in a massive demonstration "chose" Fidel, thereby abandoning the last of the bourgeoisie, the "clean bourgeoisie."

There were then three other groups contending for power, each a participant, to a greater or lesser degree, in the struggle against Batista: the Revolutionary Directorate, the P.S.P. (the old Cuban Communist Party), and the Twenty-sixth of July Movement. Of the three, the Revolutionary Directorate was the most easily and quickly diffused.

The Revolutionary Directorate was a university-based group whose legitimacy and credentials derived from the 1930s. It had carried on extensive underground work against the Batista dictatorship, including the March 1957 attack on the Presidential Palace, and had in 1958 set up a second guerilla front in the Escambray Mountains. The Directorate, following a time-honored practice in Cuban revolts, occupied the Presidential Palace immediately following Batista's exit on New Year's eve, 1958. Fully armed, with this seizure they were declaring themselves in charge. Fidel meanwhile passed triumphantly through the island to Havana, gathering a nation behind him in the course of an eight-day march. In his famed address upon arrival in Havana, held at the notorious Campo Colombia (a Batista army stronghold, soon to be converted into a school), complete with a white dove that landed serendipitously on his shoulder, Fidel took the steam out of the Directorate's demand for arms. He asked the gathered crowd, *"Armas para qué?"* (Arms for what?) *"Para luchar contra quién?* (To fight against whom?) . . . I always thought that all of us ought to be united in a single organization . . . then the people could express their wishes through a vast and powerful body which would avoid the terrible consequences of the proliferation of revolutionary groups."[41] Castro's suc-

---

*Fidel replaced him in February 1959; Miró Cardona was appointed ambassador to Spain. Osvaldo Dorticós replaced Urrutia.

cess on this score was notable and immediate: the Directorate leadership left the palace, dissolved itself, and applied for membership in the Fidelista Twenty-sixth of July Movement.

The old Cuban Communist Party, the P.S.P. (Partido Socialista Popular), was the next major potentially independent force. It had reversed its earlier refusal to cooperate with Fidel (the PSP newspaper, *Hoy,* had dismissed the Fidelista attack on the Moncada Fortress in 1953 as "putschist" and another example of the "punk gangsterism"[42] that characterized the Cuban opposition) only in August 1958, thereafter joining forces with the Fidelistas. Many—most prominently, Theodore Draper—argued that it was P.S.P. cadre who came to dominate the administrative hierarchy of postrevolutionary Cuba, a clear indication to Draper of Castro's subservience to the Soviet Union.[43] And, indeed (although for far different reasons than Draper puts forth) in the period after April 1961, that is, after the Bay of Pigs invasion and Castro's declaration that the Cuban Revolution was a socialist revolution, members of the old P.S.P. did come to monopolize positions of leadership and power throughout the higher reaches of the administration. This interlude, known as the "mini-Stalinist" period in Cuba, came to a crashing halt in 1962. The rise and fall of the old P.S.P. gives us fresh evidence of the pattern: again, Fidel, far from being used, uses a potentially competing group (the P.S.P.) for his own strategic purposes, allowing it to play itself out to a chorus of popular protest from all sides as it self-destructs.

The mini-Stalinist period saw the P.S.P. leadership appoint only its own people to office, to the exclusion of practically all the Twenty-sixth of July Movement leaders, including such beloved figures as Haydée Santamaría. With some exceptions—people it believed it could use—the P.S.P. denounced the Twenty-sixth of July people as "bourgeois" and unreliable, and indeed, reinterpreted the Revolution itself, arguing that it was not the guerrilla nor the underground city movement organized by the Twenty-sixth of July Movement, but rather the January 1959 strike, in which the P.S.P. had the major hand, that was responsible for the victory. In the course of these actions, the P.S.P. succeeded in so thoroughly discrediting itself and alienating people that when Fidel made his two famous speeches denouncing sectarianism in March of 1962, they were greeted with overwhelming popular approval.[44] The P.S.P., too, had played itself out.

What was left was the primary group—Fidel's group—the Twenty-sixth of July Movement. And it was exactly this group—and in particular the rebel army itself, the strongest among the weak—that moved in to fill the power vaccuum left by a state structure that had totally crumbled. Nelson Valdés argues:

> With the major revolutionary organizations suffering from weak cadres and lack of a well-defined program or national influence . . . only the Rebel Army had unity of purpose, a strong command structure, and experienced cadres . . . The Rebel Army had numerous assets. It could point to revolutionary experience produced in battle, a national leader who was marvelously per-

suasive and known by everyone, a disciplined vertical hierarchy of command with political homogeneity, an almost complete monopoly over weapons, and control over the key military and political posts in the country.... Moreover, the Rebel Army also possessed a most important element—support of the majority of the people. For these reasons the Rebel Army constituted the most relevant force in the country.[45]

Karol extends Valdés's assessment of the Rebel Army to the Twenty-sixth of July Movement as a whole. He disagrees, however, with his conclusion. Karol argues that, much like the P.S.P. and the Directorate, the Twenty-sixth of July Movement (including the Rebel Army) itself disappeared in the form it had existed on December 31, 1958:

> All the conditions seemed ripe for the transformation of the July 26th Movement into one vast body capable of absorbing not only the Directorio, the P.S.P. and the remnants of other revolutionary groups, but also a large number of sympathizers new to the political struggle. All the conditions, that is, save one: Fidel's wish to bring this about.[46]

It is Karol's argument that Fidel essentially destroyed the Twenty-sixth of July Movement. And it is fair to say that, as a movement, it was destroyed in the course of the mini-Stalinist period. When Fidel reassembled the most loyal of his followers after his famous March 13 antisectarian speech, he was reassembling something that was no longer the Twenty-sixth of July Movement. In 1959, the Twenty-sixth of July Movement as a whole shared with the rest of Cuba a general antipathy toward communism. In 1963, the individuals from the Twenty-sixth of July Movement who joined Fidel in the newly organized PURSC (United Party of the Socialist Revolution) joined as individuals, and as Communists. Thus, potentially sharply competing forces were dispersed, filtered, and brought together again in a different form, characterized above all by the absence of division and competition.

It was Fidel Castro, most fundamentally, who constituted the center of the drive for unity and the symbol of that unity. Che Guevara explained it this way: "The first, the most original and perhaps the most important (single factor to render the Cuban Revolution so exceptional) is this natural force named Fidel Castro Ruz."[47] Indeed, some of the most consistently loyal Fidelistas resuscitated an old Marxist controversy concerning the importance of individuals in effecting social change: thus Armando Hart's comment to Karol, "You in Europe have a tendency to underestimate the role in history of great personalities."[48] Or Haydée Santamaría's recollection of her thoughts in prison following the failed Moncada attack after seeing both her brother and her fiancee murdered: "If Fidel lives ... the Revolution lives."[49]

No observer of the Cuban revolutionary process can ignore the centrality of the figure of Fidel Castro as it loomed over the trajectory of the Revolution during the 1960s. Those sympathetic to the revolutionary process described this centrality in one way. James O'Connor, in his *Origins of Socialism in Cuba,* labeled Fidel "the institution,"[50] and thus comes very close to identifying the nature of the Cuban state in the 1960s. Richard Fagen, in an article attempting to deal with the question of Fidel's charisma, wrote that "there is no lack of reports which mention that in the early stages of the Cuban Revolution, Castro was regarded by large segments of the population as the heaven-sent saviour of the nation."[51] These accounts were echoed in the popular reaction to Fidel's declaration on April 17, 1961, that the Revolution was socialist: "If Fidel is a socialist, so are we"[52]; or in the cries of the returned literacy campaign workers in 1961: "*Comandante en Jefe* (Commander in Chief), what next?"[53]

Interpretations of Fidel Castro's centrality naturally took on a different tone among observers less sympathetic to the Revolution. The spectrum, to a fairly consistent degree, corresponded to the degree of hostility of those commenting. Valdés correctly pointed out that all these commentaries tended to focus upon some version of a cultural or psychological interpretation.[54] Following Theodore Draper's early work, the largest number of critics focused on Fidel's "thirst for power."[55] The problem with this interpretation is that there was *never* during this first decade of the Revolution, a serious challenge to Fidel's position, or a serious evaluation that denied his substantial and sustained popularity. Others stressed his "personal magnetism"[56]—that indescribable and singularly ahistorical characteristic of charisma. Still others emphasized the historical "need" of Cubans for a strong leader.[57]

Whichever of these factors might have been relevant, for us it was the overwhelming importance given to unity that explains Fidel's centrality. Yet this consideration, as Karol pointed out, did not inevitably lead to a state structure in which the only institution of any permanence was Fidel himself. Here again, he pointed to what he saw as the underlying misunderstanding of Marxist theory and goals concerning the state that has characterized the Cuban Revolution:

> It is a sad but undeniable fact that Fidel's "infinite concern" for unity did not give rise to the least attempt to create a collective leadership or to discover ways and means of establishing a truly democratic rank-and-file organization. Neither interested him, not because he was afraid of losing his personal grip on the country (there was no one to dispute that) or because he had reason to be afraid of the rank and file (he was more popular than ever) but simply because the problem of the relation between the revolutionary vanguard and the masses, or of the role of the vanguard in arousing the class conscience of the proletariat, passed him by.

Karol continued:

> The enthusiastic acclaim of the masses and the devotion of most of his companions combined to strengthen Fidel in the conviction that he alone was able to lead his people forward. It was this conviction and not his personal vanity that persuaded him to continue governing the country, always on a temporary basis, in the same way that he had previously led the July 26th Movement.[58]

If Fidel were "the institution," "the only executive organ which functioned perfectly from beginning to end,"[59] the central occupant of a decision-making apparatus that consisted of a Council of Ministers appointed by and dependent on Fidel, what then was the relationship between the state and Cuban society? Following Jean Paul Sartre during the 1960s, Western European and American intellectual sympathizers with the Revolution described with amazing naivete the relationship between Castro and the Cuban people as "direct democracy in action."[60] What exactly did this "direct democracy" look like? Again, it was Che Guevara who gave it its most suggestive definition. In *Man and Socialism in Cuba*, he wrote:

> We are using the almost intuitive method of keeping our ears open to the general reactions in the face of the problems that are posed. Fidel Castro is a master at this; his particular mode of integration with the people can only be appreciated by seeing him in action. In the big public meetings, one can observe something like the dialogue of two tuning forks whose vibrations summon forth new vibrations each in the other. Fidel and the mass begin to vibrate in a dialogue of growing intensity which reaches its culminating point in an abrupt ending crowned by our victorious battle cry. What is hard to understand for anyone who has not lived the revolutionary experience is that close dialectical unity which exists between the individual and the mass, in which both are interrelated, and the mass, as a whole composed of individuals, is in turn interrelated with the leaders.[61]

This "direct democracy," or what Che called the "dialectical unity between the individual and the mass," took essentially two forms. The first was the huge rallies held in the Plaza of the Revolution during the first decade of the Revolution, at which Fidel spoke, sometimes for hours, sometimes to literally millions of people. The second form was Fidel's constant presence, his endless pilgrimages through the island, promoting the feeling that he was everywhere, dealing with sometimes the most trivial of individual or village problems. Both elements were facilitated by the small size of Cuba, the relative homogeneity of its people, and its extensive system of communication, ironically a by-product of U.S. domination. Let us take up each of these forms in turn.

The famous—and in some circles infamous—mass rallies have been seen by some less-than-sympathetic observers as classic examples of Castro's despotism. Thus *Life Magazine,* in a 1961 report about one of these rallies, assessed Fidel as an "insane egomaniac" and the shouts of the crowd for "*Fidel, Fidel*" as equivalent to the "*seig heils*" that punctuated Hitler's rallies in Nazi Germany.[62] Yet various aspects of these gatherings belie such an interpretation. First, the general range of content of the Castro's speeches was extraordinary. The lengthy "harangues," as they were generally referred to in the U.S. press, often dealt with the most detailed accounts of agricultural developments, even down to the problems in and results of experiments in crossing hybrid cows. Visitors during the sixties frequently reported with amazement the detailed knowledge of Cuban farmers concerning these experiments in the remotest parts of the island. Nor was the subject matter thus confined: we have only to remember Castro's reply to the first O.A.S. condemnation of Cuban policy in 1960. He literally called for a National Assembly of the People of Cuba and, to an estimated one million people (one-eighth of the population of the island), read his defiant reply, a document that would come to be known as the "Havana Declaration."[63] Second, what is on one level most fascinating about the early speeches and rallies was, for lack of a better phrase, the frequency and nature of "audience participation," a participation virtually unthinkable in any contemporary political structure anywhere in the world. Listen to Lee Lockwood's account of a speech Castro gave in the pouring rain in the Sierra Maestra town of Uvero to a gathering of farmers and rural workers:

> Castro is talking about plans to increase the use of machines to cut the sugar cane in future harvests. A combine can cut thirty times as much as a *machetero* can. But they should not be afraid of losing their jobs. The combines, he says, will make more wealth and more jobs for all. There is a commotion in the front row. A Negro *machetero* with a black cigar is shouting, trying to get Castro's attention.
> Fidel pauses, unruffled. . . .
> FIDEL: Right *viejo*? You are here from the Sierra, no?
> MAN: Yes.
> FIDEL: And when did you come here, in what year?
> MAN: In 1925, Fidel. I was a cane cutter. I used to cut cane on the plantation of your papa.
> FIDEL: Really? Well, things are different now, you know. Now it's a people's farm. (The crowd laughs.) Anyway, if you worked for my father, then you helped to pay for my college education! (More laughter, followed by applause.)[64]

Or during a large mass rally on December 20, 1959:

> FIDEL: What's going on? (interrupting his speech and directing himself at someone shouting in the gathered audience.) If this man has a problem and wants to discuss it, he should come here and discuss it. I don't know what kind of problem he has, but if he has some problem and wants to discuss it, let's discuss it here.

The man explains that he has opened a barbershop and has some problems.

> FIDEL: Well, you opened a barbershop, and what problems do you have with the barbershop?
> MAN: Well, I was too close to another barbershop. They have exploited me. I opened this barbershop with the government because it is a revolutionary government.
> FIDEL: Do you think it's correct that you as a citizen with the same worries as the rest of the people, about their destiny, about their country, about the great problems we have right now should interrupt this meeting to come up here to present your own particular problem? People allow themselves to be confused, worry about their personal problems, and I

understand that everybody has their great personal preoccupations, but I believe that we Cubans should forget a little bit about our own exclusively personal problems, because, as the saying goes, "a swallow does not make a spring." The strength of the individual is in the whole—that is the strength we have.... We cannot be putting our hands in our pockets, for a handout, each time we encounter an individual problem. The nation as a whole will solve the problems of the individual.[65]

It is, further, a rather fascinating structural exercise to observe the physical relationship between Fidel and the assembled peoples at these rallies in existing photos. There was, in the early years, an extraordinary closeness, both in vertical and in horizontal terms. Fidel addressed/talked to those gathered not from on high, but at a surprisingly parallel level, and not from an enormous distance, but at a surprisingly close vantage. It is as if in the physical closeness, the absence of spatial differentiation, Fidel is trying concretely to give substance to Che's imagery.

The second form of Cuban "direct democracy," Castro's peregrinations around the island, again was widely commented on by visitors during the 1960s. His ability to seem to be everywhere at once was of course, much facilitated by the size of the island and the limited number of its inhabitants. Nonetheless, the accounts of his constant visits lent a certain color and vividness (if not accuracy) to the notion of "direct democracy." In his 1961 account of his visit to Cuba, Jean-Paul Sartre recounted an afternoon's drive around the island with Castro, a drive that, he told us, "for the first time" made him understand the meaning of "direct democracy." The first stop, he related, was a visit to a new tourist facility, which was devoid of tourists:

All three (workers at the facility) assured us with all the power of faith that they expected workers (tourists) that very day. "Many?" "A few." Castro got a little gloomy. He wanted to see everything, including the towels. He showed us, but it was his way of looking. Finally he offered us some soft drinks.

Hardly had he wet his lips with his glass than he put it down and said, in a loud voice, "This drink is warm." He remained silent, his mouth parted. He was somber, as if holding back his anger, and I understood suddenly what he was thinking: "How could they enjoy coming if you don't give them proper service?"

Nevertheless, the women (serving) did not appear to be disturbed. They saw his displeasure yet kept their manner unreserved, as if they sensed that he wasn't addressing them.

"Then there are no frigidaires?" asked Castro.

"Well, as a matter of fact, yes," said the waitress. "But they don't work."

"Have you told the person in charge?"

"Naturally, last week. And it isn't a big job, you know," she added familiarly. "An electrician would have about two hours of work fixing it."

"And no one has undertaken the repair?"

She shrugged her shoulders. "You know how it is," said she ... She let it be seen, by her tone, by her smiles, by a shrug of the shoulders, that she was without illusion. And the Prime Minister—who was also the rebel leader—

in expressing himself before her without circumlocution, calmly invited her to join the rebellion.

"He is an agitator," thought I for the first time.

"Show this to me," he said. She showed him the refrigerator. There was a bad contact, according to her; that was the cause of everything. He carefully inspected the appliance; he came near to taking it apart. When finally he turned back to the woman, he spoke severely to her, but it was obvious to all that this severity was not addressed to her.

"A negligence like this would be nothing, it wouldn't hurt anyone to have warm drinks or even to be thirsty; but it reveals a lack of revolutionary consciousness. If we don't do the maximum for the people at each beach, the people will know that we're not anxious enough to have them come, and they won't come. And I say that if someone doesn't do all he can all the time—and more—it's exactly as if he did nothing at all." He closed with this growled sentence: "Tell your people in charge that if they don't take care of their problems, they will have problems with me."[66]

Or this account of Lockwood's:

Now a very old *campesino* is helped through the crowd into the circle around Fidel . . .

"Fidel, you don't remember me because I am an old man. But I remember you."

"Now just a minute. I do seem to remember a very old man, not such a bad man. He lived in a shack by the river. But you couldn't be that one—he would be dead by now."

"No Fidel, it's me, it's me! You remember everything, even my house."

"Really, you are the same? Well, I am glad to see you alive and so energetic, *viejo*. Tell me, what can I do for you?"

"Fidel, I want a pension."

"What, at your age you don't have a pension?"

"No, Fidel. They wouldn't give it to me."

"Don't tell me! Well," Castro says, taking out a pencil and notebook, "I am going to look into this personally. Give me your name and all the details." The old man gives the information. He does not know how to spell his name.

"All right, *viejo*. But tell me, since I see that you have your health, and are living well enough, what do you need a pension for?"

"Ah, Fidel. I want it so I can start a little business with cocoa trees. They grow very well in this soil."

"What? At your age you want to go into business with cocoa trees? What madness! Listen, how old are you, *viejo*?"

"Only eighty-seven, *Comandante*."

"Eighty-seven? What sheer madness! *Viejo*, don't you know that at eighty-seven you should be spending your remaining years in peace instead of going into business for yourself? That's what a pension is for."

"But I will live many more years yet, Fidel. I feel very strong. I am all alone. I must have something to do. I don't think I will live with any more women."

"Help! No more, no more! You will have your pension, *viejo*. Ay, these *campesinos*, going into business when they are nearly ninety. They are never going to understand what socialism is all about, that's for sure."[67]

We can draw a great deal from these and endless other anecdotes. There was, as Karol reported, an amazing "closeness" between Fidel and the people: "Wherever he goes, he tries to suggest reforms and remedies." He was clearly approachable and approached. And there was, as all visitors reported, an enormous concern for even the smallest details—what Karol called "a plethora of sheer trifles,"[68] and what Sartre identified as evidence that Fidel was not only "the man of the smallest detail. Or rather,... in each circumstance he joined the detail and the whole inseparably."[69]

But if this energy, this level of communication and involvement is impressive, it gives, as well, the clearest indication of one of the major characteristics of Fidel's form of "direct democracy": an extreme and firmly implanted paternalism. Sartre himself, meaning to underline his over-whelmingly positive impression of Fidel, inadvertently captured this deep strain of paternalism. He tells us of the end of his day's journey with Fidel:

> Now, in the sweet gray of evening, I saw his large shoulders in front of me. I told myself that I had to question him myself. I asked him, "All those who ask, no matter what they ask, have the right to obtain...."... He puffed on his cigar and said loudly, "Yes. Because demands, in one way or another, represent needs!..."
>
> "And if they asked you for the moon," I said, sure of the answer.
>
> He puffed on his cigar, verified that it was out, put it down and turned toward me. "If someone asked me for the moon, it would be because someone needed it," he answered me.... "Thanks to us they dare to discover their needs."[70]

The phrase that visitors heard over and over again in Cuba among those discontent over something, "If Fidel only knew," gives a good indication of the level of popular internalization of what can only be described as a deeply paternalistic structure.

There were obvious and unavoidable weaknesses, even in their own terms, in what the Cubans and foreign sympathizers called "direct democracy" during the decade of the 1960s. Clearly, it was difficult—indeed impossible—for one man to be everywhere at the same time. Castro's familiarity with the problems of his country, his concern for detail, his constant involvement in solving problems at the local level might have worked, on one level at least, had he been able to be everywhere at once, all the time. But much more fundamentally, paternalism reinforced a structure in which the leadership—and one member in particular—initiated policy, and the population's participation came in carrying it out. Che Guevara described what he understood to be the controls on such a system:

> [T]he State at times makes mistakes. When this occurs, the collective enthusiasm diminishes palpably as a result of a quantitative diminishing that takes place in each of the elements that make up the collective, and work becomes paralyzed until it finally shrinks to insignificant proportions; this is the time to rectify.[71]

Such controls, as Che recognized, were entirely inadequate.[72] In fact, there was nothing at an institutional level that allowed for the effective expression of conflicts or disagreements with executive decisions. The mechanism might be labeled, as James Petras put it, a "command-mass participation syndrome."[73] Leadership, and particularly a single leader, initiated policy, often in essentially extemporaneous speeches whose contents, in policy terms, the ministers concerned often learned simultaneously with the population. Participation came at the level of implementation: it was at this level that the population discussed policy; it was at this level that popular and active involvement was encouraged. "Few avenues," Petras pointed out, "exist(ed) for expressing disagreement over basic policies."[74]

This state structure, or lack thereof, and its relationship with the Cuban people was mitigated by a series of factors. Perhaps the most important of these factors was the undeniable enthusiasm and dynamism generated by the Revolution among a majority of the population. The Revolution presented this majority with something to identify with that was larger than themselves—with impossible David versus Goliath victories over imperialism, with concrete international solidarity, with the notion of Cuba's own road to socialism. This sense of identification with something beyond daily life generated energy and dynamism. And indeed, as Fagen described it, this dynamism was the key element in the "Cuban political style." There was, he argued, a "flexibility" and "adaptability,"[75] a sense of endless experimentation, that permeated Cuban politics:

> Fidel and his lieutenants have taken Cuba—and at times the world—through a dizzying and often contradictory scenario of promises, programs, alliances and adventures. . . . But closer to the heart of the matter is the fact that with the exception of a few closed or non-negotiable questions and issues—national sovereignty, public ownership, the right of Castro's group to rule—almost all other aspects of both the theory and practice of revolutionary governance can be considered "up for grabs." . . . A powerful strain of pragmatism and experimentation. . . . constantly intrudes into public life. The operating rule in many policy areas—touching subject matters as different as hemispheric armed struggle and agricultural policy—seems to be, "try it; if it doesn't work, abandon it and try something else."[76]

This sense of constant, dramatic change—a kind of creative chaos—might capture the imagination and encourage motion. But it can do this only for a limited time, and inevitably, as Fagen accurately pointed out, it has its problems. Moreover, it could not give people a long-term sense that, in the absence of direct participation in determining the direction of change, the Revolution had made them the subjects and not merely the objects of their history. How could the sense of unity and unison between the state and the society that the Cuban leadership understood as the basis of their system of "direct democracy" be maintained?

Here we come to the second mitigating factor in Cuban political life in the sixties: what Fagen has labeled the "subculture of local democracy."[77] Given the general tendency of observers to focus their attention on national structures and given the fact that Fidel himself seemed naturally to draw this attention, Fagen argued the significance of this subculture was fundamentally undervalued. He defined it as encompassing "activities that are of small scale, institutions and practices which involve citizens in decisions directly tied to problems of the neighborhood and workplace."[78] He listed within the perimeters of this subculture three elements, or at least examples: the "mass organizations"; the popular tribunals, or "people's courts"; and, less tangibly, a general atmosphere of discussion and debate around issues of local and more immediate import. We add to these a further mitigating factor: mobilization campaigns. Each of these campaigns indeed had a dramatic effect—at times, particularly in the case of the first mobilization campaign, the effect was overwhelming. But each, like the institutions which comprised the subculture of local democracy, had its own limitations in terms of moderating what remained a paternalistic, supremely centralized state structure.

In the 1960s, the mass organizations were broad-based groupings centering around neighborhoods, workplaces, and categories of people—women, youth, small farmers, and so on. They shared, however, common attributes, organizational principles, and purposes. Most importantly, they were inclusive rather than exclusive. The neighborhood committees—the Committees in Defense of the Revolution (CDRs),[79] for instance—attempted to gather into their block organizations of all the residents within a delimited area. Qualifications for membership were not based on evaluations, which tend to be subjective, but on more objective categories. In the case of the CDRs, membership required merely place of residence and attainment of a minimum age of fourteen.

The functions of these organizations has been interpreted differently, varying again with the political views of the interpreter. Those sharply unsympathetic with the Revolution have labeled the CDRs as little more than agencies through which neighbors were facilitated in spying on neighbors. Others have understood them broadly to be concerned not simply with vigilance, but with organizing the population, mobilizing it to carry out specific tasks, and perhaps most critically, providing organized forums for involvement and for discussion; in short, incorporating the population in policy execution. Without entering into this dispute about their role, it is clear that the CDRs operated within a delineated circumference. Despite the role of spontaneity and despite some variation in their form, by and large Cuban mass organizations did not contrast radically with those that crystallized in the U.S.S.R. Nor did they challenge Lenin's famous view—on which Stalin capitalized—of mass organizations as "conveyor belts."

In practice, in the U.S.S.R. these conveyor belts were unidirectional. The same was true of the mass organizations in Cuba; if they generated discussion and action, such discussion and action did not have to do with policy formation. Instead the mass organizations served as channels into the population for explaining policies formed and determined by the leadership. Initially the mass organizations, and most specifically the CDRs, performed this function admirably. As Fagen concluded: [B]y the end of 1961, the leadership's most effective way of reaching quickly into every corner of the island for administrative purposes was through the CDR."[80]

It could be argued that the popular tribunals, or people's courts, were forums for direct popular participation in actual decision making. This idea gave them their structural and substantive form. Structurally, each court (there were some 500 on the island by 1969) had jurisdiction over a small delimited area (30 square blocks, or about 4,000 people in the city of Havana), presided over by lay judges who were selected by and from the local population. In this sense, as Cantor argues, it was "deemed more important that the people (knew) the judges, than that judges knew the law."[81] These judges were nominated by a coalition of the CDRs and the Party and selected, out of a field of six, by popular local vote; judges continued in their regular jobs and served without pay. Court was held in the evening, usually in a local storefront or in the open air; unless a significant percentage of the population of the specific area was present, no court was held. Discussion in the courts tended to center less on guilt or innocence and more on the social circumstances in which the alleged crime took place. The intention here was precisely to involve the local population in a discussion of these circumstances.

The courts did seem to embody principles of justice in a new and revolutionary form. They were precisely a forum for discussion, structured by the direct participation of an affected population. But their jurisdiction was extremely limited. The courts dealt only with misdemeanors, the lowest level of crime. The extent of their authority was equally limited; the maximum sanction they could apply was a six-month sentence. In short, again we have a case of popular involvement in decision making solely at the local or base level. Only here was there a direct role for the wider population.[82]

It was perhaps the mobilization campaigns that imparted on the broadest possible level a sense of popular participation and control. We can see this most clearly in the first and ultimately most successful mobilization effort, the 1961 Literacy Campaign.[83] Here, far more was accomplished than a reduction of illiteracy from 23.7 percent to 3 percent. (This, in fact, is the campaign's most questionable success; UNESCO officially calculates literacy as the attainment of a fourth-grade level. The Cubans achieved about a first-grade level as a result of the campaign.) Nearly the entire population was actively involved: 100,000 student *brigadistas*, another 100,000 adult teachers, and some 700,000 illiterate people insured that practically everyone on the island was touched by the campaign, directly or indirectly. In essence, the Revolution at this point was transformed into a mass movement. Individuals from every class and age group were called on to act. And their action gave an enormously impressive sense of the power and the vitality of the Revolution. In a sense, through this mobilization, the Cuban people on the broadest popular scale saw tangibly their own capacity to alter their own destiny through their own work. The campaign gave to them a field in which to take control of their own present, to become the subjects, rather than the objects of their history. The moment of the Literacy Campaign transformed and transfused the Revolution. The level of participation was so overwhelming that, in practice, hierarchical structures melted to insignificance. All this was, of course, to have a lasting effect in some realms. But overall, the campaign was just that: a moment—a year—and it introduced no permanent changes into the state structure. The problem remained how to extend the moment of the campaign, to extend the sense of democratic participation and control it had generated, to daily life.

Finally—and not separately from the above—Fagen drew upon his own observations to point to the less concrete, but no less visible, level of discussion and streetcorner debate that seemed to characterize Cuban life in the first decade after the Revolution:

> Whether a discussion about dormitory rules in a youth encampment, consultation to determine who should receive the new fishing boats sent to a cooperative, debate in a labor meeting over the causes and cures of absenteeism, or an open meeting of a CDR to distribute community responsibilities, there is an impressive amount of participatory activity going on in Cuba in a variety of settings.... [T]he closer one comes to grass roots decision-making—and by implication the closer one comes to the realities of the vast majority of Cubans—the more frequently this democratic-participant countertrend is found in operation.[84]

At some level this "liberation of language," this constant and maintained level of discussion, invokes images of the vivid accounts of the tone of life in Russia after the 1917 Revolution. Indeed, 1960s eyewitness accounts of this facet of the Cuban Revolution document the similarity.[85]

But it is hardly sufficient. And it is a dynamic that again needs structural supports if it is to be maintained and integrated into a system. There are dangers either way: we have no evidence from the historical experience of actually existing socialism that it could be captured within state structure and still maintain its dynamism, but "protected by no guarantees and enshrined in no constitution,"[86] it is all too easily susceptible to disappearing.

Furthermore, there is another central problem Cuban-style "direct democracy" could not combat and, in many senses, even accentuated: the problem of bureaucracy.

In the absence of solidly grounded state institutions, and in the face of the exodus of large sections of the prerevolutionary bureaucracy, administrative structure was, in the early period of the Revolution, a rather slapdash affair—a kind of *"guerrillerismo administrativo,"*[87] as it came to be popularly called. This essentially meant chaos. And chaos did prevail, in the form of inexperienced cadre, contradictory orders, and faulty communication. Even as this was gradually, although not completely, overcome, a second tendency, more disturbing in the long run, began to emerge: a mushrooming administrative sector. The saga of the Russian experience was replayed in Cuba with the same troubling results. As in the Soviet Union, the tendency toward an expansive bureaucracy was part of the heritage of revolutionary Cuba. Prior to 1959, in Cuba, as in most underdeveloped countries, the state had been the largest employer. And every major transformation undertaken by the new regime seemed to generate new waves of bureaucracy. The nationalization of the major means of production, expansion of welfare activities, assumption by the state of the responsibility for health and education, and so forth, all meant an enormously enlarged public sector. The Cuban leadership watched, with periodic bouts of concern, as the situation progressed. And tragically their understanding of the sources of the Cuban "bureaucratic deformation" differed little from what had been understood in the Soviet Union. They never looked in depth at what they themselves had created (or failed to create) to explain their problem. Nowhere was there even an inkling that the roots of the problem might lie in Cuba's unstructured "direct democracy," in the fact that officials were appointed from above, distant and hard to reach and, in the end, in no way responsible for their actions to the actual population they were supposed to serve. In 1960s Cuba, as in the Soviet Union, bureaucracy was seen as a matter of size; success in combating it meant, quite simply, reducing its numbers. That is, there was a quantitative, as opposed to a qualitative, analysis of the problem, and inevitably, the Cubans did not differ greatly from their Soviet predecessors in dealing with their bureaucratic deformation.

Thus, in Cuba's well-publicized, national antibureaucratic campaign in 1964, the Cubans followed the strategy Lenin had recommended from his deathbed and set up Commissions for the "Battle Against Bureaucracy,"[88] which were charged with reducing bureaucratic excess across the board and maintaining the reductions. As in the U.S.S.R., with its Workers' and Peasants' Inspection, Fidel Castro admitted some years later that the Commissions for the Battle Against Bureaucracy had themselves become flabby and inflated. But Cuban "direct democracy's" most potent answer to the problem of bureaucracy was, fittingly, Fidel himself. "Our best guarantee against all forms of injustices," declared José Llanusa, the minister of education, "is Fidel himself."[89] His words were echoed and expanded upon by Osvaldo Dorticós, president of the Republic. Fidel, Dorticós explained, kept in constant touch with the people in his continuous outings across the nation and took it upon himself, once he returned to Havana, to personally confront administrative agencies and personnel responsible for meaningless red tape and delays. It was for the very reason of confronting bureaucracy, Dorticós told Karol, that "Fidel was determined to combine his prime minister's job with that of the leader of the opposition. . . . He expected other officials to adopt the same methods, to head the opposition in their own departments."[90]

Moreover, Castro was forever creating his famous "special plans," projects directly administered by him or by those closest to him whose purpose was essentially to go around bureaucratic structures and the bottlenecks these structures seemed to pose. Under orders from Castro, the resources needed for these special plans were diverted to them, without intermediary complications. In effect, the centralized authority sought to circumvent the structures it had itself set up in an effort to accomplish goals those structures had made it difficult to accomplish. Thus, Fidel's answer to paternalist centralization was purer, more direct paternalism, which in practice, as we shall see, tended to aggravate problems rather than to solve them.

And thus the seemingly circular paradox of 1960s Cuba. In the absence of any serious confrontation with the issues of creating institutional forms and structures that might anchor the Revolution's emancipatory impulse and give direction and permanence to a popular sense of efficacy in effecting change that at moments so strongly characterized the Revolution, there emerged, in those years, a dynamic of seemingly irrepressible bureaucratic growth, combined with an overriding paternalism. If it was critical to the paternalism of the Cuban leadership—and particularly Fidel—to fight a never-ending battle against the windmills of bureaucracy, the fact was that a decision-making structure rooted in paternalism had inevitably to spawn exactly such a bureaucracy.

All of these tendencies in the relationship between the state and Cuban society become shatteringly clear in the last years of the 1960s. It was as if the fissures of a volcanic fault had become unbridgeable. Critical issues that had been avoided or ignored would have to be addressed, and addressed directly, after the years from 1966 to 1970.

During these years the Cuban Revolution embarked on its own road to the future by attempting to simultaneously construct socialism and communism. (Commentators have generated an imaginative rainbow of descriptions for this attempt to telescope stages: Mesa Lago describes it as Cuba's "Sino-Guevarist"[91] stage, Gonzalez as "charismatic-hardship communism."[92] We prefer to discuss it in its own terms.) In his July 26, 1968, speech, Castro declared that the Cuban people would use "political awareness to create wealth," and not "money or wealth to create political awareness."[93] In essence, he was saying that an evolving communist consciousness would be the major means by which Cuba would overcome underdevelopment and create the abundance on which the future society must be based, a task that in the historical experience of actually existing socialism had been assigned to the socialist "stage." This was what Karol, somewhat ironically, labeled Cuba's "heresy."[94] Anticipating orthodox Soviet reaction, Fidel declared: "They will call us petty bourgeois, idealists; they will say we are dreamers; they will say we are bound to fail. And yet, facts will speak for us.... because we know our people have the capacity to comprehend these road and to follow these roads."[95]

In essence, the idea of simultaneous creation of socialism and communism obviated the very need to *think* about the difficult and unanswered web of questions and problems surrounding the issue of how to structure popular democratic participation in decision making. When K. S. Karol in 1968 asked President Dórticos to help him with a "broader perspective" on the revolution, Dórticos's answer was startling: "We are about to build communism," he replied. "The aim of our revolution is not to build a socialist state, but to move with minimum delay toward full communism."[96] The dilemma of the Marxism heritage concerning the state in the transition was thus resolved, in theory as well as in practice. The Cuban refusal to put in place any form of institutionalized revolutionary democracy now had a Marxist (if hightly unorthodox) justification, which underscored the irrelevance of worrying about the state. After all, was it not a basic tenet of Marxism that in classless communist society, the state was no longer necessary? The absence of institutions that would allow for any kind of popular input in decision making, and the glaring inadequacies of the forums for participation that did exist became of minor—or, indeed, of no significant—consequence, given the new definition of the road Cuba would follow. Inevitably, then, the old mechanism would be left to function as best they could. With equal inevitability, they would be found wanting.

The belief that socialism and communism could be achieved simultaneously in Cuba had its roots, or at least its earliest expression, in the "great economic debate" of the early sixties, specifically in the contributions of Che Guevara to that debate.[97] The debate centered around Marx's concept of the law of value: did the law of value operate in socialist societies? (The law of value, using Bertram Silverman's one-sentence summary, essentially understood the operation in societies of skill and resource scarcity of an "invisible hand" that resolved the problem of how much labor should be devoted to the production of a given commodity on the basis of the criteria of profit maximization.[98]) Such seemingly abstract questions had, in fact, enormous practical consequences. What was implied in the answer was whether there were alternative routes to communism.

Marxist economists, including Charles Bettelheim and, within Cuba, Carlos Rafael Rodríguez, argued that in Cuba the law of value did indeed operate and would continue to do so as long as scarcity existed. The stage of commodity production and market relationships could not simply be willed away, and the structure of organization of the economy and state had to coincide with this level of economic reality. The socialist stage, given scarcity, was a reality that had to be gone through. For Che, on the other hand, the law of value was not simply the expression of scarcity but also an integral part of the capitalist system and was, therefore, inevitably upstaged by the elimination of this system. The pursuit of new values had to mean a direct interference with market mechanisms in the interest of social justice and equality. Communist ethics could not be rooted in capitalist market relations. In a moving expression of the humanist idealism that is one part of the Marxist heritage, Che exclaimed to an interviewer in 1963:

I am not interested in dry economic socialism. We are fighting against misery, but we are also fighting against alienation. One of the fundamental objectives of Marxism is to remove interest, the factor of individual interest, and gain, from men's psychological motivations. Marx was preoccupied both with economic factors and with their repercussions on the spirit. If communism isn't interested in this too, it may be a method of distributing goods, but it will never be a revolutionary way of life.[99]

Here we have, as Silverman notes, a reenactment, in yet another forum, of the contradiction between revolutionary will and historical reality that has never been resolved in Marxist theory or practice.[100] Che's argument led inevitably to a system in which the incentive to work would come not from market operations since the market mechanism would be fundamentally and purposely disrupted and altered by the state in the interests of the population as a whole. Rather, the incentive to work would derive from the spirit and commitment of the people as a whole to work together to resolve problems of scarcity and underdevelopment; that is, moral rather than material incentives would predominate. The paradox in his formulation was that the reliance on voluntarism, on the *conciencia* of the population, was to fuel an economic structure controlled and manipulated entirely from the center. This paradox, as we shall see, would reverberate through Cuban society.

During the actual debate, which took place via the pages of leftist journals on two continents, Fidel remained silent. In 1966, however, long after the formal debate had petered out and one year after Che himself had departed from Cuba, Fidel took up Che's position and carried it to its extreme. For the next four years the Cuban people were to pass, at a hurtling speed and under conditions of scarcity (intensified by a 31 percent reinvestment rate),[101] through an incarnation of the idea of simultaneous creation of socialism and communism with a radical emphasis on moral incentives—that is, voluntarism (which sometimes looked rather compulsory)—and on revolutionary purity and commitment. Everything was to climax in 1970 in a major popular mobilization to harvest ten million tons of sugar, an achievement that supposedly would launch Cuba onto the plain of economic self-sufficiency. The harvest was put forward by the leadership, and by Fidel in particular, as the crucial test of simultaneously constructing socialism and communism. Its failure would signal a thorough reexamination and reconstruction of every aspect of the Revolution.

And fail it did: the results, as we know, were disastrous, and not simply in economic terms. The years from 1966 to 1970 witnessed the intensification of existing tendencies toward centralization of decision making, and a further verticalization of power, which underscored the centrality of Fidel and of the unidirectional channels between the people and the leadership, as well as a deepening absence of adequate controls on administrative structures whose inefficiency skyrocketed. All this at the same time the leadership's demands on the people had been enormously heightened. Let us examine each of these factors in turn.

Increased centralization of the decision-making apparatus was an indispensable (if unspoken) component of Che's "budgetary system of finance," the system of economic organization that underpinned the idea of simultaneous construction. The budgetary system of finance required the state planning apparatus to intervene directly and continuously into every sector of the economy to allocate resources. This meant, inevitably, that an even larger share of economic decision making was concentrated at the center.

The concentration of decision making in the central planning apparatus was heightened by the 1968 "revolutionary offensive," the "opening act," as it were, of the intense period of simultaneous construction. The offensive, among other things, saw the nationalization of whatever remained of private industry and commerce: some 56,000 small businesses were taken over by the revolutionary regime. Even farmers' markets, at which farmers could sell their excess produce, were eliminated. Nowhere in any other socialist country had such a step been taken. The idea behind this final round of nationalizations was in keeping with the notion of fostering the growth of a "communist consciousness." Completely eliminating private enterprise, it was argued, would help to eradicate individual selfishness and greed. In practice, one effect was to widen the jurisdiction of central planning to include both the production and the distribution processes.

The expansion of central planning authority brought in its wake a parallel expansion of the bureaucratic ranks. It is interesting, and not coincidental, that the concretization of the idea of simultaneous construction was preceded by a second national "antibureaucracy campaign." The year 1967 saw a new attempt at consolidation and rationalization within the various ministries. By September the 31,500 jobs had been cut.[102] Bureaucracy and even bureaucratization of the campaign itself was the target of an extremely popular film shown that year, "The Death of a Bureaucrat," by Tomás Gutiérrez Alea.[103]

But it was clear that, above all, the Cuban leadership considered the *act* itself of simultaneously constructing socialism and communism to be the final answer to the problem of bureaucracy. This is articulated in a dossier on the problem published in 1967 in *Granma* (the party newspaper) and generally considered to have been written by Armando Hart for the leadership as a whole. This document attempts to lay out a theoretical basis to explain the continued existence—indeed, the growth—of bureaucracy after the Revolution. Bureaucracy, Hart argues, will inevitably grow in size, "develop and gain strength" during the first years of a socialist revolution (although it takes on a "new character") given the expansion of state activities. It is only the active drive for communism itself that will eliminate, once and for all, the bureaucratic blight:

> As long as the state exists as an institution, and as long as organization, administration and policy are not all fully of a communist nature, the danger will continue to exist that a special stratum of citizens will form in the heart of the bureaucratic apparatus which directs and administers the state.[104]

Here then, it is spelled out: bureaucracy will continue to function until communism prevails; the Cubans, by embarking upon their homegrown path of simultaneous construction, would thus give the death blow to bureaucracy.

In practice, just the opposite occurred: during the period from 1966 to 1970, the bureaucratic sector grew both in size and in its ability to generate confusion. Indeed, it can be argued that such growth was inherent in the Cuban conception of the structure of simultaneous construction. The budgetary system of finance itself, by placing all decision-making power in the hands of central planners, effectively converted plant managers into low-level bureaucrats. Their job now was not to deal directly with problems and policies within the workplace, but to execute directives from above; they were, in short, stripped of any creative capacities they might have brought to their work. They became what Carlos Rafael Rodríguez would later describe as "administrative puppets."

Even the revolutionary offensive, designed to speed up the progress toward "communist mentality," served to reinforce rather than tear down bureaucracy. The widescale nationalization of small businesses led to bureaucratic structures taking over, however inadequately, the functions of these businesses. Bureaucracy now invaded every corner store; the famous Cuban *colas,* or lines, grew. Simply acquiring the basics for survival became a difficult and time-consuming task. Moreover, whole small but crucial areas of supply disappeared with the offensive, and the government had nothing to substitute for them. For instance, brooms: prior to the offensive, brooms were the product of individuals who made them in their own shacks from wood and straw they themselves would go to the countryside to collect. The offensive closed down these small "factories," and Cubans waited broomless for five years until a plastic broom factory finally opened. Also, shoes, which were in the preoffensive days often the product of small *talleres,* or workshops. These were replaced by a plastic shoe factory bought from China, with negative effects on people's feet. The bureaucracy simply could not provide a substitute for a wide range of small businesses; even juice kiosks and street food vendors disappeared. Nor could the bureaucracy substitute for the myriad of small service providers, such as plumbers, formerly generated and trained within the private sector.

The revolutionary offensive's attack on bureaucracy through its emphasis on creating a generalized "communist consciousness" caused further chaos and confusion. Since a "revolutionary attitude" was considered critical to increased production, those with such attitudes moved into key administrative positions. Here we have the Cuban version of the "red versus expert" problem: President Dorticós himself made the Cuban choice explicit in 1969, when he stated that "(w)e don't think an economist is useful or usable if in addition to being a good technician he is not, *above all,* a good revolutionary."[105]

This emphasis on attitude over skills had manifold consequences. It helped to blur the lines of authority. The administrative structure tended to collapse into the Party structure where, logically, those with the appropriate consciousness were to be found. It influenced plant managers to color in brighter than realistic shades the information they provided to the central planning authority concerning their ability to carry out assigned tasks. Even the weak structures that had previously existed to channel information from the base to the central planning bodies collapsed, reinforcing further the top-down nature of decision making during the 1968 to 1970 period. This meant the effective dissolution of the mass organization and, in particular, the trade unions and CDR neighborhood associations. Again, we must look at the Cubans' reworking of Marxist theory concerning the transition to explain this dissolution.

Let us take, for example, trade unions. Trade unions, theoretically, exist to speak for workers' interests. Yet if a society is engaged in a transition to communism, then, according to the Cuban reading and transposition of Marxist theory, no separate, conflicting classes exist. Workers no longer have interests that pertain exclusively to them as a class. Rather, their interests, and the interests of every group in society are the same: the creation of material abundance through communist consciousness. Since, by definition, there could then be no conflict between management, government, and workers, trade unions representing workers' specific interests have no real role. And indeed, between 1968 and 1970, they effectively disappeared. Even the post of secretary general was allowed to fall vacant and was substituted basically by the minister of labor, who took direct control of the labor force. Minister of Labor Jorge Risquet described the new arrangement:

> It is no longer the case of representing work sectors or groups of workers in the struggle for economic gains. We are now involved in a decisive battle against underdevelopment. It is now the task of the workers' movement, therefore, to mobilize its forces for such a battle, to contribute to the fullest utilization of manpower, to struggle for the observance of work discipline.[106]

Within such a framework there was little room for general worker participation in the daily affairs of the work center. And the forums for even this limited and localized participation disappeared, substituted by the so-called advanced workers movement. The advanced workers movement consisted of those delegated by their fellow workers and approved by the local party cadre as "vanguard workers." In the period from 1966 to 1970, the movement grew enormously in importance and came to serve much the same function as the work plant administration and party structure itself: to channel decisions down to the workers.

The blurring of lines of authority was further complicated by the military component of the revolutionary offensive. The Cuban military was considered the one successful, efficient body in the Revolution. To deal with bureaucratic inefficiency, army personnel were moved into workplace administrative and supervisory positions. As René Dumont reports, in 1969 to 1970 it was increasingly common to find that the appointed administrator in an industrial enterprise or a state farm was both a military officer and a ranking Party official.[107]

What existed then, was a massive jumble of conflicting lines of authority between the Party, administration, and governmental structures and the mass organizations, producing chaos, confusion, overlapping jurisdictions, and an increased, rather than the expected decreased, reliance on bureaucracy. The clear loser in all this was Fagen's subculture of local democracy. The system's top-heaviness was symbolized in the military imagery of the revolutionary offensive: "combat" missions were to be carried out, not discussed, by worker "brigades." It is almost as if the Cuban leadership was giving form to Trotsky's frightening proposal during the 1920 trade union debates to organize the workforce on the model of the Red Army.[108] "All we ask for the people," declared Fidel in March of 1968 at the launching of the revolutionary offensive, "is to trust their leaders and their revolutionary government."[109]

The harvest did indeed prove a test of the ability of Cuba's provisional institutions and "direct democracy" to lead their country to socialism and communism, and they failed miserably. Above all, it was the verticalization of political power,[110] which isolated decision makers at the center and placed ordinary the people outside the decision-making structure, intensified by the attempt at simultaneous construction, that was responsible for this failure.

At the center there was no ability to realistically assess the possibility of achieving the goals set forth. Those who did try to introduce some element of reality into the leadership's assessment—people such as the minister of sugar, Orlando Borrego, a former assistant to Che Guevara—were accused of lack of faith and dismissed. In 1968, Borrego told Lee Lockwood that even if everything went smoothly in the schedule of plans for producing machines to help in the harvesting, "at best on 5 percent of the 1970 *zafra* (harvest) could be mechanized." Such statements of doubt were considered to endanger the *zafra* and were not tolerated: Borrego was shortly thereafter dismissed from his post.[111] Contrast Borrego's comment to Fidel's assertion to Lockwood later that same year: "Be assured that we will produce ten million tons. If we couldn't produce ten million tons, the Revolution would be lost, without value. We will do it."[112]

With every agency that might have produced critical feedback from below now turned to exhortation from above, the level of economic inefficiency skyrocketed. Other crops were abandoned in the completely unrealistic drive to harvest ten million tons of sugar; equipment breakdown was not taken into account, nor its extent even realized by the central planners. The reliance on voluntary labor for 20 percent of the work on the harvest disrupted and disorganized regular work plants. Isy Joshua, the French economist, captured well the essence of the system at its moment of truth as a form of "authoritarian centralization coupled with anarchic decentralization."[113] Directives issued at the center would arrive at the base without any structure to check whether they were being acted upon. The inadequacy of Fidel as the sole institutional channel between the center and the base had never been clearer: his attempts, through pet plans such as the Cordon de la Habana,* to get around bureaucratic logjams had the effect of adding to the general economic chaos.

Street language gave clear indication of how people were reacting. Edmundo Desnoes, the Cuban writer, describes it this way:

> It was remarkable that up to 1968, for example, most revolutionary slogans were accepted and repeated, interiorized; but in 1968 something unusual happened. Che had just died and the revolutionary offensive, the last radical nationalization of small businesses, had increased scarcity and to top it all off, bars and night places were closed down due to a rather ridiculous puritanical revolutionary fervor. The slogan that year launched to celebrate the centennial of Cuba's struggle for independence, insisted on our *cien años de lucha,* one hundred years of struggle. Radio and television repeated it at every break; posters and billboards with *cien años de lucha* printed large were spread across the island. The people, exhausted, foreseeing another century of struggle, turned the slogan around: It became *no cojas lucha,* take it easy, if you were agitated. Any difficulty, in work or pleasure, was met by a soothing *no cojas lucha,* don't drive yourself into struggle. And a number of medicines were invented, pills of *antiluchin,* antistruggle. . . . The point of saturation had been reached.[114]

Nor was it only the harvest and other sectors of the economy that failed. Throughout the island, "pockets of communism," as they might be called, had been set up or set in motion; in each instance, these pockets were, in effect, absorbed and destroyed by the society for which they were to serve as examples. Thus, for instance, a command post, or *puesto de mando*, was set up in Oriente Province (and in each of the other provinces) to "control" agriculture. Resources were poured into this area (to the detriment of the city of Santiago in Oriente, where lack of resources saw the almost total breakdown of the public transportation system during these years). Anyone who worked within the *puesto de mando* received everything according to the communist mandate of "need": everything— cigarettes, food—was free. The results for Oriente as a whole were disastrous. This province, which had for one hundred years been in the forefront of Cuban revolutionary struggles, had the worst production rate of all the provinces during the harvest. The situation was so bad in Santiago and in Oriente that dramatic personnel changes were made. Desnoes relates what happened:

---

*The Greenbelt around the city of Havana, in which people from the city were to grow their own vegetables. It was later said, jokingly, that the person who thought up the idea had been tried for treason.

The government, the Buro Político, then named two of its central figures to attempt to set straight what had been twisted in good or bad faith: Juan Almeida, a bricklayer who had attacked the Moncada Barracks with Fidel, and arrived in Oriente on the Granma yacht. Almeida was named direct representative of the Party in Santiago de Cuba. Armando Hart was the other leading figure sent to deal with the problem of Oriente, a lawyer who helped organize the Twenty-sixth of July Movement throughout the island and the first Minister of Education in 1959. . . . In the early days of their arrival in Santiago, Almeida's car was stopped, blocked by a group of Santiagueros, to complain about the disastrous situation of transportation. Almeida never again used his car going to or coming from his office.[115]

The attempt in some areas of production to experiment, in the communist mode, with complete equalization of salaries no matter what the nature of work produced equally disastrous results. For instance, in the Matahambre copper mines of Pinar del Rio Province, equalization of salaries had an unintended, strongly negative effect: no one wanted to work underground, where the hardest and potentially most dangerous and absolutely the most necessary labor had to be carried out.

The same phenomenon could be seen in education, where plans were made for universalizing by 1980 "schools in the countryside" at the secondary school level. Although the massive construction of these schools, where children were to study half the day and work in agriculture half the day as an integral part of the local agricultural production plan, was largely undertaken in the later period of 1970 to 1975, in their conception and in their failure as production units, they were, down to the smallest detail of a piece with the period of simultaneous construction. Thus lockers where students stored books and clothes originally had no locks, clothes and books were free. But the creation of a kind of communist oasis in the midst of underdevelopment produced the inevitable results. Stealing was rampant, lockers were broken into, clothes were continually "lost," equipment and parts, like lightbulbs and faucets, steadily disappeared. Indeed the situation was so bad that in 1975, when Mexican President Luis Echeverria was to visit the school in the countryside named for the Mexican hero and former president, Lázaro Cárdenas, the school had literally to be rebuilt. Society, characterized by scarcity, simply overwhelmed these experiments in communism, by definition free of scarcity.

Reliance upon communist consciousness resulted in sloppy worker discipline. In 1969, at Cubanacan, the Cuban arts school, students were disciplined for lateness by *not* being allowed to do voluntary work in the fields. But, more generally, "conscience working hours" as they were called, meaning that no worker had to punch in, resulted in a general lateness and slackness. The year of the harvest witnessed a dramatic increase in worker absenteeism (estimated at a whopping 29 percent),[116] and in the percentage of those permanently leaving the work force. It witnessed, as well, a dramatic overall decline in productivity in both the regular and the voluntary workforce. A time-loss study carried out in 1968 in over two hundred enterprises revealed that fully a quarter to a half of each workday was wasted, the result of overstaffing and poor labor discipline.[117] The chaos of 1969 could only exacerbate this wasted productivity.

The marriage of a radical economic, social, and cultural egalitarianism to an authoritarian and hierarchical decision-making structure had come undone. Dramatic reconsideration and basic structural change was unavoidable. Cuba's own particular route to communism, the simultaneous construction idea, was abandoned. In its wake, a new or at least a fundamentally revised state structure would have to be conceived. And in this reconception, the Cubans would once more be confronted with the unresolved issues of democracy and socialism.

5

Cuba in the Seventies: Centralized Decentralization

By 1970, it was impossible to ignore economic failure, administrative chaos, and general level of discontent in Cuba, represented above all in the 29 percent absentee rate that characterized the labor force during the very year of the big harvest. And indeed, in his July 26 summing up of that year, Fidel recognized the failure and placed responsibility for it:

> [T]he leaders of this Revolution have cost the people too much. . . . We are going to begin, in the first place by pointing out the responsibility which all of us, and I in particular, have for these problems. I am in no way trying to pin blame on anyone not in the revolutionary leadership and myself.[1]

At least in the arena of internal policy, "the Cuban heresy" was over. July 26, 1970, marked the public death of the idea so dominant in Cuban life in the late sixties, that socialism and communism could be constructed simultaneously.* In the domestic realm, in the daily life of their country, the Cubans abandoned the notion that they could find their own path to the communist future, condemning this notion with the same words that they had once warned their critics would use: idealism.[2] As Castro said in Chile in 1971, "We expected things to develop the way our imagination

---

*In another area—foreign policy—the heresy continued in some form into the 1980s. It was in its foreign policy—expressed, for instance, in the Cuban intervention in Angola in 1975—that it most discernably steered a path independent of the Soviet Union. In these and other initiatives, the romantic ideals that had characterized the Cuba of the sixties remained most alive.

pictured them."[3] And, as it would become clear, in the view of the Cuban leadership, the alternatives to the vision of "instant communism" were harshly delimited. The Cubans would turn to a more orthodox construction of the postrevolutionary transition, a construction rooted in the Soviet experience. They would adopt, in its traditional language, the four-stage theory that had become common parlance in the Soviet Union. In order to reach their ultimate goal, communism, it would be necessary to pass through the transition to socialism, socialism, the transition to communism, and finally, communism. They would define themselves as still within the first of these stages. This was to have the most dramatic of effects on nearly every aspect of Cuban life.

The Cuba of the 1960s had taken the emancipatory message of the classical Marxist heritage concerning the postcapitalist state and simply followed its spirit. The solution to the problem of its silences and contradictions and, above all, to its incarnation in the political and economic structures of Eastern Europe and the Soviet Union was, in effect, not to create any permanent state institutions. But not so in the Cuba of the 1970s. The absence of forms to insure any kind of popular input into decision making had led, by the end of the 1960s, to a situation in which the leadership—ever more concentrated around the figure of Fidel—had separated itself entirely from the population, a population that had been left virtually without a voice and without a path by which to reach this leadership. As Frank Fitzgerald has written, the leadership had spent badly its most important currency, the *conciencia* of its people[4]; that is, it had achieved, ironically, entirely the opposite goal than that which it had sought. The simultaneous construction of socialism and capitalism was to be a giant, willful leap out of Marx's celebrated realm of necessity into his realm of freedom. In fact, if anything, in 1970 the realm of freedom seemed more distant than before.

The situation clearly called for drastic changes. We will argue in this chapter that part of those changes involved, whether or not it was consciously articulated or understood as such, renewed confrontation with and appraisal of the classical Marxist theoretical legacy. This confrontation, as has been the pattern in Cuba, began expansively. Its early promise was contained in the thousands of meetings held all over the island during the summer and fall of 1970 to discuss what had gone wrong. The meetings themselves and the conclusions the leadership *seemed* to be drawing from them indicated an opening to the idea of widescale popular participation in decision making and the creation of institutions that would permit and facilitate such participation. In the end, and again, as was the Cuban pattern, something decidedly more limited was institutionalized.

There were two lines of critique of what had gone wrong and how to solve it, both of which seemed to point in the direction of an expansively participatory model. The first involved an assessment of the inefficiency of workers and the lack of productivity in enterprises across the economic spectrum. These, the Cubans reasoned, were the inevitable results of a situation in which all leadership—including the mushrooming layer of middle-level bureaucrats and administrators—were virtually free from any degree of accountability for their decisions (or indecisions). That is, the Cubans' evaluation of the failures of their own system seemed to lead them directly back to some of the key weaknesses inherent in the classical Marxist heritage concerning postcapitalist state and society: the unresolved issues of centralization and decentralization of decision making and the absence of an understanding of the need for agencies of mediation to give form and weight to popular sentiment.

The second line of criticism the Cuban leadership confronted in the 1970 discussions was the generalized discontent of the population. This discontent, as we discussed in Chapter 4, had reached a breaking point by 1970. The fact that absenteeism among agricultural workers in Oriente, historically the most revolutionary of provinces, amounted to 52 percent during August of that year—a virtual, if uncoordinated, "strike," as Jorge Domínguez labeled it[5]—provided the clearest evidence of this fact. The Cuban leadership, publicly and with startling honesty, had acknowledged the level of discontent at the base; thus on July 26 Fidel said, "Our enemies say we have problems, and in this our enemies are right. Our enemies say we have problems and in reality our enemies are right. They say there is discontent, and in reality our enemies are right. They say there is irritation, and in reality our enemies are right."[6]

Fidel's pronouncements on July 26 sent shock waves through the population: the leadership, the determining force, the element that gave definition and direction to the Revolution, was saying that it had failed. This failure underlined the general feeling of discontent and sanctioned, in essence, its expression. Its sources had to be confronted. The constant postponement of rewards, which had so characterized the 1960s, had become intolerable for the largest part of the Cuban population. The fact that the leadership had been unable or unwilling to hear this during the harvest was, again, a reflection of the population's exclusion from active decision making and the absence of institutionalized forums for popular expression of needs and discontent. Here, too, the solution that seemed to offer itself was the formal creation of agencies to give people a direct say in both formulating problems and in finding the solutions to them; that is, an expansively participatory model.

In the end, the actual results of the institutionalization process* that

---

*The process of institutionalization in Cuba involved or enveloped practically every organism that had functioned or malfunctioned during the 1960s. It encompassed a restructuring of the work process (including the introduction of norming; a return to material, as opposed to moral, incentives; and a concomitantly drastic decline in reliance upon voluntary labor); a resuscitation of the trade unions together with the remainder of the mass organizations; the reorganization of the legal structure and introduction of a new procedure for passing laws, culminating in 1976 in the enactment of an entirely new constitution; a reemphasis on the family (particularly the norm of the nuclear family) as the major agency

dominated the 1970s in Cuba dramatically narrowed the manner in which all this would be realized. This narrowing had a number of sources. Again, the effect of external threat (in the 1970s, largely in the form of a continuing U.S. embargo, even if somewhat softened during the Carter years) and, in particular, the realities of underdevelopment, played a central role. But there was a further source: the Cuban leadership, despite the initial broad-ranging discussion, fashioned its institutionalization process within the bounds of an inherited legacy, based on the very weak paradigms shaped in the name (if not the spirit) of this legacy. And the results were in keeping with this legacy: a reproduction of the tensions between centralizing and decentralizing tendencies; clear constrictions on the role of participatory structures; an implicit denial of the need for institutions that would allow expression of autonomous mandates and agendas (that is, autonomous from the Party); an underemphasis on what are generally referred to as formal democratic rights; and the steady growth, rather than decline, of a state bureaucracy, unencumbered, in practice, with accountability for its actions or its refusals to act.

To understand how and why this happened, we must begin by considering the scope of the crisis of 1970. Practically every area of experimentation, where the Cubans had ventured aggressively onto new ground, had ended disastrously. The failure of the harvest was flanked by other severe defeats. The 1967 death in Bolivia of Che Guevara marked the failure of the incredibly ambitious independent foreign policies Cuba had undertaken in the 1960s, policies that had brought it into deep conflict with the Soviet Union. And the 1971 arrest and "self-confession" of the Cuban poet-novelist Heberto Padilla, marked the failure of Cuba's aggressive use of culture and cultural figures as an arm of foreign policy; it is from the moment of the Padilla affair that the break between Western intellectual supporters of the Revolution (including, notably, the formerly effusive Jean-Paul Sartre) and the Revolution itself can be definitively marked.[7] Castro's 1971 denunciation of these intellectual "traitors," as he labels them[8] (indeed, he went so far as to cite K. S. Karol, whom he himself had invited to Cuba to write his book, as an agent of the CIA), reinforced a process already underway from July 1970; a kind of turning in of the Revolution on itself.

In this turning in, the Cuban leadership had to confront a series of dramatically stark realities. The first of these realities was the state of near collapse in the economy, a collapse well-documented by Castro, sector for sector, in his July 26, 1970, speech.[9] There was clearly no end in sight to the cycle of underdevelopment, the cycle that, as had been drilled into the

_____

of socialization within the Revolution, as captured in the 1975 Family Code; the reorganization of the Party structure and a search for a more collective form of leadership; and finally, the organization of the state apparatus itself through the introduction, experimentally in 1974 and nationally in 1976, of the system of Popular Power.

minds of the Cuban people, was to be broken definitively and forever by the harvest. "The *zafra*," said Carlos Rafael Rodríguez, "will guarantee our second liberation."[10] It did not. No amount of forceful dreaming (which in the 1960s had gone so far as to envision the imminent elimination of currency transactions not simply between enterprises but between individuals) could will away the continuation of severe economic problems. In the leadership's best scenario, the problems would still require decades to resolve, during which time Cuba would have to continue to depend on outside aid for basic sustenance. There seemed to them to be only one path: planned, systematized rapid industrial development along already tried lines that projected realistically and at long range. That is, they began to articulate a fully developed productivist emphasis.

This need to systematize and to plan was one of the defining factors that shaped the changes Cuba would actually undergo in the 1970s. The enormous push to produce was, of course, hardly a new theme in Cuba; maximization of production had been a constant goal of the Revolution. What was new was that maximization of production was now to be reached in an orderly process, on the basis of one- and eventually five-year plans, integrated in 1972 into the socialist world market through Cuba's entrance into COMECON. Further, production itself would no longer be inextricably linked to a vision of fundamental and immediate transformation in the social relations of production, as it had been in the 1960s.

The idea of the "new person" had not been abandoned, the Cuban leadership asserted; it had merely been postponed, something of the indefinite future. But with this postponement, so, too, the virtual disappearance of the ideas of Che Guevara: while his image remained omnipresent throughout the 1970s and his name evoked daily in daycare centers and schools by children reciting, "*seremos como Che*" (we will be like Che), his writings by and large disappeared. They were referred to only infrequently and, significantly enough, by revolutionary leaders attempting to show, through a questionable reinterpretation of his ideas, that the course they were now pursuing did not contradict these ideas.

There were two roads open to the leadership to achieve their economic goals. The first of these was repression: accumulation, or economic growth at the expense (at a minimum) of participation, had been exactly the path chosen by the Soviet Union. And indeed it was generally predicted by both right- and left-wing critics of the Cuban Revolution that the failure of the harvest would concretize tendencies toward repression or, at least, military regimentation in dealing with the general popular discontent.

In fact, what happened was different. Sectors of Cuban society—for instance, its writers and artists, who constituted Cuba's interface with the outside western intellectual world—were subject to discipline in terms of what was published and who traveled abroad. A military man, Luis Pavón, the new minister of culture, administered this new discipline. Further, the faculties of the University of Havana which in the 1960s had been hotbeds of radical ideas and solutions, were silenced: the social sciences were virtually banned; the philosophy faculty was shuffled around and transformed; and the journal *Pensamiento Crítico,* which the professors and students of that faculty had put out, was terminated. *Pensamiento Crítico* through the late 1960s, although orthodox in its support for the radical turn taken by the Revolution, was very heterodox in offering its readership a wide sampling of the writings and ideas of major leftist figures in the western and nonwestern world. While some professors committed to teaching something besides the formulas of official Marxism Leninism remained within the university, the organized terrain for free-ranging, informed debate clearly was constricted.

But the leadership did not, on a more generalized plane, try to physically stifle discontent. Rather they chose the second road. Their purpose was to channel discontent, to redefine the space for its expression within a framework molded, in the end, by the same paternalism that had haunted the 1960s. They seemed to recognize, following Fidel's assumption of the failures of the harvest in his July 26, 1970, speech, that they had now to respond, in some fashion, directly to the base, to the people, to get at the sources and nature of popular discontent. In long-range terms, the leadership began a process of adjusting the system to speak to the general discontent. The return to a system of material incentives (formulated at the 1973 National Trade Union Congress), combined with the gradual but constant broadening of the availability of goods, was aimed at one level of discontent. Institutionalization, which placed the resolution (or nonresolution) of certain problems into the hands of the people and attempted to regularize expectations, addressed another level. The idea was to give the people direct control over an entire spectrum of issues that had evoked daily discontent; to take these issues completely out of the jurisdiction of the top- and middle-range leadership and to involve the entire people in either seeking the means to their resolution or understanding, as active participants, the difficulties involved in resolving them.

Thus we have the lines of argument that gave definition to the Cuban system in the 1970s. On the one hand, the economic future of the Revolution inextricably wed itself to the idea of steady productive capacity growth, which required expertise, planning, and universalization and regularization of top-down control and direction. On the other hand, efficiency within the workplace, to say nothing of a sense of well-being in the general population, led the leadership to establish well-channeled structures through which people could both voice their complaints and seek resolutions; that is, structures allowing participation at the base in decision making.

The defining elements in 1970s Cuba, then, recapitulated the potentially unresolvable tension between centralizing, top-down and decentralizing, bottom-up tendencies. They embodied the problems at the heart of the Marxist heritage with regard to the socialist project. This tension helped shape the internal dynamics and structure of the economic and political institutions created in the 1970s.

There are several points that must be made at the outset of this discussion. The first has to do with decentralization itself. As Fidel's 1970 speeches regarding the then-projected system of Popular Power progressively make clear, somewhere the line between decentralization and democracy—in the sense of the people as subject, the people in power—became ever more vague; decentralization in a certain delimited area of decision making came to be used almost as a synonym for democracy. Fidel's assertion in 1974 that Cuba was the most democratic of countries because "there are so few places in Latin America or in the world where the local bodies of power have so many attributions, so many things under its control"[11] is one measure of the degree to which the process of substitution had proceeded. Yet it requires only a minimum of thought to understand that decentralization in decision making wasn't, isn't, and never will be a substitute for democracy. If decentralization is critical to any kind of scheme or model for participatory democracy, at best it has only to do with form and process and nothing to do with the key issues of content and jurisdiction.

Second, political decentralization is by any measure difficult to make complementary to the centralization that has historically proven necessary for economic growth (particularly in conditions of underdevelopment); each seems to fight against the other. And, as we have argued, the Marxist theoretical heritage strongly recapitulates and reinforces the inconsistency between the two.

Third (and perhaps most critically), it soon became apparent that none of the new forums of discussion and decision making would truly be an autonomous venue of power, an independent and separate base for the expression of views of a distinct part of the population. For institutionalization also involved the activation of Party structures that had lain dormant in the 1960s when the Party had largely been a collective fiction. The 1976 Constitution refers to the Party as "the highest leading force of society," responsible for "organizing and guiding the common effort toward the goals of constructing socialism."[12] This meant, in effect, a severe blurring of the boundaries between the Party and any other institution of authority.

Finally, the institutionalization of Fidel himself as the First Secretary of the Central Committee of the Communist Party, the President of the Council of State, the President of the Council of Ministers, and the Commander-in-Chief of the Armed Forces formalized the strain of paternalism he had embodied and inevitably played a role in the nature and the effectiveness of the structures that would now come to dominate the Cuban landscape.

These problems emerge clearly in the new institution of Popular Power as it functioned after its nationwide establishment in 1976 until 1992, when it underwent significant changes.[†] Popular Power had its roots in the series of speeches given by Fidel during the last half of 1970. Over

[†]See chapters 7 and 8.

and over these speeches emphasized the imperative of radical and democratic decentralization, of genuine control from the bottom. They evoked images of broad-scale changes in decision making, of involving the entire population in the process. Castro seemed to promise a radical revision of social relations within the society and between the society and the state, that is, a radical revision affecting every aspect of life. As he stated on July 26, "We believe [it] is a problem of the whole people! And we sincerely believe that the only way we can solve the problems we have today is by working together—all of us."[13]

How could Cubans all work together? The implication in this speech is that there would be a massive decentralization of decision making to allow for effective collective participation: "[I]t would be the neighbors who will make the decisions. And if the neighbors make a mistake, they are allowed to make mistakes. It may be hard, but it's their decision. If the workers in a factory err in deciding on a problem. . . . it is hard, but it's the people's decision."[14] This statement was given more direct and concrete form less than a month later in a speech by Fidel to the Federation of Cuban Women. The echoes of the Paris Commune rang still louder as Fidel tied decentralization of decision making to the elimination of bureaucratism:

> [W]e have scores of problems at every level, in the cities and in the countryside. We must create institutions which give the masses decision making power on many of these problems. . . . This implies the development of a new society and of genuinely democratic principles—really democratic—replacing the administrative work habits of the first years of the Revolution. We must begin to substitute democratic methods for the administrative methods that run the risk of becoming bureaucratic methods.[15]

Here we have, as Nelson Valdés points out, a major reversal of the theoretical formulations regarding the sources of bureaucratization that were put forward by the Cuban leadership in the 1960s.[16] Che had argued that the creation of formal institutions for decision making carried with it the danger of bureaucratization. This belief, as we have seen in the last chapter, came to characterize the entire leadership during that decade. Fidel here asserted to the contrary that bureaucracy grows in the absence of channels that would allow the people "ever greater participation in the decisions that affect their lives."[17] In so doing, he pointed to the errors in the 1960s of that leadership and, as well, to the huge hole in the theoretical legacy.

But what would this new formulation mean in concrete terms? Here we come, of course, face to face once more with the limits of the legacy. The breadth of the earlier pronouncements begins to narrow, significantly. Castro, in the course of the last half of 1970, began tentatively to give some indication of what he meant by the decisions that affect people's lives. Thus he said to the Federation of Cuban Women:

> Sending a man down from the top to solve a problem involving fifteen or twenty thousand people is not the same thing as the problems of those fifteen

or twenty thousand people—problems having to do with their community—being solved by virtue of the decisions of people of that community who are close to these problems.[18]

And, even more clearly in September of 1970:

Imagine a bakery in some block, a bakery that gives service to every neighbor in that block, and an administrative apparatus controlling that bakery from up above. How does it do the controlling? How can the people fail to take an interest in how the bakery operates? How can the people fail to take an interest in whether the administrator is a good administrator or a bad one? How can the people fail to take an interest in whether there is privilege, negligence or lack of feeling? How can the people fail to take an interest in the problems of production, absenteeism, amount and quality of the product? Of course they can't. Can anyone imagine a more effective means for controlling that activity than the masses themselves?[19]

The masses, then, were to have a direct, but delimited, role. Despite Fidel's assertion that "[w]e must do away with all administrative methods and use mass methods everywhere,"[20] as the speeches progressed, they seemed to clarify the realm in which the people as a whole would have direct control, and this realm was very local. We have in effect a formalization of Fagen's subculture of local democracy; at the local level the people were to be insured a role as the subjects of their own history, and in exercising this power they were to resolve the enormous inefficiencies and bureaucratic bottlenecks that had so characterized local administration, in particular, service operations. But if control at the base implied efficiency and the end of bureaucracy in certain realms, the expansion of such control into all realms would, the leadership believed, only produce deepening chaos. Introducing order into production so as to systematically maximize it and ending the wasteful aspects of the social and political chaos of the 1960s both seemed inevitably to require a rationalization and a stabilization of overall control from the center.

These tensions—the meaning of decentralization; the balance between it and centralization; the absence of political autonomy inherent in the nature of the centralization; all complicated by the continuing of paternalism around the figure of Fidel, who embodied the tendency toward centralization—were deeply embedded in the Popular Power system in its form, its functioning, and its substance.

First, the issue of structure. At the lowest level, the local, or Municipal Assembly was shaped by the direct participation of the population concerned. Here, at least in structural terms, the Popular Power system emerged as a variant of the Soviet system, as it was reestablished in the years after 1921, complete with its credentials as the inheritor of the tradition of the Paris Commune.[21] Candidates for office were placed in nomination neither by a political party nor by their own initiative; rather they were selected in meetings of neighbors, organized within barrios, or "circumscriptions" by the neighborhood mass organizations to which these neighbors belong. The operative notion here was that people should be personally acquainted with their nominee; this was the single most important criterion in selection, which was presumably based on collective evaluation of the merits of the selected person. Although even at this level Popular Power was certainly a system of representation, this criterion of acquaintance underlay the rationale for a great deal of Popular Power's local structures. Once elected (from a roster that had to include two but generally included four to seven candidates[††]), delegates' new duties were assumed in addition to their regular work. The reasoning behind this again drew directly on the notions derived by Marx from the Commune. Marx had spoken of no governing official receiving more than workingmen's wages. Here delegates remained working people. Moreover, it was assumed that if delegates no longer remained at their normal jobs, no longer lived in the neighborhoods they represented, they would be personally removed from their constituencies' needs and problems and their relationship to these problems would inevitably change since they would no longer share them. This same principle held true (until 1992) at the provincial and national levels of the Popular Power structure; only a portion of the executive committees (that is, the body of each assembly functioning on a permanent basis) at each level of the assembly structure was exempted. Further, the principle of direct participation was embodied in the rules that required 55 percent of the deputies to the National Assembly to also be delegates at the base, municipal level.

This structural decentralization of the municipal level contrasted sharply with the organization of the upper reaches of the system. In all other aspects, the structure of the Provincial and National Assemblies, at least until the 1992 reforms, embodied clear centralization principles. Selection at these levels was not the direct prerogative of people at the base, but lay with the delegates to the Municipal Assemblies. Although Municipal Assembly delegates had the right to alter or add to the lists, candidates for these higher levels of the structure were proposed by committees made up of Party officials and leaders of the mass organizations (who were likely to be Party members as well) in a given municipality. Here, then, the flow was reversed: selection, or at least determination of the candidates for selection, emanated from the center down, rather than from the base up. Thus, in the period from 1976 to 1992, the popular base only indirectly—through its municipal representatives—had any say in who was to represent them in the Provincial and National Assemblies. And, if 55 percent of the deputies to the National Assembly also had to be delegates in Municipal Assemblies, this meant that the remaining 45 percent did not have to be selected from among these delegates; that is to say, 45 percent of the National Assembly was selected from lists of individuals who had received nowhere in the system an electoral mandate

---

[††]In contrast to the Soviet Union prior to 1989, where a single candidate generally stood for election for each base level position.

at the popular level. That 45 percent included individuals like Fidel and the whole of the central governing structure since it was the National Assembly that selected the Council of State and the president of the Council of State who recommended to the Assembly the members of the Council of Ministers. There were, however some deputy appointments that were purely symbolic and in this symbolism expressed a clear lack of seriousness. Thus, for instance, until his death, the Cuban writer Alejo Carpentier, who as Cuban cultural attaché in France lived outside Cuba, would return twice a year to represent the traditionally poor La Lisa section of Havana in the National Assembly. Cubans jokingly spoke of him as the representative of Paris in the National Assembly. What we had here, then, was a structural embodiment of the pull toward control from the center.

At the same time—and here the tension between popular control and the "wisdom of the elect" becomes clear—it was this structural control from the center that allowed it to adjust, at the higher levels of the system, what were obvious injustices at the base. This was particularly apparent around the issues relating to the representativeness of the system. At the base, municipal level, 13.5 percent of those nominated and 8.7 percent of those elected in the first election, in 1976, were women.[22] In the second election, in 1979, this total did not increase; on the contrary, it diminished to 9.9 percent and 7.2 percent respectively.[23] The 1981 and 1984 elections saw some upward movement: in 1981 there were 11.4 percent nominated and 7.8 percent elected.[24] In 1984, 16.2 percent of those nominated and 11.5 percent of those elected were women.[25] In the two subsequent elections, 1986 and 1989, as a direct result, we can surmise, of a directive from the 1986 Third Party Congress to increase women's representation, the proportion of women elected to municipal assemblies was 17.1 percent and 16.7 percent respectively.[26]

It should be noted that the numbers of women nominated and elected has consistently varied widely, according to provinces and municipalities. In the 1989 municipal elections for the Province of the City of Havana, 21.6 percent of those elected were women,[27] while in the municipality of Bayamo, in the eastern part of the island, a city with strong historical traditions and a solid and developed sense of community, only 12 percent of those elected in 1989 were women. Moreover, researchers report that women in Bayamo "regularly reject their nomination publicly stating that their husbands will not allow it. While this could very well be true elsewhere, it would at least be considered less than elegant to state it in this manner in other regions of the country."[28]

Despite this variation, one thing remains clear: at the municipal level, in particular, the level controlled by the general population, there remain enormous inequities with regard to the representation of women.

These inequities lessened, although they were not resolved, at the upper levels of the popular power system; that is, as the control from the center increases, so does the representation of women. Thus at the provincial level, after the 1986 and 1989 elections, women made up 30.8

percent and 27.6 percent respectively of the assemblies;[29] and at the National Assembly level, women gained a 21.8 percent representation in the 1976 election, a 28.2 percent representation in the 1981 election, and a 33.9 percent representation in the 1986 election.[30] This, it is worth noting, is an exact reversal of the pattern that characterized state structure in the U.S.S.R. and Eastern Europe.[31]

This same phenomenon is a bit more complicated with regard to the issue of race. In the 1978 document, *Sobre la Constitución del Poder Popular* the Cubans broke down delegates at every level along racial lines. Estimates of the percentage of the population that is black or mestizo vary enormously. Government figures put it at 28.6 percent; Fernando Ortíz, the famous Cuban ethnologist, speaking of the prerevolutionary population, estimated the proportion of those with a significant African ancestry to be much higher.[32] Of those elected to Municipal Assemblies in the 1976 elections, 28.4 percent were categorized in *Sobre la Constitución del Poder Popular* as either black or mestizo.[33] At the national level, according to what she termed a mini-survey, Lourdes Casal (standing at the entrance during two National Assemblies held during the same election period) estimated the number of blacks and mestizos at about 38 percent.[34]

In these areas, then, we have the center attempting to correct to some degree what might be seen as unrepresentative decisions at the base. Had the center not had the power to do so, one can hypothesize that no such correction would have taken place. If this is then a case of progressive paternalism, it remains, nonetheless, paternalism.

The right of recall, which is built into the structure of Popular Power, illustrates on another dimension the system's inherently dual nature. The direct right of recall at any point of representatives by the people who elected them was one of the characteristics celebrated by Marx of the Paris Commune and was arguably the most important prerequisite for democracy in the system Lenin sketched in *State and Revolution*. In Cuba, the right of direct recall of municipal delegates or by a simple majority vote of the constituency concerned is the absolute prerogative of people at the base level. On the other hand, given the indirect procedure by which assemblies at other levels were formed until 1992, people at the base had no direct say in the continuation in office of any member of the Council of Ministers or the Council of State. At each level, the right of recall, ultimately the right of review, lay with the assembly that made the selection; only the Municipal Assembly could remove members of the Provincial and National Assemblies and only the National Assembly could recall members of the Council of State or the Council of Ministers. The right of recall, then, at these levels emanated not from the base, but from a far more delimited group, at each level closer to the center.

In its very structure, Popular Power embodied the ambiguous autonomy of institutions in Cuba. The overlap between the Party and the state is clearly captured by simple statistics: Of the municipal delegates elected every two and one-half years, consistently around 75 percent have been

Party members; of national deputies elected every five years, virtually 100 percent were Party members or members of the Young Communists' Union (the UJC).[35] Why this was so may be more evident at the provincial and national levels (where, it will be remembered, candidates were suggested by committees headed by the Party) than at the municipal level. Cuban researchers reported at the end of the 1980s that less than 10 percent of the people interviewed in four selected municipalities mentioned Party or UJC membership as a criterion for municipal delegate selection (despite the fact that, of the ten candidates in the four electoral districts being studied, nine were members of one of the two organizations).[36] On the other hand, they point out the

> Significant role the municipal committees of the Party play in protecting and consolidating the authority of local government. This is not only because of the great political weight that the Communist Party has, but as well, due to the more practical reason that it is the only institution at the local level whose jurisdiction extends to the entire economic system, and to national decision-making.[37]

This leads us to a second plane of analysis: if the structures of Popular Power reflected the tensions embedded in inherited Marxist models of the state, the substance and functioning of the system gave flesh to these tendencies. Here we must consider first the jurisdictional boundaries of the different levels of the system.

Fidel Castro, in marking the occasion of the 1974 experimental elections in Matanzas Province, gave some specific indication of the range of powers of the Municipal Assemblies: "All production and service units serving any given community—that is, the grass roots—must be controlled at the grass roots level," he asserted.[38] This meant, for Matanzas in particular, that 4,971 of a total of 5,597 production and service units would come under the jurisdiction of the appropriate Municipal Assembly.[39] These units included, as Castro listed them, schools, cultural centers, radio stations, sports activities, bookstores, movies theatres, restaurants, hotels, bakeries, garages, and bus lines.[40] This jurisdictional range remained constant once the system was put into effect nationally two years later. The breadth of the list seemed to indicate a true movement toward decentralization. And indeed it was, on one level. Zimbalist and Eckstein estimated that, as of 1985, some 34.4 percent of the economy, in services, commerce, and industry, was now responsible to local Popular Power.[41] Yet, it is vital to note, the range of what was controlled was limited along two lines. The "grass roots . . . must be controlled at the grass roots level" brings down, very close to earth, the earlier implications that this was to be a system in which the people made the decisions about the issues affecting them: it gives the most literal of definitions to these issues. People would indeed have the right to exercise a form of control over the things directly affecting them, things that fall within the boundaries of their neighborhood: the corner store, the use of a vacant lot, and so forth. And this is, it should be noted, hardly nothing, as various critics have implied.[42] It meant that in their daily lives, in the basic social services that are everyday matters of concern to people, Cubans potentially had a direct voice. But it also meant that they were removed from having a voice in, much less determining, a whole range of subjects and areas that on a broader plane have an effect as well on their daily lives: for instance, decisions about the overall direction of the economy; or about a particular aspect of foreign policy, such as Cuba's years of military engagement in Africa; or about matters related to the Cuban community abroad. The Popular Power system in its very structure and functioning operated to inhibit discussions that might be, as Ritter has phrased it, "ideologically contentious"[43] since such issues did not fall within the jurisdictional range of the base-level Municipal Assemblies. We shall see that in practice the built-in structural inhibitions were quite effective.

Moreover, in the functioning of the system, there was a second line that limited the scope of actual power at the popular level, one that introduced in tangible form the potential tension between control from above and control from below: this is the principle of "dual subordination." For instance, education in any municipality is subordinate to the National Ministry of Education in all aspects that apply to the entire nation, that is, curriculum, textbooks, and the evaluation system employed. Municipal Assemblies did not initiate policy in these areas; rather they supervised policies determined by the center and applicable to the whole nation, uniformly. Municipal Assemblies had essentially sole responsibility for the daily operations of any school within their geographical jurisdiction; this encompassed the supervision of all personnel, repairs, student transportation, and the like. The same held true for a local grocery store: the goods in the store and the amounts to be sold, as well as prices, are determined by a national system of supply and pricing regulated by the Ministry of Internal Commerce. But the store itself, its daily functioning, fell to the local Popular Power Municipal Assembly.

Direct power in other dimensions was significantly delimited. Power in these other dimensions lay at the center of the system and in the cases we have mentioned—foreign policy, the Cuban community abroad—formally with the national ministries whose heads were chosen by the president of the Council of State (Fidel) and approved by the National Assembly. There was only the most indirect and circuitous link between the popular base and ministries: ministers, almost by definition (even if they were National Assembly deputies), were among those 45 percent of the National Assembly who were not delegates at the base level. Therefore, at no point did they face a popular constituency in gaining or retaining their positions.

Finally, there was the role of the Party. It is hardly accidental that the Communist Party came into being (it held its first real Congress in 1975) at the same moment that the state structure was being organized and instituted. What this has meant in the functioning of Popular Power is more or less permanent ambiguity as to where power lies. This ambiguity was physically expressed by the extreme overlap between Party member-ship and delegate status, and substantively evident in the roles a Party member/delegate-deputy was obliged to perform. If Party members are bound by the decisions of the Party what does this mean for their func-tioning as delegates; that is, as advocates of the specific needs of the populations that elected them and to whom they are accountable? Where is the space within Popular Power for active disagreement with the de-cisions of the central Party organization? What does it mean to say, that in Cuba "[a]ll the power belongs to the working people, who exercise it either directly or through the assemblies of Popular Power and other organs of the state which derive their authority from these assemblies"[44] when it is the Party that "must guide, promote and control the work of the state organs"[45] and that is invested with the task of determining the direction of the Revolution? In effect, the lack of clear boundaries between administrative and political functions, which had so characterized the 1960s and whose resolution was therefore one of the goals of institution-alization, remained as tangible a problem as ever.

The inevitable result of this was a huge gap between theoretical func-tioning and actual reality. If on paper the highest governmental authority— the *jefe máximo,*—at each level—municipal, provincial, and national—was designated the president of the assembly at those levels, it was crystal clear in practice that authority rested with the head of the Party at each level.

But effectiveness, in terms of impact of the Popular Power system, cannot be determined simply by examining it as it was laid out on paper. It can only be understood with reference to its actual operation. And it was precisely in practice, as reflected in the first seventeen years Popular Power was in effect, that inherent potential tensions in the system came alive. This was evident at every level and in the way levels related to one another.

The degree to which the Municipal Assembly was invested with real power indicated one dimension of the centralization–decentralization ten-sion. We can discuss this on two different planes: the extent to which it was perceived by the general population to be a real arena in which to effect change and the actual range of its power in practice. The area in which the people exercised direct power and control, and the liveliness of this exercise, requires a more detailed investigation, in no small part be-cause it was so lightly dismissed by critics of the Revolution.

The first measure of the perceived efficacy of the system is participation at its various levels. In statistical terms, participation in the system during its first seventeen years in operation was impressive: the 1976 electoral process witnessed a 76.7 percent participation in the assemblies nomi-nating candidates for delegates at the municipal level and a 95.2 percent participation in the actual vote; in 1979 the figures were 75.4 percent and 96.9 percent, respectively; in 1981 and 1984 (after a concentrated cam-paign to get people to participate in the nominating stage of the process) the figure at nominating assemblies jumped to 91.1 percent and 91.2 percent, respectively, and in the elections, to 97.2 percent and 98.7 percent.[46]

Attendance at the rendering of account assemblies (the meetings at which delegates report back to their constituencies) was more problematic. The first years of Popular Power witnessed a decline from the early high attendance at the first rounds of meetings: reports at the June 1978 National Assembly confirm this.[47] In the rendering of accounts assemblies this author attended from 1977 to 1979 in the municipality of Central Havana, attendance averaged somewhere around 50 to 65 percent; attendance seemed to correspond to the liveliness of the sessions. In a 1989–1990 survey, attendance in a sample of four municipalities across the island (and including the chronically troubled Central Havana municipality) was put at 50 to 60 percent.[48] The downward spiral from the first meetings in 1976 indicated a growing popular perception concerning the efficacy of the institution.

The figures for municipal-level delegates recalled gave further indication of the degree of sustained interest and involvement in Popular Power and dissatisfaction with it: in 1976, of the 10,725 delegates, some 1151, or 11.1 percent, did not complete their terms in office; of those not completing their terms, 114, or 9.9 percent, failed to do so because they were recalled and replaced by their electors. In the 1979 mandate period, the corresponding figures were 1256, or 12.1 percent, and 83 or 6.6 percent.[49] According to José Arañaburo, former secretary of the National Assembly, there was something near a 50 percent turnover in delegates to the Municipal Assembly by the second and third elections; that is, 50 percent of the delegates selected in 1979 and 1981 had not served previously.[50] This figure in turnover rate held constant over time, according to a speech of the secretary of the National Assembly at the December 1991 meetings.[51]

Arañaburo, speaking in 1983, took the high rate of turnover as evidence, first, of the continued life of the system and, second, of the fact that the general population, with increased experience with the system, was more discriminating and more demanding in its choices. At the same time, he admitted such a turnover could well reflect a high level of dissatisfaction with the operation of the system.

Base-level rendering of accounts assemblies were held twice each year in each circumscription. The number of these meetings was steadily reduced from the Matanzas experiment, in which they were held every two months, to the first five years of the system, which witnessed a reduction in assemblies from three to two per year. The justification for this reduction was that the original frequency of the assemblies did not give either the delegate nor the Municipal Assembly sufficient time to study problems and work out solutions.[52] But the problem of attendance must surely have been a consideration in cutting back the number of rendering of accounts assemblies.

The tone of rendering of accounts assemblies seemed decidedly determined by the energy the delegate brought to the meeting. There was a regular order for each assembly, which again, depending on the delegate, could become somewhat *pro forma*. The delegate first spoke to the action, or lack thereof, that the Municipal Assembly had taken with regard to the issues raised at the prior assemblies. This was done somewhat mechanically and, for the Cubans, somewhat typically first in quantitative terms: how many questions/complaints/proposals had been resolved; how many were pending; how many the relevant Municipal Assembly had no jurisdiction to resolve. These were next discussed by category: repair, construction, food services, commerce. The number of sanctions and dismissals dealt by the Municipal Assembly to administrators and employees in the service centers and workplaces under its jurisdiction was reviewed.

The floor was then opened to discussion of these actions and of new areas of concern. The atmosphere was decidedly informal: meetings were held in the streets; people came together as neighbors; children circulated freely and noisily. There was a general sense of spontaneity in participation (tempered by the fact that those neighbors who were Party members had discussed, in their Party cells, which issues the Party saw as central; it was presumably their responsibility as Party members to interject these issues into the discussion. This was the only real attempt to guide these meetings, and it was not something that was publicly acknowledged nor was it visible and strident).

The range of issues raised by electors at the meetings this author attended spoke well to the concerns of the municipal level of Popular Power. These meetings were all within the municipality of Central Havana, a concentrated, populous area of fairly old housing and narrow streets. The following issues were raised at one such meeting in July 1978: the absence of street signs (which was, apparently, a matter brought up at the previous meeting); the limited play areas for children (which evoked a lengthy and heated discussion about parents' and schools' responsibilities); the creation of after-school centers; child discipline and an angry demand that the delegate resolve the problem in the face of general negligence of the schools and parents; privileges given to local store employees at the neighborhood cafeteria; the inappropriateness of the bathing suits on sale for older women; and the serious and continuing decay of homes in the neighborhood. Each issue proposed to be brought to the attention of the Municipal Assembly was voted upon.

The areas covered, then, were matters concerning public services, repair and maintenance of housing, light industry, and education; this (with some additions) seems, in other accounts of rendering of accounts assemblies in that period to be fairly typical of the range of problems raised in meetings at this level. Meetings were not lacking in humor: listen, for instance, to Marta Harnecker's account of one such meeting in Matanzas during the 1974–76 experimental period of Popular Power:

> A woman who has been busily discussing each item, now rises to speak. She does it with resolve in her voice: "I'd like to ask something. Do you

know when the garbage truck is supposed to come by? Because, as far as my house is concerned, I haven't seen one in three months. They go down as far as Tito's corner, then turn around and leave."

Someone shouts to her: "And they don't even say hello!" There is a burst of laughter.

"We left the trash in front of Pastrana's house," the woman continues, unflappable, "and sometimes three days go by, and it's still there. They just look at the cans and take off. I ask you: don't they like our cans?"[53]

Within the context of pressing neighborhood concerns, the issues that were *not* raised at the meetings this author attended were somewhat curious: the most obvious of these was public transportation—the buses—which seemed in a chronic state of crisis as they puffed along, belching black, sooty exhaust, packed to the rafters. There seemed to be two not necessarily exclusive explanations. The first of these was that the state of public transport was indeed frequently raised in the early days of Popular Power, but that the topic had faded, given the consistent lack of response. The second was that transportation throughout the city of Havana, as the country's capital, came under the jurisdiction of national, rather than municipal, Popular Power.

Bard Jørgensen's findings in his 1983 study of Popular Power put more weight on the first of these explanations, given that his examination centered on Nuevitas, a municipality in the Province of Camaguey; that is, not in the city of Havana. He described what he called

> a certain self restraint (on the part of citizens) . . . when bringing problems to the local government. . . . [O]nly problems that are considered likely to be solved are then taken to governing bodies or representatives. . . . In Nuevitas [this phenomenon is] illustrated by the fact that less than 10 percent of the issues raised in the period from January 1, 1978, to January 5, 1979, had to do with the local transport system, whereas at the same time the local transport was considered by 40 percent of the population as the least improved sector.[54]

The meetings of the Municipal Assemblies themselves ranged basically, if more broadly, over the same kind of issues. The author attended one such assembly, on the Isle of Youth (formerly the Isle of Pines) in June of 1978. In a single, daylong discussion in response to reports of the various work commissions, concerns were raised about the maintenance of both schools and houses; the shortage of housing; the problem of housing without electricity; the nature and quality of child care on Saturday mornings (58 percent of the women on the Isle of Youth worked in 1978, when the work week still included every Saturday morning); problems of both service and quality of goods in the supermarkets; medical facilities at schools in the countryside; the size of clothes stores; the problem of returning goods; the problem of unsold, spoiled goods; student transport and bureaucratic regulations that meant empty school buses had to pass crowds of people waiting sometimes up to an hour and a half for a bus.

Several things became clear, both at the level of the rendering of accounts assemblies and in the Municipal Assemblies. First, was one struck by the involvement and knowledge of relatively high officials in and about issues of seemingly minor import. For instance, at the Isle of Youth assembly, there was an animated half-hour argument of concerning the weight and price of chickens recently sold and the number of hours they were on sale, a discussion in which the president of the assembly was an active participant. Second, there was not immediate agreement on the reports given; rather, they provoked complaints, discussion, and some attempt to understand problems in a broader perspective. And finally, one was struck by the nature of the issues dealt with, and by what was *not* dealt with.

Meetings at the level both of the rendering of accounts assembly and the Municipal Assembly gave a clear indication of subject parameters: of which issues fell inside and which outside of the jurisdiction of the most local level of Popular Power. These issues were not minor and unimportant, as critics asserted. This was not participation minus substance: housing, the provision of services, the quality of education, repairs in the neighborhood are all matters of critical importance in daily life. At the same time, they were all issues that, taken individually or collectively, would not determine the basic direction the Cuban nation would take.

Perhaps we can see this with more clarity if we focus on two such issues: first, the determination of foreign policy and, second, the way in which the Popular Power system was supposed to, and has in actuality, interacted with the formulation of national plans.[†]

Foreign policy matters were, it seemed, structured to fall within the realm of the National Assembly, whose task it was to deal with matters applying to the nation as a whole. Even had the Assembly effectively determined such matters, given the way in which the Assembly was composed until 1992, it would hardly have reflected popular participation in making policy. However, what became apparent in the course of the four sittings of the National Assembly the author attended (June and December 1978, December 1982, and July 1983—the Assembly met in plenum twice a year, for two- or three-day sessions) was that even at this level such matters were dealt with only formally. Of the seventeen issues up for discussion during the June 1978 meeting of the National Assembly, the single time foreign policy issues were discussed was in a report on the international activities of the National Assembly. These reports turned out

---

[†]The author speaks here with reference to the years 1976 to 1991. After this point, the end of the cold war and the severe economic crisis following the collapse of the Soviet Union led to dramatic changes in the nature and direction of both foreign policy and economic planning. With relation to foreign policy, in January 1991 Fidel declared the definitive end of Cuba's support for revolutionary movements elsewhere in the world. With relation to economic planning, the enactment of a "special period in peacetime" in August of 1990 radically altered key aspects of economic planning. See Chapter 8 for a fuller discussion of the special period in peacetime.

to be exactly that: Raúl Roa, then vice president of the Assembly, and Aleida March de Guevara (the widow of Che Guevara), then head of the Assembly's Foreign Policy Commission, summarized three meetings to which they had led delegations. These were presented in a nonsubstantive, descriptive fashion; they evoked no response and were approved without discussion. The whole matter took no more than a half hour to complete. There was, in practice, no discussion of the foreign policy decisions, initiatives, and directions being implemented by the Revolution, presumably supervised by the Ministry of Foreign Affairs (which is, of course, formally responsible for its operations to the Council of State). This same procedure was true of the other National Assemblies I attended.

There is theoretically no reason why there is not a fuller discussion of foreign policy issues in the National Assembly. Nor, according to everyone this author talked to in the Popular Power structure itself, from the national to the local level, was there any reason why there should not be discussion at the lower levels.

But given the tensions inherent both in the structure of the state and its substantive operation, it was difficult to imagine that such discussions at the local level would go beyond a basically informational function. The very "localness" of the local level of Popular Power would have to have been subverted, as would the structures at the highest level, which put matters of foreign affairs into the hands of the same few people who have managed foreign policy for the thirty-three years of the Revolution and most specifically, Fidel. Moreover, the questions concerning what a foreign policy shaped by direct popular input might look like seem wildly abstract given international political realities; the Cuban leadership would argue that external threat, in the nineties as well as in the sixties, seems inherently to determine the need for direction and control, for organization and agility of response. All of this militates against any real decentralization in matters related to foreign policy.

In foreign affairs, for the populace as well as for the ministers, the model we described of the 1960s—one of leadership alone determining and population following—held firm. There was an overwhelming perception that Fidel was setting the course and a basic acceptance of this course. In short, with the exception of occasional words from returning *internacionalistas,* the direction of foreign policy did not seem a concern of people at the base; the sense was that the introduction of discussion of foreign policy issues—injected, it should be noted, from the top—would be formalistic and certainly not determinative in nature, given the structure and the substance of the system, the historical patterns of the revolutionary Cuba, and the force of international realities.

The issue of national planning was a substantively parallel matter. Here, too, the tensions inherent in the Popular Power system tended to collapse authority in one direction: it remained by and large a centralized affair. It should be said that everything in pre-1991 Cuba tended to make it so: the newness of the notion of long-term economic commitment in

Cuba, the pressures of specialization of knowledge in a modern economy, the traditions of actually existing socialism, and the Marxist theory in which such planning was rooted. There were some efforts to decentralize planning at the workplace level, which parallel the decentralization of the Popular Power system in many ways.[55] But the structure through which the people were to have their most direct say in the shape of the national plan—at least with regard to the 34.4 percent of workplaces under its jurisdiction—was to be the Popular Power structure.

Proposals for the relevant parts of the national plan entered the Popular Power system not at the base level, but at the national and provincial levels; that is, at those levels where selection of representatives was indirect and subject to significant influence from the center. The detailed discussion at the national level happened not in the plenary itself, according to national Popular Power officials, but within a work commission of the Assembly, made up of key figures from Junta Central de Planificación (JUCEPLAN), from the Secretariat and the Finance Committee of the National Assembly, and from the State Committee on Statistics.[56] The closest thing to a direct route to the base came in the form of deputies who were base-level delegates, and of the head of the Office for Attention to the Local Popular Power, an office, as we shall see later, created to attempt to bridge a part of this gap between the levels of the Popular Power structure. But it was to the provincial level that proposals for short- and long-term economic plans went first: it was this level in the overall scheme that was responsible for directing, gathering, evaluating, and assessing in depth the discussions and recommendations made in workplaces and in the Municipal Assemblies of each province. This, then, became the channel for popular, albeit indirect, input from the base.

And, with relation to the Provincial Assemblies' role, all the evidence points to the fact that effective participation at this level either did not happen or was clearly inadequate. Jorge Domínguez mentions Cuban newspaper accounts of the critique of the provincial process at the January session of the 1980 National Assembly, at which it was revealed that, in this first attempt to incorporate the provinces into the discussion and formation process of the plan, the deliberations actually went on in the executive committees of the Provincial Assemblies, rather than in the full assemblies.[57]

The minutes of the National Assembly meeting for July 1982 filled out the picture, and gave some notion of progress in this matter, or rather lack thereof, over a two-and-one-half-year period.[58] In the course of the rendering of account report by the Province of Camaguey to the National Assembly, it became apparent that there remained the same problems related by Domínguez. The report itself placed blame on the center for what clearly was this province's continuing inability to fully discuss the national economic plan. Deputies, in an argumentative exchange that was recorded in the minutes of the Assembly, spoke at length of "the late arrival of basic figures, principally, investments, the weakness in the participation of the Management Councils from the workplaces, the deadline failures of central state agencies, which in turn affected the possibilities of analysis with the workers and of providing answers to their questions."[59] The sense of the Assembly's discussion of the Camaguey report was that the problem could be generalized nationally. Substantive provincial-level discussion and participation in planning was not going on. The old Cuban Communist Party leader, Carlos Rafael Rodríguez, himself no stranger to the planning process, captured in 1980 what this meant for Cuban attempts to structure democracy: such a failure, he declared, effectively "transform(s) democracy into technocracy and allow(s) a group of people to decide everything." It threatens to "turn . . . the dictatorship of the proletariat into a dictatorship of the Secretariat."[60]

There was another matter that blocked participation at the base in the economic planning process, one of the central chords of the decentralization–centralization pull: the issue of education. As one delegate/deputy stated in 1982, the discussion of the economic plan proposal, even when it did arrive at the assemblies, remained basically formalistic: "There are no possibilities of discussion because the *compañeros* do not sufficiently know the problems."[61] This statement underlined the enormity of the educational effort required to give individuals enough grasp of a complex modern economy to understand the overall meaning of differences in percentages and to contribute concretely and formatively to a discussion of the national plan. At that point, such a capacity clearly did not exist, nor did the structures that would enable such a discussion: the overall direction and intent of national planning of both the one- and five-year varieties remained very much the prerogative of the center.

Discussions of territorial economic plans fared no better, it would appear, when they began to reach the Municipal Assembly. The explanation given for this by Cuban researchers in a 1989 study underscored some of the same problems. They pointed out that delegates were not elected on the basis of their "efficacy or expertise" and that "the most sophisticated aspects of government"—the discussion of the economic plan or the profitability of large factories—were "incomprehensible or at least very unappealing."[62] They cited two aggravating factors: first, the delegates' short term in office (two and a half years), which meant that a delegate was just beginning to get a grasp on things when her or his mandate came to an end; second, the unclear role of the executive committees, which were composed, in part, of professionals dedicated full time to the system. In practice, these committees, which proved the most stable and continuous institutions in the system, often overstepped their prerogatives in decision making.

The question then emerges: are we speaking of a system in which there was effective disconnection between the different layers, which was, in reality, horizontal? Such a separation would indeed raise fundamental doubts about Cuba's seriousness in using decentralization as a means for achieving participation in real decision making. To what degree *did* the demands at the base affect decisions at the upper levels; that is, what was the degree and the rapidity of responsiveness of the center to the base? This question leads us back into the arena of the National Assembly to a case study. The case study we will use is the issue of housing and housing maintenance and repair: first, because across the island it was the major issue brought up in the initial years of the national Popular Power system and remained or (depending upon whether the municipality is urban or rural) resurged in the post-1986 period as *the* critical issue in the system; second, this author was able to observe in her fieldwork the way, up and down the system, in which this issue was dealt with in the early years of Popular Power.

In the period from 1977 and 1979, the base-level rendering of accounts assemblies the author attended were overwhelmed by questions related to the repair and maintenance of housing and neighborhood facilities and to the shortage of housing. One-half to two-thirds of all the problems posed by electors had to do with these issues.

The intense focus on such problems might have been determined by the fact that the majority of base-level assemblies the author attended were in Havana, particularly in the populous neighborhood of Central Havana where the population crush and, therefore, housing problems are most severe. In 1989, the total population of the municipality of Central Havana, which comprises an area of 3.5 kilometers, was about 164,000 persons. Most of the housing in the area is at least fifty years old, and there had been virtually no serious repair of this housing.[63] But, it quickly became apparent in the course of the author's research that housing repair and maintenance, as well as new construction, was a problem of national proportions, dominating assemblies throughout the island. This was true even on the Isle of Youth (formerly the Isle of Pines), a region developed only after the Revolution took power, where the overwhelming proportion of housing was, when the author visited in 1978, no more than eight to ten years old. In an interview that year, the president of the Municipal Assembly on the Isle informed me that some 75 percent to 90 percent of the complaints brought up at both the base-level rendering of accounts assemblies and at the weekly *dispacho* nights[‡‡] had to do with problems in housing maintenance.[64]

Housing, then, appeared clearly to be one area in local government in which the population was demanding that their needs not be sacrificed and postponed to the future, but met in the present. And at least from the end of the 1970s until perhaps 1986, significant movement by the center on the issue did indeed develop rapidly. The author marks this response from the June 1978 National Assembly she attended, during

---

‡‡*Dispacho* nights were nights set aside for individuals to speak to their delegates in those delegates' homes. Formally, one night a week is set aside for such meetings, although this particular formality appeared to have eroded, unevenly, across the island.

which there took place what amounted to a dramatic and virtual confrontation between the base and the center over issues that focused on the
matter of housing construction, repair, and maintenance.

The strains built into the system materialized in the National Assembly. It was here (again, during the first seventeen years of the system)
where deputies who were also representatives at the base deliberated on
common ground with those who represented the center. The potential
this difference in orientation—that is, the conflict between centralizing
and decentralizing tendencies, had for producing tension—was perhaps
never more clearly illuminated than at that June 1978 session of the National Assembly. On the second day, in the ordinary course of business,
Faustino Pérez commented on the report of the recently formed Office of
Attention to the Local Organs of Popular Power, which he headed. This
office had taken shape in May of 1978 in an effort to create more direct
channels of information flow from the base level to the top of the structure,
the very need for which gives some indication of blockages in those channels. Pérez basically sought to evaluate critically the functioning of the
local base-level structures of Popular Power; he pointed specifically at what
he saw as a "lack of initiative on the part of delegates at the base level."
Pérez noted a significant decline in the numbers of electors attending the
rendering of accounts assemblies and the *dispacho* sessions delegates hold
for their constituents at the base level, as well and the steady and regular
decline in public attendance at many Municipal Assemblies. Pérez asserted
that this drop in numbers might well "indicate a loss of confidence in the
initiative of the delegate" and noted that

> [w]e have seen badly organized rendering of accounts assemblies, character-
> ized by poor attendance, little participation and less enthusiasm, where the
> delegate limits himself to reading a statistical account of his actions and the
> replies received to the complaints of the electors, which are often formal and
> do not convince anyone.... [Poor public attendance indicated that] [t]heir
> content and the form in which they develop is not able to awaken the interests
> of the people, despite the fact that it is in these assemblies, supposedly, that
> the most daily and immediate problems which affect these same people are
> discussed."

Diminished interest at the base level would affect, Pérez said, the future
operation of the entire system; it was "essential" to eradicate it. Why?
Because, he argued, it is vital that we "keep in mind that the two basic
links, [through which] the masses can make most real, most effective their
participation in the government of the society, are in the circumscriptions
and in the Municipal Assembly." Without these links, it is thus implied,
direct interaction between the people and the system of government is
broken.

If the situation was to be corrected, Pérez urged, the delegate's job
was above all to find solutions to problems and not simply to explain why
they could not be solved. "We must prevent a situation in which, because
they become solely messengers who deliver the explanations of the work

centers and their administration, delegates are converted into 'lawyers' for administrative inefficiency, against the just demands of the people."[65]

We have quoted at length from Pérez's statement because it so clearly brings up key questions. First, it points to the extreme importance the leadership placed on the base-level operations of the system, and to their understanding that it was only at this point that there was, in fact, direct popular participation. Second, it points to the fact that at a level significant enough to provide such a critique in 1978, only two years after the Popular Power system was put into place nationally, all was not well. Pérez confirmed the general sense this author got in informal conversations with Cubans that the level of participation and interest in Popular Power had diminished substantially a short time after its introduction. And third, perhaps most important, despite the report in the newspaper, *Granma,* the next day that the speech was "well-received,"[66] in fact, it produced a heated debate that lasted until 7:30, well beyond the usual recess hour for the Assembly, and evoked discussion of a wide range of problems that characterized (and continue to characterize) the functioning of Popular Power at the local level.

This debate focused on the issue of the responsiveness of administrators and bureaucrats and the center itself to the needs and demands of the base; the chief example throughout was housing and housing repair. The reaction from the floor was overwhelming; forty-seven deputies—all but two from Havana,[§] almost half women, and all from among the 55 percent of delegates from the base—stood up vehemently to disagree with the clear implication of Pérez's report that the blame for the situation of declining interest lay with delegates at the base. One after another, speaking from their experience as base-level delegates, they rejected wholeheartedly the idea that municipal delegates were not working hard enough at their tasks or were working with minimal enthusiasm. It was fine for those at the center to be making such assessments, one delegate/deputy asserted; they did not, like the delegate at the base, have to face these problems concretely and directly. Fault, they argued passionately and sometimes angrily, did not lie with individual delegates. Rather, it lay primarily with the continuing scarcity of resources, with the lack of materials, and even when materials were finally available, with the lack, for instance, of means of transport or efficient workers needed to resolve urgent problems relating to housing maintenance and repair, problems that loomed ever larger in discussions at the base level.

And, above and beyond the *falta de recursos,* there were the continuing problems of getting administrators even to reply to requests about what was available or to reply within a reasonable amount of time. One woman delegate/deputy, emphasizing this point, related that she had received the

---

[§]Although deputies from elsewhere did stand up to confirm the housing problems in their circumscriptions and municipalities.

day before a response from the Ministry of Transportation to a query made at the first Municipal Assembly meeting, held a year and a half earlier. Delegates reported having to repeat requests three and four times, with either no response or with responses that, if they had been given to the electors, "would be rejected immediately."[67]

The delegate/deputies suggested the need for mechanisms that would insure quick and adequate response to a given issue and allow sufficient time for it to be discussed in the relevant Municipal Assembly before it was brought back to the rendering of accounts assembly in which it had been initiated. One delegate called for making it obligatory for administrators to attend Municipal Assemblies when discussion concerned them. Another pointed to the fact that, since delegates work at other jobs all day, they could only get to the work centers involved by taking time off or by going at night or on Sundays, when the director was usually not there. Some delegate/deputies argued that the recalls that had already taken place at the base were due not so much to any failing on the part of the delegates, but to the electors' lack of understanding concerning available resources and unresponsive administrators. If all of those who could not solve problems were recalled, it was argued, an entirely new election at the base would be needed. More attention and more resources had to be given to the municipalities, two of the delegate/deputies cautioned; failure to do this would inevitably result in a ever-increasing cynicism among the electors concerning the viability of the system as a whole.

Nor were all the problems a matter of lack of resources and the refusal of administrators to take municipal delegates seriously. There were, as well, severe problems in the attitudes of workers in productive sectors who "failed to come through" to produce the promised resources and of workers in the service sectors who continued to provide an "infinity of bad services": the trade unions had to be urged to deal with this. And if attendance at meetings was indeed diminishing, more support was needed from the neighborhood organizations (the CDRs), whose job it should be to "guarantee attendance": Popular Power delegates, who worked all day, could not be responsible for this. Again and again, delegate/deputies pointed to their inability to respond concretely and effectively to their electors' demands. They spoke of the "traumatic moment" when electors are told to come forth with their demands, and they argued that the problems cited could in short order bring about a loss of electors' confidence, not only in individual delegates but in the Popular Power system as a whole—an attitude of "Why should I speak about whatever problem if it can't be solved?"[68]

Several points critical to a discussion of the tension between the decentralizing and centralizing impulses of the Popular Power system became clear in the course of this extraordinarily heated debate. First, the base appeared to be demanding that the center—too removed from the problems to understand them—recognize the delegates' situation and provide them with the means for dealing with it. Only this would validate the center's repeated assertions that the base was the most important level of Popular Power. Those who represented the decentralizing tendency, then, challenged the centralizing tendency, which they implied had the actual authority and resources to help resolve the problems rendering delegates so ineffective. Second, the discussion gave evidence of a clear differentiation between those deputies who were as well delegates at the base and those who were not. Delegates at the base seemed far more militant. By the nature of their duties, they were advocates for decentralization; they identified themselves (at least to some degree) against the center, as represented by the remainder of the deputies and by the Council of State, none of whom were delegates at the base. And third, it underlined starkly the primacy of the housing issue.

The response of the center was revealing. First, the emotional argument by one woman delegate/deputy that there were mechanisms for solving the problems in the system and that the solution was simple and available to every delegate at the base ("if every workplace director has to be replaced, then every one of them *will* be replaced because directors must act in the interests of the people!"[69]) was given enormous attention and clear, high-level approval. (Fidel, on stage, nodded his head throughout this deputy's intervention, which was interrupted by three bursts of general applause. Further, it was greatly played up in the next day's newspaper account of the discussion.) Second, the session, which remained heated and showed no signs of abating, was brought to a somewhat abrupt close by the National Assembly President Blas Roca (an old-time PSP member), who attributed the whole problem to "the constant threat of imperialist U.S. aggression" in collaboration with Peking.[70] Third, Fidel (who refused Roca's offer to comment, stating that "he, too, needed time to think") did respond, in an hour-long intervention the following morning.

Fidel's intervention came during the opening hour of the next and final day of the National Assembly session, in the course of another heated discussion—this one about electricity rates. It was a spontaneous, unwritten response. He dismissed Blas Roca's explanation out of hand:

> I'm going to say something—with or without the blockade, we will still have problems another twenty years at least. We still have many problems, but for at least twenty more years we have to realize (that) these are problems of poverty, and it is clear that imperialism is trying to make our development even more difficult. . . . But if tomorrow the blockade were lifted . . . we would be at least twenty more years with many difficulties.

His answer stressed, over and over again, that the source of the problem was not decisions taken at the center, but rather the inability of both delegates and electors to comprehend the correctness of these decisions. "Our people," said Fidel, "have, in a sense attained a political culture but not yet an economic one, not a culture about the economic problems of the country in concrete and clear conditions." And the problem, Fidel asserted (in clear reference to the delegate/deputies who had spoken so passionately the preceding day), encompassed not simply the electors, but, "meditating over the things I heard here yesterday," the elected as well:

> I see the need for a very serious job beginning now and in the years to come, concerning the education of the electors, but in addition, in order to educate the electors we must put into action a serious process of education of the elected because if the delegates lack sufficient . . . knowledge and education about the problems of the country then it would be impossible to educate the electors, and I came under the impression yesterday that we, all of you, ourselves are far from having a good education about the fundamental economic problems of the country.

Fidel argued repeatedly that both the elected and the electors must come to understand that the heart of the problem—in Fidel's words, "the entire rosary of complaints"—was underdevelopment and that Cubans could no longer simply will themselves out of underdevelopment, could no longer make impossible leaps into the future, no longer "reach communism before constructing socialism." Here the Fidel of the seventies contrasts starkly with the Fidel of the sixties, for whom the impossible was simply another barrier to be overcome. Cuba was no longer carving its own route to the future through the socialist maze, but rather traveling down a road already clearly mapped and marked. Neither the direction nor the nature of this road was open to debate: "We are faced with the realities of constructing socialism first, with all the laws and principles which adhere to the construction of socialism." Economic development could no longer be improvised, as it was in the sixties. Now it entailed the entire apparatus of one- and five-year plans, of carefully studied allocations of resources:

> Yesterday it seemed to me that the importance of the idea of economic planning, even if it came up, was not understood. Everything can't be done in any way: we've made many mistakes while trying to do things too quickly, without investigation, without enough studies done. . . . We cannot simply do things because the electorate says it's best, that it is good, really beautiful. There are many beautiful things in the world that have to wait to be realized. Unquestionably there is a yearly plan of work, construction, and when this plan is made, the wishes of the electorate cannot be taken into account. . . . It must be the statistics and the concrete necessities which determine where a hospital must be built.

Above all, Fidel argued, if the "problems of the country were not to be eternalized," then resources must be increasingly invested in economic and industrial development. This was an absolute; the priority given to such investments was not open to discussion or questioning. Fidel emphasized that both delegates and electors must differentiate between what he labeled as subjective and objective problems. Objective problems lay outside the realm of concern of Popular Power; these problems could only be overcome through development. The implication here was clear: Popular

Power must focus on the array of questions he described as "subjective," those dealing largely with the nature and provision of services. The Cubans had traveled a long way from people determining the policies that affect their own lives.

There was, as well, another element that crystallized in Fidel's words and underscored the tone of paternalism permeating his intervention. It emerged in his discussion of the population's incapacity or confusion in coming to terms with the differentiation between subjective and objective problems. Here we have confirmation of one key aspect of continuity between the sixties and the seventies; in somewhat the same words over which Sartre had so marveled, Fidel told the assembled delegates, "We must understand that we are now faced with humanity and its infinite desires, needs and problems," and, in an aside, he compared those infinite desires, needs and problems to his own wishes as a child for specific gifts at Christmastime:

> On Christmas even, when I was a child, even though I wasn't born to a poor family, I was sometimes poor for one reason or another. When Christmas came around—I really should have been a musician—I was sent to live with a family in order to study and I really had a rotten time. At Christmas I asked for a locomotive and millions of things. I used to make a long list, but instead, I was given a cardboard trumpet. Then came the next year and I repeated the same thing. I got some grass and I put it in a little glass of water and put it under the bed for the camels of Baltasar, Melchor and Gaspar and the others. But I was given another trumpet, half cardboard and half metal. The next year came around and because there were three kings, I wrote three long letters more eloquent and detailed, in order to convince them, but they gave me another trumpet—three in total. This one was made of aluminum.... In a country such as ours, where so much poverty has accumulated, so much misery, the Revolution is often seen as the bad king.

The image here is powerful and unmistakable: it is an image of the people as children with demands that are childishly unrealistic dreams and fantasies, who conceive of the Revolution as the all-powerful king who grants wishes and gives them gifts according to his whims. It is an image that contrasts sharply with faith in and reliance on the people. And this contradiction weighed heavily upon the leadership, reinforcing its tendency to keep ultimate decision-making power concentrated at the center of the system, even while creating structures intended to disperse this power.

Fidel went on to distinguish between those problems requiring material resources and those resolvable without resources: "There must be a distinction between these two things, which are the problems with an objective base and which are those with a subjective base: this must be known by every elector and every delegate, one can't be confused with the other."

The "rosary of calamities, called poverty," as he identified it—the lack of wood, steel, cement, and so forth—have an objective economic base, and echoing words he had used since 1970, "it would be a great idealism, an incredible idealism, to believe that we can resolve essential objective problems without development.... Maybe one of the problems of the Revolution is that it has tried to resolve more problems than it is able to resolve."

Within this categorization, housing construction (new construction, in 1978, seemed to be the Cuban leadership's main solution to housing problems) was clearly an objective problem. Fidel's direct response to the critical housing issue was framed in terms of planning:

> Now, the investment in housing construction is still low, ... [but] [w]e're hoping to reach 50,000 a year at the end of the five year plan. You all know we are finishing very important industries for building materials, including two large cement factories which will double cement production.... The social investments that must increase [in this five-year period] are in housing, the solution to hydraulic and water problems, etcetera, in order to build 100,000 [houses] which is considered the minimum necessary to solve the problem. We'll be able to reach the 50,000 goal by 1980.... Investments between 1980 and 85 will increase annually the number of houses constructed by 10,000, so that in 1985, 100,000 houses will be built a year and then this level will be maintained.... Between 1985 and the year 2000, the housing problem[§§] will be solved by 85 percent.[71]

The immediate response of the center, then, to demands from the base was projections of rational, planned progress.

At the same time, the heated nature of the discussion at the Assembly, and its immediate and intermediate aftermath, give us perhaps the clearest evidence of the degree to which the center was willing and able to adjust itself, its plans, and its vision to respond concretely to the explicit and implicit demands of the base-level delegate/deputies. If the severity of the housing crisis dominated the heated discussions of the June 1978 Assembly, housing was the central focus of reports at the December 1978 Assembly. Here, it became apparent that even in its own terms, the center could not fulfill its promises. Total plans for 1978 had called for the construction of some 24,500 new homes; in fact only 16,700 had been completed.

This failure was taken up in some detail in Marta Harnecker's unusually extended interview with Humberto Pérez, the head of JUCEPLAN, in the pages of *Bohemia* in February of 1979.[72] The interview was intended to open and channel, within acceptable bounds, public discussion about general discontent with the Popular Power system and to provide the center's response to this discontent; that is, it was intended to be a vehicle to move the discussion out of the closed arena of the National Assembly, at the same time defining the terrain of this discussion.

[§§]This was based upon UNESCO figures that calculate the need for new housing at 10,000 per one million in the population.

On the issue of housing, the interview was particularly revealing; the center acknowledged the inadequacy of its policies. In this sense, the interview takes on critical importance, representing the first indication of the center's movement in the direction of demands of the base on this issue. Harnecker phrased her questions to emphasize issues of housing maintenance, around which we have said the majority of concerns at local level Popular Power meetings centered. Harnecker began by underlining the severity of the housing maintenance problem: "In a study of one of the commissions of the Assembly, it was affirmed that around 25,000 houses are destroyed each year for lack of repairs. These figures are alarming. They mean that last year less houses were constructed than destroyed."[73]

Pérez's reply was revealing: he not only acknowledged the extent of the failure; more importantly, he indicated the degree of impact the demands of the base were having on the center. At the same time he laid out the newest directive in the 1979 plan that 70 percent of total monies for construction going to local Popular Power be spent on repair and maintenance, he acknowledged that up until that moment—that is, the moment at which demands from the base of the Popular Power structure made the issue highly visible—"we have not had a policy with respect to repairs."[74] And further, he indicated stepping up construction of new housing was now a central priority. "From 1981 on [i.e., the beginning of the next five-year plan]," he stated, "we are planning to give a very complete response to the demand, given the growth planned in general in the industries of construction materials, primarily cement."[75]

In fact, there would be rapid movement on this issue—far more rapid and more radical than that envisioned by Pérez here. The issue of housing, so central to discussion at the base of Popular Power during its early years, was, in a sense, a test of that system at two levels: first, the ability of the base level to fulfill its stated role of meeting the demands of its constituency, that is, its capacity, or lack thereof, to prove to people at the base level the efficacy of using its structures to meet their perceived needs; and second, the responsiveness of the center to the base, that is, the possibility of resolving the June 1978 Assembly debate. In the case of housing, the attempt at resolution was notable for its flexibility as well as its speed.

By 1982, although the housing problem was still terrible, the number of new houses constructed per year had doubled, as had the resources devoted to maintenance of old housing.[76] But far more important in terms of solutions, the structured, public discussion of the issue had generated a variety of measures designed to alleviate the severity of the problem, which in turn, gave new authority to local Popular Power, at least in some regions of the country, as a source for real solutions to real problems. Provisions were introduced and approved that allowed individuals to build their own houses on land granted to them by the Municipal Assemblies, and with materials purchased through those assemblies.[77] These measures had, of course, their greatest impact in the countryside, where land was more abundant; during the three years from 1979 to 1982, the countryside went through a visible change. An examination of one of the fourteen provinces—the Province of Havana—and one municipality within this province, provides some insight, albeit limited and particular, into the meaning of these changes in housing for Popular Power at the provincial and base levels.

The Province of Havana encompasses the area surrounding the city of Havana, but does not include the city itself. It is a rich province both in the potential of its agricultural lands and due to the fact that it supplies the city of Havana with the majority of its foodstuffs. This presumably meant that, with the introduction of private farmers' markets and parallel state markets in 1981, the potential for enrichment for the farmers of the province escalated. Indeed, this escalation might at least in part have been responsible for the enormous amount of private construction going on in various of the municipalities of the province from 1981 to 1986. In the municipality of Güira de Melena, there literally seemed no street on which construction was not underway.[78] The provincial executive committee (an unusual executive committee, given that it was the only such committee in all of Cuba in 1982 whose president was a woman) confirmed that here, as elsewhere across the island, the overwhelming majority of demands at the base level during the early years of the Popular Power system had to do with new housing and repair and maintenance. Although they could show this author no official records for the prior years, by 1982 housing concerns had receded. According to their records, *gastronomia* and *comercio*, categories that included restaurants and food services in general, dominated the discussions. They asserted that this change had gradually taken shape in the 1979–82 period, that is, since the new regulations had been put in effect and new housing opportunities had developed. Thus in the first round of local rendering of accounts assemblies held in March of 1982, of the 9,281 questions/complaints/issues that delegates brought to Municipal Assemblies throughout the province, some 2,524 were related to food provision and restaurant services, while issues of construction and maintenance fell to sixth on the list, following questions about communal services (1,349), transportation (960), public health (591), and education (556). In October 1982, at the year's second round of rendering of accounts assemblies, of the total of 11,242 issues brought from the base to the Municipal Assemblies, 3,036 fell within the category of food and restaurant services, and construction (at 420) again ranked after communal services (1,884), transportation (1,137), and education (746). The pattern continued into March of 1983. Of the total of 9,371 issues, construction maintained its sixth-place status behind food services, restaurants, communal services, transportation, health and education.[79]

The same pattern held true in Güira de Melena. Here, of the 308 issues raised in the course of the March 1982 base-level rendering of accounts assemblies, 106 had to do with food and restaurant services, 55 with communal services, 44 with transport, 32 with education, 28 with construction, 16 with health, 16 with sports, and 11 with culture.[80]

In the City of Havana (which constitutes by itself a province in the administrative division of the country) and in other large cities, where there are clearly not ample supplies of land to give away, the introduction in 1982 of a new national housing law, which gave individuals the right to sell property and houses to other individuals, was in like manner aimed at generating individual initiative in acquisition and repair of housing. Further, individuals who wished to work on their own to provide services such as plumbing or electrical repairs were now to be licensed by the state. In essence, the state was legalizing what had been underground activities and at the same time claiming a channel of response to the problems of deteriorating housing. (Both of these reforms would be suspended in 1986, as we shall see in Chapter 7.) Here, with relation to housing, was one indication of the ability of the base to influence the central decision-making structures in what was, relatively speaking, a short period of time.

This same flexibility by the center in responding to demands of the base was shown (again, until 1986) in the area of food services, a prominent arena of local attention in many areas of the country (and since 1982, according to figures in the Province of Havana, the major issue at base-level rendering of accounts meetings in that province). The 1980 introduction of free peasants' markets in cities throughout Cuba represented an effort to ameliorate the ration card system and the scarcity that rationing indicates. (Cuba was remarkable among socialist countries in not allowing any such expressions of private enterprise.)[81] The runaway prices in these markets led, in December 1982, to the setting up of state-controlled parallel markets, whose prices, while well above those of the *libreta*, or ration book, were generally half those of the free peasants' markets.

These efforts with regard to provision of food paralleled the reforms with regard to housing. As with housing, they were attempts by the center to find a means to respond immediately to the demands of people at the base level. They represented in this sense a commitment to taking these demands seriously.

In 1960s Cuba, the absence of formal political institutions which might serve as forums for discussion, debate and accountability, and the tension between a disorganized and chaotic decentralization, operating within the context of an overcentralized command structure, was directly tied to the issue of ever-mushrooming bureaucratization. Elsewhere in those countries which called themselves socialist, bureaucratization, as we have seen, was the ultimate product and reflection of ossification, stagnation and corruption: it was, simultaneously, the means by which such countries managed to function and not function, the final expression of popular alienation. The Cuban leadership in their 1970 (re)engagement with the Marxist theoretical legacy concerning the postcapitalist state seemed to avoid any direct or articulated confrontation with, or reflection upon, this reality. Rather, they transplanted the principles legitimized by the Marxist heritage and its interpretation—fusion of executive and legislative power, the instant recallability of those elected, continued work at workingman's wages—and built them into the Popular Power system. The results were clear in a very short space of time: if, as the leadership had asserted throughout the 1970s, the new state structure was to eradicate the problem of bureaucratization, in fact, it did not. Indeed, the prevailing mood around Havana as early as 1978–79—that is, two to three years after the new system was established nationally—was that, if anything, everything had become *more* bureaucratized.

That this sentiment was fairly universal is reflected in the fact that Marta Harnecker brought it up in her public airing of the problems interview with Humberto Pérez. Harnecker queried, "There is a generalized sense that the process of institutionalization, instead of lessening bureaucratic impediments, have increased them. What do you think of this?"[82] The fact was that the leadership didn't quite seem to know what to think. Pérez himself gave an entirely mechanical answer to the question. He basically argued that by *definition,* the system was antibureaucratic, that, in short, the structure itself, and in itself, could not possibly be the source of bureaucratic excess in any form. Any idea, he stated, that bureaucracy had grown with institutionalization "would not be just. . . . To the degree that there are bureaucratic impediments, it cannot be due to the process of institutionalization because, entirely to the contrary, this process creates the conditions to eliminate these impediments."[83] Indeed, having said earlier in the interview that some of the people working in the various new structures, including Popular Power, were so "impregnated with old centralizing and in many cases bureaucratic habits" ingrained in them by years of experience, he went so far as to suggest that perhaps these same bureaucrats, for their own purposes, were spreading nasty rumors.

The mechanical nature of Pérez's argument was nowhere more apparent than in his justifications. First, since with institutionalization one whole level of administration—the regional level—had been done away with, this meant that any given problem, even one needing resolution at a national level, had substantively fewer hurdles to get over and therefore less bureaucracy. And second, according to Pérez, the fact was that local Popular Power had control "in an immediate manner over the majority of activities having to do with the satisfaction of the needs of the population"; therefore, by definition, there was less bureaucracy. Where bureaucracy remained, he argued, the responsibility for it lay largely in any given municipality, which had, again by definition, the structural means for eliminating it by the right of recall.

The problem with Pérez's analysis is that it was entirely static. Pérez did little more than take Popular Power as it was laid out on paper and say that such a structure, as given, *could not* but reduce bureaucracy. There was no deeper examination of the sources of bureaucracy: rather, the paper structure itself becomes the means to avoid this discussion. To argue that a structure is by definition antibureaucratic and that bureaucracy continues to the degree that the mechanisms of the structure are not being fully employed did little to respond to the multitude of complaints Harnecker's question *had* to represent; indeed, its tautological nature, if anything, sought to obfuscate the problem, to undercut discussion at any real depth. And he, of course, never questioned, even indirectly, the adequacy of inherited Marxist wisdom on the subject.

This was not the answer of the entire leadership. José Arañaburo—to whom we have also referred above—was far more contemplative in his response to similar questions in interviews in 1978 and in 1983.[84] He acknowledged that, in fact, bureaucratization could and did increase in the first years of the system, that this was bewildering to the Cubans, that it was a complex and contradictory problem requiring "mechanisms that we have to be constantly revising." Arañaburo, at least, indicated a sense of dynamic, a need to adjust and readjust. And indeed, the debate at the June 1978 Assembly actively underlined the refusal at the base to accept mechanical answers and inherited wisdom on this subject.

However, as subsequent history would illustrate, the core of the problems that were so well illustrated by that Assembly have yet to be resolved. As various delegate/deputies predicted, their limited roles, aggravated by Cuba's declining economic fortunes in the mid-1980s, served to undermine both the efficacy of the Popular Power system and people's belief in it as an agency of effective change.

6

The 1980s—Unchanging Change: Cuba in the Era of *Perestroika*

During the last half of the 1980s, the Cuban Revolution, in accounts by commentators from the right to the left, emerged as the negative or flip side of what was portrayed as a far-reaching movement toward democracy going on in the Soviet Union. In this comparison, Castro became the "fossil marxist"[1] or, alternatively, the "aging hippy"[2] "at the tail end of the communist movement...totally isolated from outside realities."[3] If Gorbachev was pragmatic, then Castro was intransigent. If Gorbachev was future-oriented, then Castro was backward-looking. If Gorbachev was credited with heralding, or at least facilitating, the end of the cold war, then Castro was seen as "acting more and more like a Cold Warrior."[4] The collapse of command socialism in Eastern Europe generated ever more nasty epithets for Castro; thus *New York Times* columnist William Safire, following Susan Kaufman Purcell, labeled Castro the "Ceaucescu of the Caribbean."[5] And in keeping with the times, during the 1990–91 Persian Gulf crisis, critics turned to citing the Cuban leader as the "Caribbean Hussein."

In moments of intense comparisons, such as those afforded by Gorbachev's March/April 1989 visit to Cuba, the contrast emerged with particular starkness. Here, the comparison between Castro and Gorbachev was extended to encompass the ongoing processes in the two countries. The Soviet Union's march forward became the measure of Cuba's obstinate and retrogressive refusal to do so. The gulf separating Russian experimentalism, reflected in its programs of *perestroika* and *glasnost,* and Castro's enforcement of what was labeled an old-fashioned, dogmatic Marxism

134

Leninism appeared virtually unbridgeable. It seems a strange fate for a revolution that was, at an earlier point, deemed a heresy, and even more ironic given that the policies inherent in the "Rectification Campaign" Cuba was pursuing at the time were, at least in part, the policies that originally had fueled that heresy.

Once again at a key point of transition in Cuba, the general image in the West of the Cuban Revolution was being shaped not primarily by an understanding of the internal logic (or illogic) of the dynamics of the Revolution, but by factors external to it. And, as we have argued in these pages, it is impossible to understand the Cuban Revolution through such external lenses; just as they have proven themselves misleading in the past, so too, here, they could only obfuscate. Fidel was certainly critical of Gorbachev's attempts at political and economic reforms and was perhaps even more sharply critical of their ramifications in Eastern Europe, and the tempo and tone of his criticisms became increasingly pointed and intense over time. Indeed, in response to events in Eastern Europe, Fidel chose to label himself an "inflexible socialist."[6] It seems important, however, to untangle the web of factors that underlaid his critique and to locate its roots within what was transpiring in Cuba itself. The world, observed with Cuban eyes, is a much different place than the world observed with American, or for that matter, Russian, eyes. In part, our task here will be to understand those differences and to use them as a framework within which to return to this study's larger themes concerning democracy and socialism. For if, as Fidel himself tirelessly asserted, there were vast contextual differences between Cuba and what was until recently the Soviet Union or the Eastern Bloc, they shared, in certain respects, a common landscape. Most fundamentally, all had (or have) to come face-to-face with a legacy that continues to be haunted by key unanswered questions, which revolve around the central issue of democracy in the political and economic organization of the transition. In the end, in Eastern Europe and the Soviet Union this confrontation brought into question every aspect of the existing structures and models. It is, as yet, far from clear how deeply the Cubans are prepared to engage (or to resist engaging) these issues.

"*Perestroika*," Fidel asserted several years ago, "is another man's wife. I don't want to get involved."[7] His analogy here is less than fortunate; but it points to the differences separating Cuba and the Cuban Revolution from its Eastern European and Soviet counterparts. These differences involve historical as well as political, economic, strategic, and demographic considerations. They justified and explained in the minds of the Cuban leadership Cuba's refusal to step into line with what was transpiring in the rest of what was the actually existing socialist world.

First, the Cuban Revolution was a genuine mass uprising with wide-scale popular support; it was not imposed from above by occupying armies as was the case in Eastern Europe. If the rhetoric and, in certain periods, various models propounded by official Marxism-Leninism found their way into Cuba, nonetheless, the Stalinist yoke that strangled the Soviet Union and Eastern Europe and contributed so directly to their disintegration had and has no real hold over Cuba. If nothing else, the history of the Revolution and of its various experiments and heresies demonstrates this.

Second, if Poland's enemy has traditionally been Russia or the Soviet Union, this is not true of Cuba, even if relations with the Soviet Union were not always cordial. Cuba's enemy, at least from the end of the nineteenth century, has been the United States; it was to this that Castro was referring when he asserted that Cubans "must never forget where we are located. We are not in the Black Sea, but in the Caribbean Sea. Not ninety miles from Odessa, but ninety miles from Miami."[8]

The threat posed by the United States further underlines Cuba's understanding of the world and of its place in that world. Cuba identifies itself with the Third World. If, as it could be argued, Eastern Europe as a whole and the Soviet Union in the era of the Russian Revolution shared many characteristics with Third World countries, nevertheless, there was no conscious or proud articulation of this. As a Third World nation located on the American continent, Cuba necessarily sees the world quite differently than Hungary or Czechoslovakia. Given a historical interaction with the United States that has been marred by an almost classical relationship of economic and political domination, revolutionary Cuba could never look to U.S. capital to "bail it out" as does Poland, or have any expectation of U.S. goodwill in doing so. Nor could it identify itself with those countries in the world—the industrialized, capitalist countries—which it understands as the source of human misery, impoverishment, and underdevelopment in the Third World.

Finally, Cuba is a 700-mile-long island of 10 million people. If it does not have to deal with multiple nationalities living within the confines of a single nation, at the same time it does not enjoy the abundance of natural resources that might enable it to go it alone if necessary.

But these differences alone cannot explain Fidel's overt hostility toward the processes underway in the late 1980s in the Soviet Union and Eastern Europe. The notion of some commentators that it was Fidel's concern over retaining concentrated power that motivated his rejection of these processes is as wrongheaded as it was when some of the same commentators pointed to this concern as the source of earlier dramatic positions he has taken. Despite hoopla in Miami and bumper stickers (already several years old) proclaiming "Next year in Havana," and despite the fact that by the end of the 1980s Cuba's increasingly dire economic situation had certainly resulted in an unprecedented disenchantment with the leadership and pessimism (particularly among residents of the island's largest cities), Fidel's position was not seriously in question.

Rather, Fidel's problems with *perestroika* must be traced to three fundamental factors. The first of these was the very real commitment of the Cuban Revolution to a high degree of economic egalitarianism and the understanding that any widespread introduction of market mechanisms and private property would inevitably undermine the foundations of such egalitarianism. But the limits that the Soviet leadership was willing to place on the reintroduction of market mechanisms and private property were never entirely clear. On the issue of private property, Gorbachev himself proposed a framework that recognized all forms of ownership—state, cooperative, and individual—as equally valid.[9] He gave little clarity to this in his 1989 statement to the Congress of Soviets:

> We are in favor of the creation of flexible and effective social relations, in regard to the utilization of social wealth; each form of property should demonstrate its power and its right of existence in the course of lively emulation and just competition. Only one condition is required: that exploitation and the alienation of the worker from the means of production should not be permitted.[10]

Legislation passed by the Soviet Congress allowing the purchase of land by individuals, as well as the right to pass such land along to one's children or heirs, gave some indication of the direction in which the Soviet Union in its final years was moving and the degree to which the contradiction between private property and socialism had dissolved in the minds of Soviet leaders. The implications of such actions were clear: as Abel Aganbegyan, a close economic advisor to Gorbachev, explained, "We do not talk about a 'state of workers' as before. . . . We now talk about the nation as a whole and the middle class as the main class."[11]

This analysis of society had far-reaching reverberations in terms of projections of what economic stratification might look like in the future. As Robert Davies reported in 1990, the majority of the Soviet reformers saw egalitarianism as one of the sources of the Soviet economic conundrum:

> They believe that earnings should be differentiated more sharply and purport to believe that this is compatible with socialism. While privileges based on office should be swept aside, they should be replaced by differentiation of earnings, based on the value of the work as measured on the market. In his report on the occasion of the anniversary of Lenin's birth, V. A. Medvedev[*] emphasized that "the differentiation of incomes will obviously increase. . . . Demagogic calls for equalizing incomes of everyone and everything are alien to socialism."[12]

Tatyana Zaslavskaya, following in this vein, suggested that a 10,000 rouble per year ceiling for earnings should be set.[13]

Such stratification would simply not have been tolerable to the Cuban revolutionary leadership. They derived their staunch adherence to a relative egalitarianism as much from Martí as from Marx; it had always been at the core of the social project within which the very legitimacy of the

---

[*]Chief of Ideology in the Politburo until the July 1990 Party Congress.

Revolution was rooted.** We hear their rejection of economic and social inequality echo through the decisions in 1986 to end the five-year experiment in free peasants' markets and to suspend the 1982 law allowing the purchase and sale of housing. Both the peasants' markets and the housing law were of a piece with the late 1970s. Both sought to introduce flexibility into the effort to solve pressing problems: in the first instance, food availability and distribution; in the second, the housing shortage that, as we said earlier, had come to dominate discussions of problems of daily life in Cuba. The bitterness of Fidel's denunciations of peasants who were making 50,000 to 60,000 pesos a year from a single hectare of land planted in garlic[14] and of other 100,000 pesos a year "hole in the wall operations"[15] had particular resonance here. So did the contrast between the rapid growth of unemployment in Eastern Europe and Fidel's detailing, given during the August 1990 meetings of the Federation of Cuban Women, of what life might look like in Cuba during what he called a "special period in peacetime" brought on by shortages resulting from nondelivery of goods from Eastern Europe and the Soviet Union, increased economic pressure from the United States, or any combination of these. (In September 1990, Fidel called this period in effect.[16] We will discuss it, in some detail, in Chapter 8.)

> The general principle would be, at least, that whatever we have we distribute evenly among everyone. Not even in the special period will we have beggars here, because there won't be anyone without food. Whatever we have will be distributed among everyone: electricity, everything. We may have a labor surplus, but no one will be left out on the street.[17]

Fidel's second major concern about *perestroika* centered around Gorbachev's dealings with the West. Here he was not alone in marveling at Gorbachev's willingness, for whatever reasons, to accommodate to Western, particularly U.S., demands. Fidel would have had few disagreements with the analysis of Michael Howard, former Regis Professor of History at Oxford University and a frequent commentator on strategic security issues, who wrote in 1988 that

> Gorbachev's technique is now clear. It is to ask us to state our demands and then simply to meet them. We demanded that the Soviet Union should leave

---

**Indeed, one of the most deeply felt results of Cuba's progressive economic crisis has been the separation of the country into what some Cubans label the *pais* and the *diplopais*, that is, the country and the dollar country. The intensified drive for hard currency has greatly exacerbated the division of the island's economy into three layers: the dollar economy, the peso economy, and the black market economy. The dollar economy is visible everywhere, in *diplo* shops, where food or goods nowhere else available are sold (theoretically to non-Cubans) for dollars, and at dollar hotels, where tourists (including visiting Cuban exiles) bask in luxury that contrasts sharply with surrounding conditions. Such stark contrasts, however excused by Cuba's economic situation and future prospects, must serve to gradually erode the legitimacy of the Revolution by challenging its egalitarian ideal.

Afghanistan. He has done so. We demanded that he should scrap the SS20s and their smaller adjuncts. He did it. We demanded that such scrapping should be verified by intrusive on-site inspection. He agreed. We demanded that troop reduction in Europe should be asymmetrical. He has agreed to that as well. We demanded that the offensive deployment and training of Soviet forces in Eastern Europe should be abandoned for an overtly defensive posture. He has made his military reexamine their doctrine. What can one do with such a man?[18]

The question for Cubans had to be what if Cuba became the next demand? How would Gorbachev react if the West, specifically the United States, began to make Cuba, and a revision in Soviet-Cuban political and economic relations, the next prerequisite to continuing arms reduction and other negotiations (as indeed the United States did in the summer of 1990 when it refused the Soviet Union much desired most-favored-nation status until it ended its special economic relationship with Cuba). Despite Gorbachev's sustained resistance, prior to the 1991 attempted coup, to calls for the diminution, if not the elimination, of all foreign aid, most pointedly in the famous 500-Day Plan, it is unlikely, given the highly volatile situation in the Soviet Union as well as bitter Cuban memories of the Soviet/U.S. resolution of the 1962 Missile Crisis, that Fidel's suspicions were ever completely put to rest.

The implications here were both strategic and economic. They went beyond dealings, or potential dealings, between the Soviet Union and the United States. They pointed to the heart of the Cuban critique of the dramatic changes occurring in Eastern Europe and the Soviet Union. Where, the Cubans asked, in Gorbachev's vision of a "common European home," was the Third World? This query echoed through all of Castro's comments on the new East–West spirit of detente. Thus, in his 1989 speech marking the thirtieth anniversary of the Revolution, Castro observed:

> There are two kinds of survival and two kinds of peace, the survival of the rich and the survival of the poor; the peace of the rich and the peace of the poor. That is why the news that there may be peace, that there may be detente between the United States and the Soviet Union does not necessarily mean that there is going to be peace for us.[19]

Or again, in his comments at the burial of Cuban soldiers killed in African wars:

> The elimination of nuclear weapons is an excellent idea. If it were more than utopian and could be achieved some day, it would be of unquestionable benefit and would increase world security—but only for a part of mankind. It would not bring peace, security or hope to the Third World countries. . . . [I]n many of those [Eastern European] countries no one speaks about the tragedy of the Third World. . . . What resources can the Third World—in which billions of people live in subhuman conditions—expect from such developments?[20]

The virtual exclusion of any discussion of the Third World in the intense processes of change going on in Eastern Europe was indeed notable. In the Soviet Union, whatever discussion did take place tended likewise to deemphasize and devalue Soviet–Third World relations.

Castro's assertions did not come in a vacuum, nor were they simply a comment upon the reintroduction of capitalism in Eastern Europe. In part, they were a bitter response to what he understood as the likely consequences of these events for the Third World in general and for Cuba more specifically. Gorbachev's 1989 letter to Bush announcing a cutoff in military aid to the Sandinistas was seen as one such consequence.[21] Discussions in the Supreme Soviet concerning the need to reduce Soviet economic aid to Latin America in general were another.

Such discussions, of course, had great immediacy for Cuba given its reliance on the Soviet Union for both aid and extremely favorable terms of trade. Nor could Fidel have been much assured by the January 1990 COMECON meetings in Bulgaria and the proposals (made first by the Czechs) that future dealings with the bloc take place on a strict market basis, with payments made in hard currency.

But perhaps even more critical, in the sense of the immediacy of the threat, Fidel sees himself as living in a world that has changed drastically in the shadow of a superpower that has not changed at all. From Fidel's point of view, for the Cubans, *perestroika* did not trigger movement into the future; rather, it meant a return to the past. In his view, it strengthened rather than weakened the sinews of the cold war. It was, after all, the bipolar world that created the space in which the Cuban Revolution could survive. The U.S. invasion and occupation of Panamá and its economic and military stranglehold on Nicaragua, which effectively forced the Sandinistas to cede political power, fostered in Cuba a sense of isolation and provided convincing proof of increasing U.S. militancy in its drive to dominate Latin America. United States intransigence about broadcasting Television Martí into Cuba, as well as the various bills aimed at intensifying the embargo that were circulating in the U.S. Congress in 1991 and 1992,[†] have been understood in this light. They have served, at a minimum, to justify the leadership's renewal of a state of siege mentality, leaving little space in which to discuss or even consider alternate opinions. In such an atmosphere, simply stated, socialism becomes synonymous with nationalism, and unity—a closing of ranks—as the Cubans have understood it since José Martí's efforts to forge a single Cuban movement to drive the Spaniards from the island becomes the tried and true strategy.

---

†We refer here to the Mack Amendment, which was vetoed by President Bush in 1991, and the Cuban Democracy Act (or the Torricelli Bill), which was signed into law by the president in October 1992. The Torricelli Bill forbids subsidiaries of U.S. companies operating in third countries to do business in Cuba.

This, then, is the framework within which we must situate the "Campaign to Rectify Errors and Correct Negative Tendencies."

The Cuban Rectification Campaign was formally introduced in 1986, almost at the same moment that *glasnost* and *perestroika* were becoming household words in the Soviet Union. These words came to have distinct meanings. By comparison, the meaning and content of the Rectification Campaign have never been quite clear, even to those involved in it.

Some Cubans initially saw the campaign as a series of readjustments of the economic mechanisms within the Management and Planning System (SDPE). Some have seen it as a catch-all label for political and economic measures that had to be taken in the aftermath of dramatic decreases in foreign exchange earnings in the mid-1980s. Some have understood it (not without reason) to be the means by which Fidel could rid himself of those around him—the technocrats—who were bothering him. By contrast, others, at least in its early days, saw in it the initiation of a period in which everything is once again up for grabs, that is, a critical point at which the basic structure and workings of the Revolution would be reexamined. This seemed to jibe with the stirring statements made by Fidel in launching the campaign. In speech after speech during 1986, Castro's rhetoric recalled the dramatic tone of the late 1960s experiment and evoked the 1970 promises of far-reaching popular control. Over and over again, his words about the power of moral forces and the weight and centrality of popular intervention seemed to hold the expectation (perhaps for some the threat) of a renewal of the seed of radical Marxism that had always seemed embedded somewhere in the core of the Revolution. Thus Castro's remarks at a July 1986 conference on enterprise management:

> What has made us powerful and invincible in the face of economic and political aggression and military threat? Moral force! . . . Morale, an unselfish spirit of sacrifice, altruism; that was the raw material that made our people, a virtual colony of the United States, a socialist and communist country. . . . It is more important to safeguard the consciousness of workers and act honestly than to meet the plan.[22]

Or his diatribes against money, juxtaposing the drive for "profits, profits, profits" with the very meaning of the Revolution.[23] Or his evocation of widespread popular mobilization that seemed just beneath the surface of his declarations at the 1986 commemoration of the invasion of Playa Girón. While denouncing those who diverted public resources for private consumption, he returned, albeit with a qualifier, to the images of the central, controlling role of the base population that had so characterized his 1970 talks in the aftermath of the failed harvest:

> We aren't advocating a cultural revolution here; we don't want to use extremist measures to solve problems, or throw the people against those responsible for such irritating acts. . . . Can anybody here engage in shady deals without

the people finding out? We don't want to unleash the masses, I repeat, against the guilty parties for them to stop such activity on their own.[24]

Yet, as practice unfolded, the question of whether the Rectification Campaign would address, either directly or indirectly, issues of popular empowerment and democracy remained unanswered. Nowhere in the revival of late 1960s values and slogans was there any discussion of the very undemocratic nature of this period. Its evocation was always qualified by saying it was an era that suffered from certain problems of "idealism." If the precise definition of this idealism was never given, it was nonetheless clear that the label did *not* encompass a deep-reaching critique concerning the absence of structures by which the people might have exerted control or authority over the leadership's decisions and policies. Nor was there any discussion of the need for, or the means by which to encourage, the revival of the kind of effervescent, far-ranging informal discussion and debate that did characterize that first decade and was terminated in the aftermath of the failed 1970 harvest.

What became increasingly evident was that no one in Havana really knew what the Rectification Campaign would in the end encompass. As a Cuban friend aptly remarked, "Everything new is suspiciously reminiscent of something we have already tried that didn't work. And then we tried the opposite, and that didn't work either." On the street, Medea Benjamin reported, the Rectification Campaign came to be labeled the *espera estoica,* the long stoic wait[25]—a play on the word *perestroika.*

In the wake of the 1989 trial, conviction and execution of General Arnaldo Ochoa and the de la Guardia brothers on corruption and treason charges (rooted in their alleged participation in drug trafficking), Cuban social scientists have sought to lay out a logical progression of events beginning in the early 1980s—that is, before the Rectification Campaign was announced—perhaps as part of an effort to explain or rationalize the Ochoa affair. In doing so, they have tried to emphasize the coherence of the process and to portray an ever deepening, ever broadening questioning of the status quo that moved along a trajectory from the military sphere, to the ideological sphere, to the economy, and finally to political institutions and structures.

Their argument is that the 1986 formal announcement of the campaign can no more be taken for its commencement than could Fidel's 1961 declaration that Cuba was socialist be taken as the moment at which socialism began in Cuba. Further, in underscoring the idea that Rectification actually began in the early 1980s, that is, prior to Gorbachev's accession to power, their intention is to press the point that Rectification was not a Cuban reaction to *perestroika* and *glasnost,* but the expression of, and reaction to, specifically Cuban needs and problems and was generated from within the Revolution itself. Perhaps most critically, their argument positions them to identify the October 1991 Fourth Party Congress as a profoundly significant moment of realization and change for the Revolution. It therefore behooves us to explore this trajectory.[26]

Their basic thesis is that Rectification was a full-scale attack on the 1970s and, most particularly, on borrowed institutions, ideology, and methods of procedure. In this perspective, then, Rectification becomes "Cubanization" and underscores the appeals to nationalist sentiment that are, and will continue to be, increasingly intense in the wake of Cuba's growing economic and political difficulties.

The original impetus to Rectification, in this analysis, was the 1983 invasion of Grenada.[27] Here the absence of a Soviet response made it crystal clear to the Cubans that they were on their own in facing a far more hostile and actively aggressive White House and that this required a structural rethinking of military strategy. The new strategy was designed around a concept of *guerra popular:* the organization of massive numbers of people into territorial militias (involving something more than 2 million people, that is, roughly one-fifth of the island's population) rather than sole reliance upon a professional army.

The dramatic nature of this change was evident on a number of levels. First, given their experience with "people's war," Vietnamese military advisors were substituted for their Soviet counterparts. Second, the people's war strategy fell under the direct jurisdiction of the Party rather than the army. All this, Cuban analysts argue, tended to undermine the position of an elite of military officials and soldiers that had developed during the 1970s. It also provided the basis for Fidel's response to the queries concerning the absence of democracy in Cuba—for instance in Brazil to a gathering of church people:

> [W]e don't just have the vote, we have the weapons in the hands of the people. Can a people who have weapons in their hands be enslaved? Can a people who have weapons in their hands be oppressed? Can a policy be imposed upon a people who have weapons in their hands? And how can such a miracle be possible unless there's a total identification between the people and the nation, between the people and the Revolution?[28]

The second moment identified by Cuban social scientists as a milestone in the evolution of the Rectification Campaign centered on the issue of ideology. Here again there was a structural outcome: in December 1985, the enormously powerful ideological apparatus of the Party, which was widely seen within the Party itself as a stronghold of conservatism, was dismantled. Tony Pérez, the Politburo member who had been secretary of ideology on the Central Committee, was dismissed from his post and the ideology section, which within its jurisdiction had controlled the departments of science, culture, education, and revolutionary orientation, was broken up. The impetus for this dismantling seemed to come out of critiques of the manner in which those in charge of ideology had enforced the application of a kind of dogmatic Marxism-Leninism in various areas, beginning with the manner in which Cuban history itself was taught and learned in the school and university system. The application of schematic, preset formulas about "worker's states," through which Cuban history was strained and reshaped, meant that the actual dynamics of that history had been lost, replaced by an artificial, superficial, and distorted assemblage. This same rigidity and dogmatism was interpreted as the source of the closing of the faculties of sociology in Cuban universities and a general deterioration and devaluation of the social sciences, leading to further erosion in the way in which Cuban reality and the history of the Revolution was taught and studied. Castro himself, in his lengthy 1984 interview with Frei Betto (published in English under the title *Fidel and Religion*), did in for Cubans one key element of what had always been a rigidly held Marxist formula: scientific atheism.[29] (The issue of religion, and the Revolution's changes of policy with relation to it, would continue to reverberate, as we shall see in the Chapter 8.)

In 1986 the economic crisis hit full force, exacerbated by the rise in strength of the dollar in international markets, the decline in oil and sugar prices, and the resulting dramatic halving of Cuban foreign exchange earnings. This crisis, and Fidel's disagreements with the solutions proposed by key JUCEPLAN figures, led directly to the declaration of the Rectification process and to its first targets, which involved the structure of the economy and the stated intent (although in practice still not carried out) to virtually dismantle the economic mechanisms that had been put into place during the 1970s to regulate that economy. In particular, the focus was on the organization of work, the determination of salaries, and the level of economic decentralization.

From this moment (marked by the Third Party Congress) the leadership, particularly Fidel, began to stress once more key features of the 1960s: voluntarism, the moral impetus to work, the capacity of the masses to accomplish the seemingly impossible, combined with an ever increasing emphasis upon efficiency in production to make maximum use of scarce resources. It was at this point that the thinking of Che, and particularly his economic thought, was revived and used both as a critique of the 1970s and a justification and occasional guide to the policies of the 1980s and beyond. Yet, noticeable once more for its absence (despite claims to the contrary) was any full and open discussion of democracy either in the workplace or in the society as a whole.

In presenting the Rectification Campaign as a logical historical progression, Cuban social scientists point next to the aftermath of the Ochoa and de la Guardia trials,[30] when, they argue, it became clear that the Party itself and political institutions as a whole needed to be reexamined. The 1991 Party Congress becomes in their analyses, a transcendent event, the expression of an expanding reevaluation of the Revolution. In this context, the March 1990 "Call" (the announcement of the beginnings of preparation for the Congress) is given its most radical reading. Statements in the Call about the "unreal quest for unanimity, which is often false, mechanical and formal," and the need for "democratic discussion in the Party and the Revolution, as part of the quest for solutions" have particular resonance here.[31] They point, further, to the fact that, for the first time, the framework for the discussions within Party cells that led up to the Congress was not set out in declarations or foregone conclusions, to be accepted and adopted, but rather, in terms of themes and questions to be debated.

Even if this trajectory were valid, it is apparent that at every turning point it identifies, it was Fidel who initiated the change. This simply reinforces the clear sense one got that ordinary Cubans were waiting, as they always have, for Fidel to sketch out the direction, the framework, and the scope of the Rectification Campaign. Indeed, the campaign was marked by the ever more tangible presence of Fidel. As in the 1960s, he was constantly initiating new schemes to achieve seemingly impossible goals. The revival of the microbrigades is one example of this. The creation of the work brigades in construction and agriculture—groups of workers (by 1990, 40,000 out of a force of some 4 million) who labor twelve to fifteen hours a day in Stahkanovite fashion, living in groups in facilities equipped and provisioned at a level far higher than that of the general population and receiving pay some 60 percent higher than the national mean salary—is another.[32] So, too, his plan, in the face of dramatic declines of food imports, to organize the entire population into *mobilizaciones* (usually for two-week periods) to do voluntary work in the countryside planting and harvesting.[33]

The weight of Castro's increased public presence was captured by his continual appearances on television; one felt again, as one did in the 1960s, that Fidel almost sought to convert himself into a material force in development. Although some of those committed to the Revolution began, particularly in the wake of the Ochoa trial (which no one on the island appears to have accepted at face value), to question Fidel's leadership in private, it is finally Fidel who will determine the definition and parameters of "democratic discussion in the Party and the Revolution."

In doing so, he faces a set of critical problems, a key moment in the Revolution, that resembles in more than one aspect the problems and the moment that confronted Gorbachev in the Soviet Union. Some might argue that the manner in which Gorbachev dealt with these issues (or unloosed the reins containing them) contributed directly to the collapse of the Soviet Union. This, without doubt, is Fidel Castro's interpretation. And it has reinforced his natural instincts to hold on tightly to the reins—that is, to contain, channel, and control. We will examine here two common issues.

The first of these issues—and in the long run the most critical for Fidel—is a generational one. It revolves around young people and the hold that aging leaders and the evocation of a history shrouded in myth have on them. Early analyses of *perestroika* pointed to the dimensions of this issue of young people for Gorbachev. As Boris Kagarlitsky wrote in 1987:

The country which Gorbachev has inherited is already not the same one that came into Krushchev's hands. It is an urbanized society with a large number of hereditary townspeople and skilled workers.... Young people have no memory of the poverty of the forties, but react acutely to any threat to lower their present standard of living. Problems of personal freedom and responsibility have come to the fore.[34]

The importance of these concerns for young people was quite clear even prior to Gorbachev's accession to power; it accounts in part, for instance, for the wide popularity of Vladimir Vysotsky, the poet-rock singer and the leader of the "bard movement," whose songs, often banned during the Brezhnev years, circulated on pirate cassettes numbering in the millions.[35] When Vysotsky died in 1980, tens of thousands of people sought to attend his funeral, occasioning what was, in effect, the largest mass demonstration in the Soviet Union since 1927 (and only overtaken by the Gorbachev-era demonstrations). Even ten years after Vysotsky's death, his anniversary was loyally observed by thousands who moved patiently past his graveside in a procession that lasted from dawn into the night.[36] Vysotsky would be followed by other, wildly popular rock musicians, who, like him, became almost spiritual leaders, or at least the "custodians of popular conscience,"[37] charged with expressing popular disillusionment and personal aspirations.

Rock music as a genre functioned in the Soviet Union much as it did in the West in the 1960s, as a vehicle for widespread communication of independent and radical ideas. By the 1980s, lyrics evidenced a strong distrust of authority and a tone of "muted anarchy,"[38] which measured well the distance between young people and the Communist regime. A young American caught the flavor of the moment in his description of his 1985 journey to the U.S.S.R., a few months after Gorbachev took power, in a 1990 Op-Ed piece in *The New York Times:*

> I was struck by how profoundly changes were occurring in the Soviet Union at the social and cultural level. Here were kids growing up in the cities with creature comforts never known by their parents, yet acting with the same rebelliousness as their peers in Eastern Europe and America. They were experimenting with marijuana flowing in from Afghanistan, listening to rock music, dressing in new wave styles and dabbling in counterculture or health culture activities like jogging, massage and psychic healing. And despite all of their ideological training, they were embracing Lennon—not Lenin.[39]

Nothing brought the centrality of the issue of young people's allegiances more clearly into focus than the reported youthfulness of many of those gathered in front of the Russian Parliament during the days and nights of the aborted August 1991 coup.[40]

The descriptions of youth in the Soviet Union in its final years have real resonance in Cuba, despite the obvious historical, cultural, and geographical differences. Here, too, is a population of young people, fully half of them born after the Revolution, with no personal memory of life before 1959 and no knowledge of a time when free education and health care and job security were not readily available to everyone. It is to this generation that an increasingly aging leadership must appeal, and the shape of this appeal is not at all clear. Cuban youth of this third postrevolutionary generation clearly share concerns with their Soviet counterparts about personal freedom and individual expression. The fate of the Revolution will depend on the degree to which the young feel enfranchised in a system that speaks, and permits them to speak, to their own concerns.

The Cuban response thus far to the "youth problem" has been far more conservative, limited, and of a qualitatively different order than that of the Soviets.

In order to understand the nature of these differences, we must situate them in a discussion of the nature of the relationship between civil society and the state in the two countries. For, what *glasnost* in the Soviet Union allowed, in fact, facilitated and speeded along, was the beginnings of a (re)definition of civil society as distinct from the state, a (re)emergence of a terrain on which the terms of discourse are not given, controlled, and defined by the state. Within the civil society, the Gorbachev period witnessed the formation, for instance, of a remarkable variety of political groups and clubs or, as Ernst Mandel has termed them, "social mini-milieus,"[41] representing views ranging across the political spectrum, from Pamyat (memory), which embodied right-wing, nationalist, and anti-Semitic tendencies; to a constellation of small, constantly regenerating left-wing groupings organized loosely into a Federation of Socialist Clubs; to a growing movement of issue-oriented groupings centered around ecological concerns.

The formation of these clubs was paralleled by an incredible boom in the publication of journals and bulletins of all sorts, as well as an opening in Soviet newspapers and magazines for critical articles and commentary. Former state publications like *Moscow News* (once directed at foreign audiences, but by the late 1980s published in Russian as well), *Ogonyok* (Light), or *Vek XX i Mir* (Twentieth Century and Peace) or literary journals like the famous *Novy Mir* were literally snapped up by the Soviet population (to such an extent that Kagarlitsky reported in 1988 that families joined together in "consumer cooperatives" in order to be able to share the expense of subscribing to the many publications of interest).[42]

But more than this, the penetration of the political into every arena of life for seven decades generated, perhaps in reaction and perhaps more pervasively, the flourishing of the *not* political. The opening provided by *glasnost* went in all kinds of directions. The sudden availability of novels, poetry, or historical accounts that had been banned in the 1920s and 1930s, or even in the 1960s and 1970s (most prominently, Pasternak's *Dr. Zhivago*), was intertwined with an intense interest in other sorts of texts. For instance, from 1990 to 1991, the top-selling book in the U.S.S.R. was Dale Carnegie's *How to Win Friends and Influence People*. Its major competition came from a variety of "popular autobiographies" (also part of the how-to-make-good category) such as Henry Ford's *My Life and Work* and Lee Iacocca's *Iacocca: An Autobiography*. What wasn't selling was everything tainted by the legacy of orthodox Marxism-Leninism: in its place, its most obvious opposites—idealist, existentialist, and religious tracts—flourished.[43] In 1991, Kagarlitsky reports, hawkers on the Moscow metro were doing a heady business in vampire literature and artifacts.[44]

What this meant for young people was captured impressionistically by our young American on his second trip to the Soviet Union in June of 1989:

> I returned, startled not only by how quickly change has come since 1985, but also by the leading role now played by young people. In Moscow's city squares, young pamphleteers arc calling for multiple political parties. In Leningrad, young environmentalists are demanding the cleanup of the water system. In Gorky Park, we joined a thousand young Soviet kids dancing to anti-apartheid songs from Paul Simon's album, "Graceland."[45]

Cuba, in contrast, has experienced no such uncontrolled resurgence within the civil society. It would be almost impossible to imagine in Cuba the proliferation of the political clubs that sprung up seemingly in every context in the Soviet Union, even those defining themselves as Marxist. Indeed, resumed publication of a journal like the 1960's *Pensamiento Crítico* is inconceivable under the present circumstances.

If in the *glasnost*-era Soviet Union, young people (among others) began to look to new arenas for expression on various levels and in multiple contexts, in Cuba these possibilities remain far more limited and limiting. Rather, the Cubans have sought to deal with the youth issue by encouraging the incorporation of more young people into existing governmental and Party institutions and by emphasizing the importance of their role in these institutions. Thus, within Popular Power, there has been a conscious and concerted effort to increase the number of young (as well as black or female) delegates and deputies. In this same vein, the role of the Young Communists' Union (UJC) as the central pillar of the Revolution and its voice to young people in general has been underscored. The age at which one can become a member of the Party was lowered from thirty-five to thirty, and the head of the UJC, Roberto Robaina, was elevated to the status of member of the Politburo.[†]

Indeed, in the late 1980s Robaina's name came up usually within the first five minutes of any discussion with Party cadres of the issue of youth. He was described as an iconoclastic and charismatic leader, respected by young people both within the UJC and outside it. If these adjectives sound familiar, one might recall that such terms were, and still are, used to describe Fidel. One got the sense that Robaina's rapidly growing po-

---

[†]Robaina's star has continued to rise. In April of 1993 he was appointed minister of foreign relations.

litical stature had everything to do with the belief that, in him, the Revolution had found, in the short run, the Fidelista link to the third generation and, in the long run, a possible substitute for Fidel in a post-Fidelista Cuba. And all this without having to reconsider the terms and the *meaning* of the basic manner and form in which political power has been invested in the thirty-three years since the Revolution's accession to power.

Calls to young people to participate in the Revolution have been phrased in the hauntingly familiar terms of sacrifice and struggle filtered through an all-encompassing nationalism that were evoked for an older generation. But within the distinct reality of this younger generation, to what degree do such pleas have an appeal?

And if the rhetoric of the appeal to sacrifice is the same, so, too, is the paternalism, with specific reference to young people, that has been such a powerful component of the Cuban Revolution. The 1989 banning of two Soviet magazines, *Moscow News* and *Sputnik,* provided one indication of this (*Moscow News* had become a hotly sought after source of information about changes going on in the Soviet Union; it would disappear from Cuban newsstands moments after its appearance and circulate at many times the official price on the black market). In an editorial explaining the banning of these magazines, the Party newspaper, *Granma,* denounced those in the Soviet Union who "deny the guiding role of the Party and demand a multiparty system, advocate the free market, exalt foreign investments, have rediscovered popular participation and question internationalism and solidarity aid to other countries." The editorial stressed that

> [w]e now lament the negative consequences noticeable as a result of the dissemination among us of these distortions, confused ideas and fabrications. . . . [W]ith pain and bitterness we have had to confront the consequences of this confusion, of all these ideas, in young people who have been poorly informed in terms of ideology and history, a state of affairs for which we are responsible.[46]

This statement *must* raise questions about the leadership's view of Cuban youth and about its faith in young people's abilities to sort out their thinking with regard to a revolution with three-decades-old roots. The attempt to exclude ideas seems, at best, a futile way to influence people's thinking or correct for weaknesses in the Revolution's own mechanisms of socialization. At worst, it underlines the paternalism that has always characterized the top leadership of the Revolution, and most particularly, Castro himself.

This same deeply ingrained vein of paternalism feeds the Revolution's seemingly unquenchable need to channel and, thereby, contain and control. With youth, as with virtually all other aspects of life on the island, the Revolution seeks somehow to encompass any potential rebellion or protest, in effect, to co-opt it before it escalates. Thus cognizant of the fact that popular music has been throughout the world a vehicle and a mouthpiece for youthful expression, the Revolution has tried to incorporate new musical trends into celebrations of itself. On the occasion of the April 1990 celebration of the Day of Youth, army helicopters flew over Havana inviting young people to "come dance lambada and reaffirm your commitment to the Revolution." Even the visual accoutrements of youthful rebellion have been adopted and adapted: in recent demonstrations (around such events as the March 1990 return to port of a Cuban fishing vessel attacked by the United States), headbands, worn across the forehead in the style young people have employed in the past few decades in protest demonstrations (most recently, by Chinese students occupying Tienanmen Square), were handed out bearing declarations such as, *Yo me quedo* (I am staying here) or *Cuba sí* (Cuba, yes). Further, areas have been, in effect, cordoned off and given over to young people in the major locales—the city of Havana most prominently—where they might pose a threat were they more generally dispersed. For example, in May of 1991, the beach strip closest to the heart of the city of Havana became a designated area for young people to gather, complete with concessions, blaring music, and a very visible contingent of police guarding its periphery. Whereas on one level this move is intended as a response to the shortage of outlets for youth in the cities, on another level it could be understood as the geographical representation of the leadership's instinct and desire to contain potential sources of protest within boundaries it can control.

Finally, the age at which Cubans are permitted to travel abroad has been lowered; in August of 1991 it was reduced to twenty.[47] While this can be interpreted as a response to popular desires, since many who have traveled recently do not return, it can also be seen as a measure (effectively used earlier by the Revolution) to ease the departure from Cuba of those who are the most discontent and, therefore, potentially disruptive.

Given this drive to contain everything within itself, the terrain of civil society contracts and the mildest forms of youthful expression have the potential of escalating or being made to escalate, into signs of antagonism unacceptable to the leadership. Further, it plays directly into what Nelson Valdés describes as the "dichotomous terms" that have traditionally characterized Cuban political reality. Valdés, writing with great insight about the constant reference to "betrayals" in the rhetoric of Cubans, observes:

> The right to competing and distinct political perspectives has not gained acceptance in Cuban politics. As with other social relations, politics appears to be based on total, complete and absolute loyalty to an individual or a set of "morals." Politics, hence, requires unconditional loyalty, trust and faith. These then become an index of political commitment.... Cuba before 1959 was a society filled with discord, with no fundamental community of interests, and it could not foster a culture of tolerance and diversity. The revolutionary experience, after 1959, heightened the divergence and the polarization. The political categories of the nineteenth century continue to this day, in Cuba as well as in the exile community.[48]

The degree to which the leadership is willing to release its grasp and able to move beyond this rigid dichotomy in judging individual activity and expression will measure its ability to continue.

Cuba shares with the former Soviet Union a second, perhaps more immediate dilemma that plagued actually existing socialism since its early years. It must deal in some way with an entrenched bureaucracy whose interests and existence militate against change or reform of any sort. The autonomy of this bureaucratic stratum, the fact that it is responsible to no one, becomes most visible in the corruption it so inevitably spawns.

In various retellings of the chronology and sources of his initiatives, it was Gorbachev's inability to push forward his plans for economic change in the face of overwhelming bureaucratic resistance that made both *glasnost* and democratization necessary: a political and cultural loosening was required to begin to stir people at the base to identify and attack bureaucratic strangleholds.

Gorbachev's initiatives against the vast middle and lower levels of the entrenched Soviet bureaucracy took a variety of forms. *Perestroika* began from the top down. It was heralded by outright dismissals on a wide scale at the beginning of Gorbachev's regime. When these efforts failed to dislodge the huge body of inherently conservative administrators and party *aparachiks, glasnost* became his means to attempt to accomplish his goals from the bottom up. *Glasnost* quickly engendered a disparate movement for democratization. Among the most telling results of *glasnost* and democratization were the April 1989 elections for a newly revitalized Supreme Soviet.[49] Further, various analysts have speculated that the flames of nationalist conflicts, such as that between the Azerbajani and Armenian Republics, were fanned by bureaucrats threatened by or already ousted as a result of Gorbachev's reforms; their actions were an attempt to put a halt to these reforms by undermining Gorbachev himself.[50] Gorbachev's waffling on this issue during his final two years in office, his turning back to the old-line Party bureaucrats as his mainstay, certainly contributed directly to his demise and to the dissolution of the Soviet Union.

The Cuban attack on what they refer to as their "bastard class" has been far more circumspect and has broken no new ground, either in analysis of its origins or in prescriptions for dealing with it. The source of this swelling bureaucracy is clear to the Cubans; like much else in the Rectification Campaign, at first, Fidel pinpointed the Planning and Management System as the personification of the villain: "In 1973, there were 90,000 administrative personnel in the country and by 1984 the figure had risen to 250,000. In other words, prior to the implementation of the SDPE and the reforms, we had only 90,000 administrative personnel and now we have two and one half times that many."[51]

Over and over after 1986, and more intensively in the wake of Eastern Europe occurrences, Fidel Castro's speeches were punctuated by attacks on "some people, supposedly very theoretically knowledgeable

[, who] . . . forgot the true path, the really revolutionary path to build socialism" by using "methods . . . which were actually capitalist methods."[52]

The idea, now broadened to encompass political as well as economic entities, is that the source of the bureaucracy is the institutional structures copied from the Soviets during the 1970s. These models are not understood as Stalinist in nature, but they are seen as involving the most negative aspects of the Soviet system and enshrining a political elite that is not composed of the best and the brightest but, particularly at the intermediate level, the most compliant and the most career-oriented, and therefore, the most conservative. This elite is seen as the most stubborn bulwark against effective change. Rectification, within these parameters, becomes, at least on paper, a virtual coup détat against the enshrined party and state bureaucracy.

There are several key issues that such an interpretation raises, or at the least, does not resolve. First, it points to Fidel as the solution. As initiator of the coup against an inherently antidemocratic bureaucracy, he is once again seeking to resolve societal problems through personalistic measures. Fundamentally antidemocratic, paternalistic means are being used to combat antidemocratic formations as part of a cycle of actions and reactions that has been repeated in Cuban revolutionary history since 1959.

But equally important here is what the Cubans are ignoring by tracing the source and nature of bureaucracy in Cuba to the error of having mistakenly borrowed bad models from other countries. What they forget is the long history of bureaucratic strangleholds that have at other moments enmeshed the Cuban Revolution, even during periods in which "capitalistic methods" had been most thoroughly rejected. Forgotten as well is the Revolution's equally long track record of failure in dealing with these strangleholds. The top leadership has seemingly always sought to deal with bureaucracy as a matter of numbers. This continues to be true in the present crisis; thus Castro announced in September 1990 that

> [w]e must reduce by 80 percent the office workers in those agricultural enterprises, 80 percent! Yes, this must end once and for all. And those who keep asking for reports to be filled out, let them beware because we'll see to it that wherever there are 100, less than 20 will be left; and not only there but in the rest of the country as well, less than 20! No one knows the amount of people who have ended up in the offices.[53]

The figures are dramatic and will become increasingly dramatic as Cuba fights its way through its "special period in peace." In part, they are dictated by the nature of the current crisis, most particularly, the need to cut back on public transportation and workdays to save energy and to close workplaces due to energy and resource shortages, as well as the pressing need for agricultural labor given the current drive for food self-sufficiency. But nonetheless, the methodology is achingly familiar. In the absence of a thorough analysis of the roots of the problem, not only now but throughout Revolution, even the most severe number chopping is doomed to failure.

The heart of the problem—that officials in every political and economic structure must answer only to those above them, if at all—evidences itself everywhere. If we take, for the moment, the 1989 trials of Ochoa, the de la Guardias, and former Interior Minister Abrantes at their face value— that is, if we accept the official Cuban presentation of them—they indicate some measure of the degree to which, in Cuba as in the Soviet Union, high-level officials were responsible to no one for their actions and could do whatever they liked with impunity. And, as in the Soviet Union, the inevitable benefits to those who enjoy this lack of accountability are privilege and corruption. According to Fidel himself, the de la Guardia brothers "lived like tycoons, spent money, showed off and led a life that was different from that of anyone else."[54] One must wonder why, if as Fidel says, "everyone knew" how the de la Guardia brothers lived, no one did anything about it or apparently even questioned it. The answer again is unfortunate: only Fidel was in a position to question it; nothing happened until he did.

Moreover, popular reaction to the trials revealed the degree to which it is perceived that the same corruption generally characterizes those who hold any sort of position of power in the Revolution, even at the lowest levels. In Santiago during the 1989 Carnival rehearsal, celebrations that coincided with the Ochoa trial and his subsequent execution, this refrain passed among the *trovadores*:

> *Pidiendo clemencia para Ochoa*
> *Después de todo, cada cual*
> *Se corrompe según el nivel que tiene*
> *Pues hasta Cachita la del Comité*
> *Se vende por un bistec*[†]

The focus of Fidel's interpretation of what went wrong in Eastern Europe and the Soviet Union tends to move away from systemic analyses and toward a belief in individual "errors." Events in the Soviet Union for him comprised a sort of "suicide at the center"[55] and are not a sequence he wishes to emulate. The lessons he draws from this assessment necessarily heighten his instinct to control, not to allow the beginning of a process that will, in his understanding, lead inexorably to the unraveling of the fabric of the Revolution. In declaring Cuba the final bastion of socialism, he continually evokes what we have cited as the very real differences between the Cuban experience of socialism and that of the countries of

---

[†]Asking for clemency for Ochoa/After all, each/corrupts himself according to his position/down to so-and-so of the Committee (Committees in Defense of the Revolution, or C.D.R.s, which are neighborhood organizations)/Who sells herself for a steak.

Eastern Europe and the uniqueness of Cuba's paths and decisions over the past thirty years. He is right in stressing these differences, but they must not blind him to certain evident parallels and to the lessons that the wrenching transitions of the Gorbachev years offer to Cuba. For, as Roy Medvedev and others have made clear, what happened in the Soviet Union was indeed systemic and cannot be seen as a result of the actions of a single individual or individuals. Thus, while Gorbachev's actions certainly facilitated the (re)awakening of civil society in the Soviet Union, it occurred in large part independent of him: "The situation in the country," says Medvedev, "became so bad that the people simply spoke out, and could not be stopped. He gave people opportunities which they took in ways that surprised him and displeased him."[56]

To the degree that the Cuban leadership chooses to ignore processes already underway on the island or to believe that it can control these processes for its own, predetermined ends and by its own traditional means, it must fail. And this would be true even if the collapse of socialism in the rest of the world had not left Cuba bereft of the material bases of its existence. We turn to exactly these events and their impact on Cuba in the chapters that follow.

7

Popular Power: The Reckoning

Given the limits in its jurisdiction, it seems almost inevitable that a downswing in the economy would seriously undermine the functioning of the Popular Power system and, most importantly, the degree to which it was perceived by the public as an effective institution. By the late 1970s and early 1980s there were harbingers of the severe critique to which Popular Power would be subjected in 1990 in the course of preparations for the Fourth Party Congress.

This critique proceeded over the years along two veins. The first concerned the system's ability to "deliver the goods." As we have seen, as early as the December 1978 National Assembly, delegate/deputies had articulated the problem at a national level by describing the direct connection between local delegates' ability to come up with the means to resolve problems and the prestige of the institution of Popular Power as a whole. To the degree that jurisdictional limitations fed a popular perception (particularly in urban areas) that delivering the (material) goods was what Popular Power was about, the economic downturn that began in the mid-1980s would underscore the failures of the institution. We can measure this to some extent, by returning to the issue of housing maintenance, the mini–case study examined in Chapter 5.

The economic crisis meant inevitably that material for housing repair would become even more scarce. According to the official statistics for 1988, while the total amount of pesos spent nationally on materials for

155

maintenance* grew steadily in the first half of the 1980s, it began to decline after 1986, so that by 1988, it was somewhere near the 1983 figure. This pattern repeated itself in the value of maintenance materials alloted to the two provinces we examined in the earlier case study. In Havana Province, the decline in absolute investment in maintenance began in 1987, and by 1988, maintenance expenditure was approximately 62 percent of the 1986 figures. The City of Havana Province followed along the same lines: spending by 1988 is 74.5 percent of what it had been in 1986.

These general declines were matched by parallel drops after 1986 in the resources for maintenance work controlled by Popular Power. Nationally, Popular Power in 1988 was alloted only 77 percent of the amount in absolute peso value that it had at its disposal in 1985. And again, this same pattern of declining resources was reflected on the provincial level. In 1988 the peso value of resources for maintenance and repair controlled by Popular Power in the Province of Havana declined to 79 percent of what it had been in 1986. The equivalent figure for the City of Havana Province was 68 percent. These figures, along with the general decline over the 1981 to 1988 period in the percentage of total maintenance funds given to Popular Power (from a high of 91 percent in 1981 to a low of 76 percent in 1988, with only slight fluctuation in the intervening years), indicate that after 1986 Popular Power, in the highly visible arena of housing maintenance, was left with fewer and fewer resources and could presumably resolve fewer and fewer problems.[1]

By the time of the December 1989 National Assembly, the housing crisis, particularly in Havana, had intensified to the degree that, by official estimates, of the 528,000 dwellings in the capital, only half could be said to be in good condition; another 23 percent were classified as in fair condition; a further 23 percent were in bad condition. The Assembly was told that some 3,000 people were living in homeless shelters, while 16,000, who should be living in shelters, chose to "continue living in their precarious homes at their own risk." Another 205,000 were living in 7,000 "tenement areas"; 63,000 lived in 60 neighborhoods and 96 small areas considered "unhealthy"; and 284,000 lived in "slums, unhealthy areas or homes in a very poor state of repair." (The difference between these categories was not spelled out.) And these figures did not take into account the vast numbers of people living in severely overcrowded conditions.[2]

Castro traced the severity of the crisis to "negative tendencies and wrong ideas."[3] Whatever the source of the problem, it was crystal clear that Popular Power had done little to resolve it. The escalating incapacity

---

*This category, in Cuban accounting, includes housing maintenance, which generally amounts to approximately 13 percent of total maintenance expenditures. It includes as well the maintenance and repair of schools, health centers, industrial and agricultural plants, electrical and telecommunications facilities, oil and gas pipelines, roads, railroad systems, and maritime, hydraulic, and mining facilities.

of the Popular Power structures throughout the country to deal with the material problems of daily life surely contributed to a growing popular disenchantment with the system as a whole. But this disenchantment was fed, as well, by a second vein of critique, which had much more to do with the political limitations of the structures, particularly as they were experienced at the local level, and a sense (much accentuated in urban areas) that Popular Power was not a viable arena of political discussion, input, influence, and popular control; that is, what was being questioned was the very legitimacy of the institution.

Certainly, on both scores, economic and political dissatisfaction, experiences varied tremendously from one municipality to another. The complex and aggravated problems of living in the municipality of Central Havana always contrasted starkly to life in rural municipalities like Güira de Melena. Cuban researchers[**] examining the local structures of Popular Power in four municipalities across the island, including Central Havana, in the late 1980s pointed to the sources of this contrast: the concentration of population in Central Havana, the number of institutions or entities not under its municipal control, the daily influx of people who are not residents in the locality, the age and dilapidated condition of buildings, the wear and tear of traffic on streets and sidewalks that are already in bad condition, and the more intangible anomie that always affects crowded urban communities. As a result, they concluded, "It was here (in Central Havana) where the indices of conflict and dissatisfaction were sharpest, and where local government enjoyed the least legitimacy."[4] Elsewhere, members of the research team noted, on a more generalized level, the range of relative efficacy of the institutions of Popular Power was revealed in the very language by which people refer to it; *habañeros,* they pointed out, had continued for fifteen years to use the official label, "Popular Power"; by contrast, in the interior of the country, "the government" has in many places replaced the official designation.[5]

These two veins of critique came together in the course of the islandwide Party meetings during the summer of 1990 held in workplaces in preparation for the Fourth Party Congress. The meetings—89,000 of them—were open, in the expectation that non-Party workers would attend and participate. It is fair to say that Popular Power, along with the Federation of Cuban Women (FMC[†]), were the two institutional structures subjected to the most vociferous criticism. The public critique was provided by a series of articles in the magazine *Bohemia,* which focused in

---

[**]The work of this research team represented the first serious systematic effort by Cuban social scientists not employed within the institution of Popular Power itself to examine the system in the field. As such, we will refer to it extensively in the pages that follow.

[†]In the case of the FMC, the debate concentrated on eliminating it altogether, or at least eliminating it formally on the base level. The argument was not that it had succeeded too well, but that it in essence had lost its sense of purpose and in actuality was not functioning at the base level.

three successive issues in July 1990 on Popular Power at the local level, seen first from the vantage point of the electors, then of the delegates themselves, and on an examination of public perceptions of the functioning and failures of the National Assembly.

These articles are revealing on a number of levels. First, they clearly articulated the general consensus that local, municipal-level Popular Power had eroded as a forum for effective popular participation. Two-fifths, or 40 percent of those surveyed by *Bohemia*, felt that they played no role in the governing of their country. The same number of people registered their lack of confidence in their local delegate. Almost 50 percent agreed that their delegates did not have the authority to resolve the problems with which they are confronted. One-fourth, or 25 percent, could not name their delegate. And only 31 percent stated that, if nominated, they would stand for election to delegate in their circumscriptions.[6] Delegates were seen as little more than messengers between people in neighborhoods and unresponsive administrative personnel over whom they had little to no effective control. A friend related that in her circumscription, their delegate was regularly referred to, not by name, but as *voy a tomar nota* ("I'll make a note of it"). *Bohemia* gave anecdotal substance to the seemingly widespread conclusion among electors that if the delegate were "the first link in the chain" of government, the only representative directly elected by the people, s/he was also the weakest link.[7] One respondent from Granma Province related that in his barrio, a new suburb built without a water supply,

> [f]or five years, we had a problem with the water and nobody did anything about it. We've been promised many things, but there are always delays. I stopped going to the *rendición de cuenta* sessions from the moment in which my delegate argued that we had to be satisfied with the little we'd gotten, because even that was acquired through begging and asking for favors.[8]

Nor was a delegate's lack of authority always linked to questions of availability of materials. A second respondent from the Province of Havana complained:

> In several *rendición de cuenta* meetings we asked that the bus schedule be changed to allow a bus to (start operating) before seven in the morning so that children and workers were not late. The delegate went to the terminal and made the request but nothing changed. And here the solution doesn't depend on scarce resources because we weren't asking for more buses. What authority does the delegate have?[9]

For their part, the delegate interviews revealed that delegates did not themselves understand precisely what they were supposed to be doing, "governing or transmitting." As one delegate commented: "In converting himself into a transmitter of problems, many times the delegate lets himself be used by administrators to justify unjustifiable things to the people he represents."[10] Partly at least, they argued that this was due to the fact that delegates across the system were not prepared to carry out their mandate:

"Some who are elected have only a superficial understanding of what they represent and how to efficiently carry out their job. The orientation seminar they take is a slapdash affair."[11]

The work commissions introduced a further ambiguity in the functioning of the assemblies at all levels. Work commissions, made up of delegates and "experts" in a given area and appointed by the relevant assembly, were intended to inform the work of assemblies at all levels of the Popular Power structure. They meet on a continuous basis to study given issues and to report their findings and recommendations back to the assembly. For instance, attached to the National Assembly are twenty commissions that focus on issues such as child care and women's rights, culture and art, youth, defense and internal order, constitutional and legal affairs.[12] Archibald Ritter, in his 1985 examination of the National Assembly, cited the work commissions as "one encouraging feature," which permits "a type of scrutiny of a particular aspect of Cuba's socioeconomic system [which] may be invaluable as a means to put the pressure on parts of the economic bureaucracy in order to improve economic performance from the standpoint of citizens in their positions as consumers." Optimistically, Ritter concludes that "The commissions may come to play an important role in permitting the views and interests of the public on specific issue areas to find expression in the National Assembly."[13] Dilla and González, in their study, portray the work commissions at the municipal level as "successful examples of connecting the population to the tasks of fiscalization" and calculate that, nationwide, they incorporate, some 20,000 regular citizens into the governing structures. (As an example, they cite one municipality's commission on gastronomy that, aside from three delegates, is comprised of nondelegates, including two retirees with more than thirty years experience working in restaurants and cafeterias.)[14]

In the *Bohemia* articles, however, delegates spoke of the obscurity of the work going on in these commissions and of how assemblies tended mechanically to rubber stamp the work commissions' studies and proposals, without substantive critique or in-depth discussion, either out of habit, fear, or ignorance. From this, one deputy from Santa Clara concluded, "Popular Power assemblies provide no real countervailing force."[15] This was felt to be particularly egregious at the national level. The electorate, which saw the deputies to the National Assembly merely approving reports or voting unanimously for the passage of laws, "[felt] a certain lack of concern on the part of deputies with the manner with which their problems [were] dealt."[16]

Finally, the weaknesses of the municipal-level assembly structure were magnified by the ambiguous relationship between the executive committees and the assemblies they were intended to serve. Both the *Bohemia* articles and the Dilla/González study underlined the tendency for the executive committee, which was to serve as the subordinate administrative arm of its assembly, to replace the assembly as the actual and perceived governing body. This was made even more problematic, particularly at the municipal level, by the fact that executive committees were not directly chosen by the electors, but elected by the assembly itself from a list of candidates provided by the Municipal Electoral Commission, over which the Party presided. Since it was the executive committee that functioned continually in between assembly meetings and since its president, vice president, and secretary (elected by each executive committee from its own ranks) served as professionals (that is, with salaries) and could therefore devote their full attention to their work, it is easy to understand why this substitution took place and what its impact would be on the perceptions of an electorate to which a given executive committee had no direct links, nor any responsibility to give account of its actions.[17]

The second level of critique raised by the *Bohemia* articles was perhaps more important in terms of its implications for the future. Embedded in the responses of both the electorate and the delegates were a series of suggested reforms that looked toward a restructuring of Popular Power, largely within the confines of the present system. Occasionally, suggestions went beyond these confines to challenge the conceptualization of the system itself and the qualitative narrowness of its jurisdiction. Dilla and González, drawing on their fieldwork, develop in greater depth these two categories of reforms.

In the first category (that is, reforms that did not challenge the boundaries of the space within which Popular Power has thus far operated), electors suggested that delegates (as well as National Assembly deputies) should operate as professionals during their terms in office. The implication is that as professionals they would have both the time and the prestige to more seriously carry out their obligations and more effectively influence recalcitrant administrators.[18] Further, and very much related, electors (and the research study) noted that delegates hardly had a chance to familiarize themselves with the issues they must grasp to be able to operate effectively when it was once more election time. These observations, as well as the remarkable and consistent 50 percent delegate turnover in each municipal election, pointed toward extending the delegates' terms in office from two-and-one-half years. (The most common projection seemed to be to double terms to five years.)[19] Professionalization, as well as lengthened terms in office, might at least to some degree ameliorate the fact that few delegates or deputies had the time or the training to grasp the complexities of issues under discussion: their ignorance inevitably limited their participation in discussions and left virtually all authority with nonelected specialists to shape both the parameters and the content of discussion in the assemblies.

A second category of suggested reforms did begin to challenge, at least potentially, the confines within which the system has operated and to speak to a qualitative shift in its bases of power. The articles and studies looked to correct the situation that most people living in a given municipality hadn't the least idea who represented them as their deputy in the National Assembly[20] through direct elections of deputies by people at the base. The sense that short biographies were insufficient as the basis for choosing between municipal candidates implied rethinking the issue of campaigning. Dilla and González stress the inadequacy of the present system:

> According to our inquiries in Santa Cruz, only 9 percent of those interviewed considered the biographies as an effective means of information, and something less than one third had read them before voting, which certainly means that the basis of voting relies on the circulation of information through primary links among neighbors with probable unwanted consequences in terms of the transmission of traditional and conservative stereotypes.[21]

Perhaps most serious in the context of immediate goals and needs, reliance on biographies, which as the Dilla/González study points out, was intended to "equalize" people's chances for election, had in practice done just the opposite: these biographies militated in favor of older males at the expense of both women and younger people—two categories of individuals whose participation in governance is a critical goal of the leadership. Older males were likely to have a longer list of public achievements, such as prestigious international service, while women and younger people were likely to be less politically visible.[22]

Was it possible to envision a type of campaigning that would avoid, as Dilla and González put it, the "demagoguery and commercialization of suffrage, and the fragmentation of the individuals to Party loyalties or *caudillos?*"[23] The necessity for rethinking the issue of campaigning was certainly implied in their conclusion that the system's "unilateral projections of a sum of values and political conduct has generated serious obstacles to the emergence of a dynamic representative leadership capable of meeting the challenge of power."[24] It was directly articulated by one respondent in the *Bohemia* articles, who suggested the need for "pre-electoral meetings" where those nominated could "express their ideas about their mandate."[25]

The final category of suggested municipal-level reform focused on the issue of jurisdiction. If, as we have argued earlier, Popular Power at the base continues to operate within a limited space that focuses exclusively upon local issues and people's material needs, then its escalating inability to meet these needs inevitably made it seem a less-than-efficacious forum, thereby eroding its potential as an important legitimating and legitimate institution. If its scope of operation were substantially broadened, then the measure of its efficacy or its power would have to be qualitatively different. A few respondents among both the electorate and the delegates in the *Bohemia* articles began to consider this issue. One delegate, for instance, stated that "discussions (in the *rendición de cuenta* meetings) must not be limited only to local concerns. These meetings must serve as the primary tribunals which question the inadequacies of the Popular Power system itself or deliberate over other matters of national policy which are now generally ignored."[26]

The Dilla/González study recapitulates this idea at a generalized, if somewhat vague, level, when it speaks of the need for "greater autonomy for political associations" and "more ample and systematic spaces of public debate."[27] The president of the students' union in the economics department of the Cienfuegos Technological Institute was more explicit in this regard; he suggested to his *Bohemia* interviewer that Popular Power, to have any credibility and, by implication, legitimacy, must become more autonomous from the Party. "It must," he asserted, "make its own decisions. Presently," he added, "many Party militants (within Popular Power) consult the Party about everything."[28]

Bohemia's examination of the National Assembly began with the common image of the invisibility and passivity of the National Assembly deputies. Here it was perhaps even harsher than in its critique of Popular Power at the municipal level:

> Anonymous or nonexistent? Both are suggested by the apparent silence that encases the work of the deputies. Comfortably installed in the Palace of Conventions, they meet two or more times a year to debate about and decide upon national policies, but it is the voices of functionaries and government leaders which dominate the interventions.[29]

One National Assembly deputy from Holguín went farther, arguing that what goes on is "really not democracy": "The National Assembly is monotonous. There are almost never objections (and) almost nobody ever opposes anything: the conformity is overwhelming. Deputies are aware that some things are no good, but are afraid to say anything."[30] He drew back, however, from concluding that the absence of democracy in the National Assembly had structural origins in the system itself. Rather he concluded that the blame rests in individual cowardice: "It's not a question of asking for more liberty; it's a matter of needing more political courage. This I've said in the Municipal and the National Assemblies."[31]

The reform implicitly suggested here is that the National Assembly be a real forum of debate (as it perhaps was in the June 1978 meetings) and that, as Dilla and González phrase it in their comments on the municipal level of the system, "conflict as a moment in the construction and direction of consensus" must be recognized.[32] While this would not necessarily expand the jurisdictional space of Popular Power, it would at least look toward blurring the boundaries within which it was contained.

Efforts to reform or correct poorly functioning aspects of Popular Power were underway well before the Fourth Party Congress. One indication of the leadership's intention to renew the system and begin to restore its importance was the appointment in February 1990 of Juan Escalona as president of the National Assembly,[33‡] the office that, jokingly,

---

††Following the 1993 postreform elections, Escalona was replaced by the far better known and well-liked Ricardo Alarcón. This appointment has escalated hopes that the new National Assembly will indeed have power. (A second interpretation is that Alarcón, who was Minister of Foreign Relations, has been demoted.)

had come to be perceived popularly as a place for retirement and death (since no president had lasted more than two years in office before dying). Escalona, the minister of justice, was extremely visible the summer prior to his appointment as he prosecuted General Ochoa and the de la Guardias in a nationally televised trial.

More substantively, in October of 1990 (surely as an attempt at an intermediate solution to the functional incapacities of Popular Power, particularly in the City of Havana), ninety-three *Consejos Populares*, or Popular Councils, were formed in different municipalities in the city.[34] The idea of popular councils was actually not new; according to Gina Rey, head of the Committee for the Integral Development of the Capital, they first took shape in 1983 in various municipalities across the island, largely at the initiative of delegates who represented towns or barrios within municipalities that were not the headquarters of these municipalities (that is, where the executive committee was based). The distance between a barrio and its municipal center made difficult daily or frequent delegate interaction with a given executive committee, which, as we have said, governed the day-to-day functioning of the system, including decisions about the allotment of resources. Thus, in the Province of Havana in 1983, delegates in the town of La Salud (whose municipal center is San Antonio de los Baños, some nine kilometers away) organized themselves into the equivalent of a popular council in order to try to resolve the problem of slow response to the demands and questions of their electors. Rey's argument is that these councils formed around preexisting neighborhoods, in which historical ties and social and familial connections antedated and postdated the 1976 administrative division of the island into circumscriptions. Shared understandings of mutual problems and familiarity with neighbors seemed to enable far more rapid solutions. The success of the councils elsewhere, she asserts, led to their establishment in the City of Havana itself. From a central nucleus in Old Havana, the city had grown over the centuries in concentric circles to include vastly more area, while distinct neighborhoods or barrios continued to retain their own identity in much the same way as in smaller towns in the interior. But, Rey points out, in the 1976 administrative division of the island and the subsequent establishment of Popular Power, each municipality in the city (therefore, each Municipal Assembly) grouped together, on the average, ninety circumscriptions, not necessarily taking into account existing differences or ties between barrios or neighborhoods.

In 1988, the Provincial Assembly of the City of Havana approved, on an experimental basis, the formation of four Popular Councils in barrios that were not municipal centers: Campo Florido, Calabazar, Punto Bravo, and Playa de Guanabacoa. In actuality, even prior to the Provincial Assembly's stamp of approval, delegates representing various barrios in Havana, such as Santa Fe and Cojimar, had begun spontaneously to organize themselves into what were, in effect, neighborhood groupings in an effort to resolve problems that assemblies or executive committees in municipal

seats seemed unable to resolve. Therefore, according to Rey, the establishment of the ninety-three Popular Councils in the City of Havana in
1990 was a formal declaration of the effectiveness of what she understands
as a process of both decentralization from above and spontaneous neighborhood organization from below.[35]

A Council is composed of the relevant Popular Power delegates, along
with representatives from the various mass organizations and social service
agencies within the given barrio under that Council's domain. Council
presidents are professionals; they receive a leave of absence from their jobs
and continue to be paid at the same salary while devoting their full-time
attention to Council work—this, presumably, to give them a force and a
presence the delegates themselves do not have. Further, Rey notes the
establishment of eight experimental *talleres,* or workshops, made up of
architects, engineers, sociologists, and social workers who are residents in
the specific barrios involved and who work on a salaried basis, in an effort
to resolve some of the problems that have been so severe in the City of
Havana. For instance, four of these workshops are located in Marianao,
where in the face of the now almost total elimination of state provision
of cement for repairing individual housing, architects and engineers have
been exploring the use of a kind of dirt, common in the barrio, as a
substitute. The idea, said Rey, is to use the barrio as a kind of laboratory,
to attach to it people who both know the barrio and have the professional
skills to begin to deal with problems that have seemed impervious to
resolution.

But the Popular Councils raise as many questions as they resolve.
First, given the severity of the current economic crisis and the concurrent
decline in resources available to local governing structures, it is hard to
imagine that any intermediary reform aimed solely at resolving material
problems (like housing), which everyone knows are only likely to get worse
in the foreseeable future, could evoke widespread enthusiasm or, for that
matter, reinvigorate the system.

Second, Popular Councils were established outside the framework of
the Popular Power system itself; if they managed in the interior, due to
their roots in district barrios or villages, to successfully integrate themselves
informally into the structures of government, this was hardly the case at
least initially, in Havana. The ninety-three Councils set up in 1990 were
clearly imposed from above as an emergency response to the perceived
and actual inefficacies of Popular Power itself. In a familiar pattern, the
center has imposed a solution to get around the failures of the system it
itself had created to disperse some of its power. In their first years, some
Councils, according to one observer, had a destabilizing effect on the
established Popular Power structures in the municipalities in which they
were located. The president of each Popular Council worked on a full-
time basis, in contrast to the local delegates, and although each Council
was theoretically subordinated to the Municipal Assembly that subsumed
it, its power and authority rested outside the electoral structure of Popular

Power. Reports that some Council presidents saw their authority as derived directly from Fidel and acted themselves as local "little Fidels" within their area of operation gave a sense of the problems the Popular Councils posed to the structure of Popular Power as long as they remained unintegrated into the electorally based institutional framework of local government.[36]

But more importantly, as the major pre-1992 reform of Popular Power, the Popular Councils emphasize the very limited nature of the system as a whole as a forum for broad popular expression and debate. They point again to that confused line between decentralization and democracy in Cuba. The Councils seem, at least on paper, to represent an attempt to further decentralize the structures of government in a logical manner in order to speak more directly to a series of neighborhood problems that remained unresolvable (or were perhaps even aggravated) after the countrywide 1976 administrative division was implemented. But if attempting to resolve these problems has everything to do with making daily life more bearable, it clearly has nothing to do with restructuring a system to allow forums for debate concerning decisions being taken, or directions being followed, by the leadership.

8

Into the 1990s: Socialism on One Island — or, Cuba in a World Without Alternatives*

The 1990s in Cuba dawned on the grimmest possible scenario: the collapse of the world of actually existing socialism left the island isolated as it had never been before. In a sense, the moment is 1960/61 again: the U.S. blockade has been fully implemented, but now there is no longer the possibility of a Soviet lifeline. In another sense, the moment is new and far worse: the boundless hope of Cubans in the years immediately following the Revolution—their belief in being able to accomplish the impossible, their commitment to something larger than themselves, linked with an almost universal faith in the revolutionary leadership and in the Revolution as a project for social justice—has significantly eroded. The essential question is well posed by Cuban-American sociologist Marifeli Pérez-Stable: In this most difficult of moments, "is the revolution thirty-two years ago sufficient to legitimate the current Cuban government.... [Are] the politics of consensus born out of the social revolution [still] ... effective for a more complex, diversified society?"[1] The answers to these questions are not at all as clear as the leadership might assert.

Nor has the response to the concerns, problems, and disquietude of

---

*The title is borrowed from Zygmunt Bauman's 1991 article, "Living Without an Alternative," which appeared in *The Political Quarterly,* January–March 1991, pages 35–45. (Bauman, in turn, borrowed his title from a 1956 piece by Leszek Kolakowski.) We will return to Bauman's article in the Conclusion.

the Cuban people provided by the much awaited 1991 Fourth Party Congress been reassuring.

It is hard to be very optimistic. I mean this not simply because of the dire economic straits in which Cuba finds itself, although these problems are, quite literally, catastrophic. They were spelled out in grim detail by Fidel Castro in December 1991: of the 3,763 billion dollars in imports agreed to with the Soviet Union for that year, only 1,673 billion dollars arrived.[2] This 62.2 percent shortfall had drastic effects on the everyday life of most Cubans; it is expressed best by the frustration and anger of people waiting on line after line to receive rations of basic goods, which sometimes never arrive or arrive months late. Fidel gave a concrete accounting of the shortages in his October speech to the Party Congress: As of September 30, 1991, of the amounts agreed on with the Soviet Union for that year, Cuba had received none of the caustic soda and sodium carbonate (used in the making of soaps and detergents); none of the wood pulp (used to make paper); none of the cotton and textile goods; none of the rice (in 1991, Cuba produced most of the rice it consumed, relying on China and the U.S.S.R. for the remainder); one-sixth (16 percent) of the vegetable oil; less than half of the butter; one-tenth of the condensed milk; one-fifth of the powdered milk; one-tenth of the fresh and dried fish; one-fifth of the canned meat; less than half of the agricultural machinery; and virtually no spare parts. While as of September 30, 1991, almost all (95 percent) of the agreed-upon oil had been received, almost no other petroleum products had arrived.[3] Nor in the end did the remaining 1991 allotment of Soviet oil. What this has meant, among other things, is that many enterprises work now until 3:00 PM in order to eliminate distributing the normally provided lunches; many work a shortened week to save energy and transportation costs; others have closed altogether; the hours of television operations have been shortened, again to save energy and operating costs; and electricity for domestic use has been severely rationed. Regular blackouts have become part of the daily routine of most Cubans. Given the breakup of the Soviet Union, the dissolution of COMECON (which accounted for 85 percent of Cuba's trade turnover in 1988[4]) and the termination of Soviet aid, the immediate economic future looks even bleaker. The decline in gross social product totaled 3.1 percent in 1990, 25 percent in 1991, and 14 percent in 1992.[5] Given drastically reduced oil imports for 1992, national bus schedules during that year were reduced by 40.5 percent and train schedules by 38.4 percent.[6] In Havana, where transportation has traditionally depended on buses, the 53,000 daily passengers on the *ruteros* have seen the number of these buses slashed, so that they now serve only about 60 percent of their usual passengers.[7] Waiting for a bus can now literally be a three-hour task. To alleviate the situation, hundreds of thousands of bicycles have been distributed, and they have become the major means of transport for people in all age groups.

Finally, unemployment, virtually unknown in Cuba until 1986, has increased dramatically. Cutbacks of workers in Havana, due to shutdowns and layoffs, have amounted to 29,348 by the end of 1991. While some of these "redundant workers" have been "relocated"—part of a major effort to resettle Havana residents in planned "new agricultural communities" in the countryside—many remained, for various reasons, unemployed.[8] By early 1992, 22,000 employees of the Ministry of Agriculture, that is, 52 percent of its work force, and 46,000 Ministry of Construction employees had been laid off.[9] This situation is not likely to improve much in the future. And it has hit and will continue to hit young people entering the labor force hardest; a generation of highly educated and skilled youth will have real difficulty finding work appropriate to their actual qualifications and training.

It is largely in this context that Cuba made operative a "special period in peacetime" in September of 1990. The "special period" encompasses an ambitious range of policies whose purpose is to put Cuba on stable economic footing within a short period of time.[10] The first set of policies seeks to foster self-sufficiency in food consumption through intensive development and use of land, involving selective modernization of irrigation and drainage, the resettlement of surplus urban residents in new towns being built in the countryside, and the mobilization of the population for two-week stints in planting and harvesting crops. In Havana and particularly in the cities and towns in the interior, available pieces of grassy land are now planted in vegetables. And further, in the effort to maximize food production, workers on state farms have been allowed for the first time to have their own plots of land for purposes of self-provisioning.[11] (Since some of this food production is clearly making its way into the black market, this has renewed discussion about the need to legalize private sale.) This is happening in concert with a movement toward decentralization of the management of state farms.[12]

The second set of policies reorganizes the distribution of scarce resources through the reintroduction of widescale rationing (extending even to items such as bread, which has not been rationed since the 1960s).** and a drastic cutback in the consumption of oil and energy resources.

Third, an all-out effort is being made to locate sources of hard currency by emphasizing three prongs of targeted development—sugar, tourism, and biotechnology—and by encouraging foreign investment in the form of joint ventures, profit and production sharing. As Julio García Olivares, the former head of the Cuban Chamber of Commerce, asserted in 1991: "We have to think like capitalists but continue being socialists."[13] (Olivares, a year earlier, envisioned 100 percent foreign ownership.)[14] By January 1992, there were fifty-five joint venture or production-sharing operations underway. The majority were in tourism, but during 1991, they expanded

---

**Rationed goods comprised one-fourth of family consumption during the 1980s (*Cuba Business,* October 1990, page 7).

into biotechnology, pharmaceuticals, nickel, oil, textiles, construction, sugar derivatives, transportation, cosmetics, and food processing,[15] and one hundred more such ventures were under negotiation.[16] The possibilities, according to Fidel Castro, are wide open: "There are no rigid precepts. We are ready to consider any kind of proposition."[17] In effect, what these policies amount to is a de facto transition to a mixed economy.

Finally, the Cubans are reforming the management and work process in an effort to facilitate Cuba's re-entry into the world economy.[18]

These provisions of the special period, looked at from one angle, deal directly with exactly those areas of the Cuban economy that were already chronically problematic: food production and distribution, work efficiency and redundancy, transportation. In this sense, one could well argue that the special period masks problems whose main source is hardly the present crisis.

And if this is true of the economic arena, it is at least as true of the political realm. Here this author would argue that there would have been a severe crisis even if the dramatic events that dismantled the world of actually existing socialism after 1989 had never occurred. This crisis has everything to do with the absence of democracy in the structures of decision making and the ramifications of a system that, in practice, allowed those in charge the freedom to act (or not act) without having to answer to anyone.

The crisis was not abated by the Fourth Party Congress, which was held in October of 1991 after several postponements. If the Congress was initially anticipated as the moment when a new course would be articulated, that promise faded, due to a general impression that in the end nothing truly pathbreaking was likely to occur. And indeed, the themes of the Congress echoed the traditional themes of the Cuban Revolution—unity, sacrifice, and struggle—at a time when, in the face of a very different world and a radically transformed internal situation, such themes by themselves rang hollow, and even unbearably archaic, for large sectors of the population, across all age groups or political dispositions.

The 89,000 preparatory meetings to the Party Congress held across the island during the summer of 1990, give some indication of the extent of the problem. What emerged from these meetings was a litany of complaints about ridiculous inefficiencies and horrifying and stultifying bureaucratic strangleholds and procedures, as well as a harsh critique of the institutions that were to be the means by which people participated in the decisions affecting their lives; in short, an outpouring of tales. The accounts of these meetings echo, in some respects, the critiques that followed on the failure of the harvest in 1970. And in these echoes are the reminders of the limited response those critiques, in the end, evoked. The solution that by its very repetition found its way to the center of every discussion, whether about a workplace or a political institution, seemed to be decentralization.

But the issue of decentralization raises practical, historical, and ideological questions. In a practical sense, the stress upon decentralization in the political sphere comes into conflict with the need during the special period for centralized direction of economic policies. (This is probably the reason why, by the time of the Party Congress, the rhetorical emphasis upon decentralization had faded.) Moreover, we would do well to recall that decentralization is not a new concept in Cuba: perhaps ironically, given the current critique of the 1970s, it was a word very much at the heart of the 1970 discussion. And the institutionalization policies enacted in the wake of those discussions clearly demonstrate that decentralization in and of itself is not a solution. Decentralization, as we have argued earlier, is not a synonym for democratization, nor for that matter, is increased participation.

On the question of democratization, the answers provided by the 1991 Party Congress and the political climate of the special period remain ambiguous.

In the political arena, the Congress initiated a series of reforms within clearly delineated boundaries. In the Party there was an attempt to stream-line the top layers by eliminating the Secretariat as well as "alternate member" status in the Politburo and the Central Committee. But perhaps more important, the Congress made potentially deep-reaching changes in the nature of the Party, specifically, the composition of its membership. It confirmed the use of direct secret ballot elections in the selection of members and appointments to committees at all levels. (Direct secret ballot actually became the rule in inter-Party elections soon after the 1990 Call to the Party Congress and resulted in the removal of more than one-half of the party secretaries at the local level and three of the fourteen provincial-level secretaries.) It marked a 53 percent turnover in Central Committee membership, evidence of the leadership's efforts to incorporate new faces, most particularly, younger people. The Party seems to be moving in the direction of becoming a far broader entity, more rooted within Cuban traditions—a *partido criollo,* heir to the organizational legacy established by José Martí rather than to international models. Its membership numbers 600,000. The Congress's official elimination of atheism as a requirement for membership constitutes one further step in the direction of a more inclusive membership.[19]

This movement toward a more inclusive reconceptualization of Party, state, and society is reinforced by the changes in the Cuban constitution adopted by the National Assembly in July 1992. These changes include the removal of all reference to the "dictatorship of the proletariat," the substitution of the adjective "people's" for the adjective "workers' " in describing the composition of both the Cuban state and society, and a decided shift in emphasis in tracing the basis and roots of the Cuban Revolution from Karl Marx to José Martí. Reinforcing the "Cuban-ness" of the revised document, the country's integration into the Caribbean and Latin America, that is, its more natural geographical and historical context, has replaced all references to its integration into the now defunct socialist bloc.[20]

But, Cuba will remain a one-party state; Fidel has made this crystal clear in his denunciations of multiparty systems as "imperialism's great instrument to keep societies fragmented."[21] This, in and of itself, does not spell doom for any movement toward democratization, just as the existence of two or more parties in other countries does not guarantee it. Rather, what is critical in this regard is the Party's continuing effort to confiscate the political arena. No form of nascent, in any way organized opposition outside the Party will be tolerated: the leadership's harsh (and, many observers might argue, given their size, extremely foolish) treatment of the tiny human rights groups that began to form in the 1980s makes this clear. But even more than this, there will be little, if any, officially sanctioned room for any sort of groups that are distinctly autonomous (that is, not subsumed by the Party/state), which might provide the platform for genuine popular dialogue.

Nor is it clear in the end that the decision-making structure will in practice be much altered or that the Cuban leadership's call for democracy within the Party will bear much fruit. Political parties are hardly ever models of democracy; history has demonstrated, in both capitalist and socialist societies, the difficulties in maintaining, as one Cuban analyst put it, a party structure that is *unido pero no uniforme* (united but not uniform). And, of course, the international pressures on Cuba to drop the second half of this formula (as well as the traditions of the Revolution itself and of its Marxist heritage) are and will be immense. Further, the creation of a National Defense Council, which is charged with "directing the nation in conditions of a state of war, during war, or general mobilization or a state of emergency," underscores once more the Revolution's tendency at moments of crisis to concentrate power in and around the person of Fidel Castro: as president, of course, he heads the new council.[22]

The second set of major political reforms recommended by the Party Congress and adopted, in part, by the National Assembly at its July 1992 meeting involves a substantial revamping of the Popular Power system, which after sixteen years in operation was as one Cuban friend put it, "neither popular nor powerful." (The Party's recommendations were made to the National Assembly, which has the power to accept or reject them. The National Assembly voted a set of changes into law in its July 1992 sitting.) These reforms alter some of the structures of Popular Power, and in this sense, they hold a degree of promise. They fail, however, to change certain basic aspects of the system and, therefore, must be regarded as highly limited.

First, province-level delegates and national assembly deputies are now to be elected by direct popular vote. Castro represented himself as mildly opposed to this reform when it was presented to the National Assembly at its December 1991 meeting. Ironically, he based his opposition on his

belief that a system of direct elections would make those elected accountable in a far more abstract, generalized way and would therefore increase
their power:

> Election by a collegiate body, by an assembly is much more democratic, and
> much more practical because the individual who is elected by direct ballot
> has enormous power, that person can be idolized and feel above everyone
> else. That person is invested with power in an election after which he or she
> is responsible to no one. . . . I have the deep conviction that what the people
> with a lot of responsibility in the government and the state need in a socialist
> and democratic country is not an excess of power but limited power.[23]

However the form in which this decision was embodied in the November 1992 Electoral Law limits both its potential impact and, indeed,
popular perception of it as a reform altogether. Candidates for provincial
and national assemblies are not nominated, as are municipal candidates,
from the base. Rather, they are proposed by candidacy missions and selected by the various Municipal Assemblies, which put forth as candidates
exactly the number needed to fill available slots. The electors' right to
choose directly is thereby limited to their ability to vote for none, some,
or all of these candidates (each of whom must receive at least 50 percent
of the vote in order to be elected.[24] In essence then (and despite Fidel's
heated assertions to the contrary),[25] the recommendation of the 1991 Party
Congress for direct elections from the base of provincial and national
Popular Power delegate/deputies has been encapsulated in a system that
channels choice, applying to it qualitative controls that effectively negate
the "directness" of the electoral process.[†]

Second, the term of Provincial Assembly delegates will be extended
to five years.

Third, consideration was given to clarifying and enhancing the power
of municipal-level delegates. Proposals to extend delegates' terms in office
from two-and-a-half to five years (in order to allow them to build some
degree of expertise) and to professionalize them (in order to allow them
to focus their attention full time on the districts they represent) were, in

---

[†]The first direct elections to the National Assembly took place in February 1993. As
dictated by the new Electoral Law, voters were presented with a single slate of candidates.
Given the low voter turnout in the municipal elections two months earlier, there was a
tremendous campaign to encourage people to vote—and to vote the "united list"—that is,
to vote for all the candidates. This campaign was spearheaded by Fidel Castro, who threw
himself into this effort during the three weeks prior to election day. Anti-Fidelista broadcasts
from Miami were urging people not to vote, or to nullify their ballots; on both sides of the
straits of Florida, the decision to vote and vote the list was portrayed as a choice between
Miami and the Revolution. The voter turnout was high, and overwhelmingly, people voted
the list. Despite Fidel's statements in various interviews that he would probably retire after
his next five years in office, the vote surely must serve to reinforce his traditional sense of
himself as the key to resolving Cuba's problems. And indeed, it is hard to imagine a Cuba
in which Fidel Castro lived and did not have his hand close to the levers of power.

the end, rejected by the National Assembly. But executive committees, which, it was argued, had in many municipalities effectively replaced the assembly itself as the governing bodies, were eliminated. They will be substituted by a committee no longer made up of elected delegates, but appointed by each assembly and, therefore, clearly subordinate to that assembly in much the same manner that work commissions are at present. The reform is intended to underline the purely administrative nature of these bodies and the sovereignty of the municipal assemblies themselves as the governing bodies. To reinforce the subordinate and purely administrative nature of the new committee, the president of each assembly will serve as the committee's president.

Fourth, the Popular Council experiment (Popular Councils now number 900 across the island)[26] was hailed as a great success and incorporated as an intermediary level in Popular Power, between given barrios and the municipality to which they belong.

Finally, the Party as Party will no longer participate in nominating candidates for the Provincial and National Assemblies. This acknowledges, in a limited fashion, the problems arising from the manner in which the Party is interwoven into the structure of Popular Power.[27] But it hardly begins to address the chief ambiguity and perhaps the major factor undermining the authority of Popular Power as a genuine institution of popular government—the fusion of Party and state. The overlap between Party and state, succinctly captured in the fact that virtually every National Assembly deputy has been a Party member, remains unrecognized as in any fashion a problem by the leadership. This is one of the major unresolved dilemmas of the Revolution, which will continue to haunt it.

Other reforms that might have moved toward a clear separation of Party and government, potentially increasing the government's authority, were rejected. The issue of campaigning is instructive here. The nationwide discussions of Popular Power, as well as the study we discussed in Chapter 7, underscored the inadequacy (and even the misleading nature) of structuring competition between candidates based simply on their past achievements. The system tended to militate against the election (or even the nomination) of women and of young people, who the Revolution is so earnestly trying to draw toward its center.[28] The idea of campaigns might have been reformulated and transformed; they might have been rethought as genuine opportunities for popular debate concerning national and local issues. Rather, they were narrowly interpreted as inherently and inevitably corrupt. Thus, at the December 1991 National Assembly, Fidel described campaigns as "really vicious" things of the past from which Cubans have "liberated" themselves.[29]

These changes in the political arena, taken together with alterations in the economic arena, suggest that the country is at another moment of transition, of redefinition. In moments of transition, outcomes can never be seen in beginnings; the paths at this stage lead off in a number of directions. The politics of the special period seem by definition to push for stronger measures against even mild expressions of dissent or differences in opinion. While war footing—essentially what the special period means—is never a good setting for individuals' civil rights, in this context it provides renewed justification for already existing tendencies in Cuba. The leadership's de facto banning of the ICAIC (Cuban Film Institute) film, *Alicia en el Pueblo de las Maravillas (Alice in Wonderland)*, is one very small indication of what the immediate future holds. Following a vigorous protest by ICAIC, the film was allowed a four-day run in June of 1991. After this, it officially disappeared (although it circulated widely underground on videotape). Far more ominous were the leadership's attempts to organize what it called "rapid response detachments" to meet vaguely defined internal disturbances. Such detachments had been formed previously in Cuba, but always in response to a specific event or crisis, such as the 1980 Mariel boatlift. In the summer of 1991, they were formed on the eve of the Panamerican Games, but they were clearly intended to remain organized and ready for action after the games with no specific event in mind. It is these brigades that have been employed in dragging from their homes and beating various spokespeople for the human rights groups. But it should be noted that at the time of their formation the popular response was largely negative: in both Party cells and in neighborhood CDR meetings, the purpose of the detachments was widely questioned. Original requirements that Party members sign letters agreeing to participate were dropped. There are further indications that the political parameters of the special period are being drawn in a manner that makes *all* critiques counterrevolutionary. In this vein, Carlos Aldana's speech to the December 1991 National Assembly[††] during a discussion of the rise in crime across the island is particularly chilling. Aldana moved from evoking the image of a not very attractive "austere communist future" to presenting evidence of CIA links to what he classified as the two streams of the human rights movement. He concluded with a more general discussion of what must now be considered counterrevolutionary: it encompassed virtually all criminal behavior. Aldana created a new category of people, the "lumpen antiproletariat," and suggested that

> we would be committing an error if we thought that counterrevolution in our country boiled down to this type of group and these types of activities. I believe that we are obliged to reflect, in the light of the situation in which we find ourselves, about current realities and the diverse new phenomena that we must confront.[30]

[††]Aldana himself will have no major role in his "austere communist future." In October of 1992, he was removed from all positions of power and soon thereafter expelled from the Party. The scuttlebut about his demotion involved charges of corruption for having received electronic equipment from a Japanese businessman (who, in turn, was reputed to be a CIA agent). It certainly did not appear to have anything to do with official disapproval of this December 1991 speech.

The extent to which, two years after its March 1990 issuance, the call for open discussion both within the Party and without has eroded is marked by Armando Hart, the minister of culture (and old Twenty-sixth of July member). Hart, reverting to an old and much replayed formula, declared that the time for being a "critical intellectual is over. Now it's a moment of participation."[31]

The problematic illuminated here remains dauntingly clear. It involves, above all, the fragility of the terms of discussion and debate, and of the spaces for organized expression of ideas.

Our point is not that there are no roots from which a renewed popular dialogue, neither elicited from the center nor charted or confined by it might grow. To the contrary, despite the fracturing of the intelligentsia in the early 1970s and fifteen years of virtual silence around key issues of socialism while official Marxism-Leninism ossified further, these roots do exist. They were planted firmly in the early revolutionary period and were cultivated and nourished, as we have argued, by the promise of other key moments of crisis and transition. Paradoxically, as a direct result of the economic crisis gripping Cuba, there has been an opening to the outside world not simply in economic terms, but in intellectual and political terms, marked in academic spheres, for instance, by requirements for outside financial support that both direct and encourage Cuban intellectuals to engage with their counterparts elsewhere in the world in a more free-ranging dialogue concerning contemporary issues. Further, there has been an incipient revolution at the universities, particularly in terms of what is being taught. The re-establishment, in the late 1980s, of departments of sociology and the reorganization, in 1991, of interdisciplinary faculties for the study of women (independent from the F.M.C.) are just two indications of the changes that are taking place in the intellectual realm. A vacuum has opened up: the old, imposed, rigid theoretical models are being discarded and experimentation with new ideas, methodologies and approaches has become, increasingly, the order of the day.

Movement toward a more expansive plane of discourse is, of course, tentative; its development is shadowed by multiple threats. On one side, there is the ever-present thread of paternalism in the Revolution, its instinct to channel and control, which has at other moments reined in, narrowed, and contained the realm of what is acceptable. On the other side, with a terrible and tragic irony, there is the continuing U.S. obsession with the Cuban Revolution and its attempts to strangle it by isolating it and forcing others to act in like manner; a policy, we might note, that has been for thirty-three years nothing if not counterproductive.

These forces determine at least a part of the present impasse in Cuba: here, where in the 1960s, Marxism seemed to take new life, the very content and form of discourse, the very language of the possible, which had become trapped and closed-ended, must once more chart for itself a new path upon a terrain mined with difficulties of every conceivable variety, both internal and international. It must find a way back to its beginning, while moving clearly beyond a futile re-evocation of the ideas and visions of the past. It must draw on these beginnings to locate voices that both recognize and have resonance for a whole new generation of Cubans. In a society where scarcity inclines individuals toward retention of anything that might have future use, trash cans across the island are filled with the old manuals of official Marxism-Leninism. The question remains: What will take their place?

Conclusion

There was, perhaps, nothing so remarkable about the demise of the states of actually existing socialism than the ease with which they collapsed. In the case of Eastern Europe (with the exception of Romania), the collapse came in response to peaceful gatherings of hundreds of thousands of people. In the case of the Soviet Union, it came after a few hundred youths in Moscow stood down some tanks. Zygmunt Bauman has captured the implication of this well:

> What discredited (these) state(s) more than anything else...is that they revealed an unbelievable inner weakness: (they) surrendered to an unarmed crowd while ostensibly threatened by no more than that crowd's resolute refusal to go home...Can one imagine a similar effect of a public gathering at Trafalgar Square? Or the Champs Elysées?[1]

Bauman sees the answer to his question in what he labels the "overprotectiveness"—we might term it the extreme paternalism—of the now-defunct socialist states. These states, he observes, were the incarnation of the notions of modernity that began brewing with the French Revolution and the onset of industrialization. He writes:

> Throughout its history...communism was modernity's most devout, vigorous and gallant champion—pious to the point of simplicity.... [I]t was under communist, not capitalist, auspices that the audacious dream of modernity, freed from obstacles by the merciless and seemingly omnipotent state, was pushed to its radical limits: grand designs, unlimited social engineering, huge and bulky technology, total transformation of nature. Deserts were

irrigated (but they turned into salinated bogs); marshlands were dried (but they turned into deserts); massive gaspipes criss-crossed the land to remedy nature's whims in distributing its resources (but they kept exploding with a force unequalled by the natural disasters of yore); millions were lifted from the "idiocy of rural life" (but they got poisoned by the effluvia of a rationally designed industry, if they did not perish first on the way).[2]

Since the state strove to encompass civil society, it set itself up as the (rightful) target of all discontent. Capitalism, by contrast, has shown real genius in its remarkable adaptability. Bauman points, as an example, to what he calls the "privatization of dissent," the result of capitalism's recent inclination away from governmental control which has so effectively dispersed potential opposition into seemingly separate niches organized around single social issues. The West, he asserts, has thereby "succeeded in reforging its discontents into the factors of its own reproduction."[3]

Bauman leads us back, then, to the specter of statification that has haunted throughout this century those engaged with the socialist project, centering around what we have identified as the single most critical silence within the classical Marxist tradition concerning socialism: its refusal, or its inability, to consider the boundaries between civil society and the state. Marx, in his focus upon the dis-alienation of humankind, surely expanded the definition of democracy from one of formal rights and obligations to encompass the age-old dream of social justice and substantive rights. Yet, in the same moment and so very ironically, given his virulent hatred of the boa constrictor state, Marx's vision failed to understand the continuing need for borders between civil society and the state. As Agnes Heller has observed, these borders "had no relevance for [Marx] at all. . . . In the realm of freedom, you cannot raise questions about freedom."

The contours of this issue go to the roots of political theory itself. Generations of Marxists, who throughout this century watched with varying degrees of horror as the idea of society absorbing the state was turned on its head, have sought to reinvent the boundaries between state and society within the Marxist paradigm itself—unsuccessfully. It was exactly the matter of relocating these boundaries that Rosa Luxemburg spoke of when, in her critique of the Bolsheviks, she wrote, "Freedom only for the supporters of the government, only for the members of one party—however numerous they may be—is no freedom at all. Freedom is always and exclusively freedom for the one who thinks differently."[4] Her voice was taken up by a long list of succeeding Marxists, but the dilemma of the paradigm, confounded by the practice of socialism in this century, has never been resolved and may, indeed, be unresolvable.

What does all this mean for the Cuban Revolution? In Russia, Antonio Gramsci pointed out long ago in a now famous metaphor, that civil society at the moment of the Revolution was amorphous, "primordial and gelatinous," grounded in a powerful statist tradition, and therefore unable to defend itself.[5] Yet even here, a project anchored in the drive for total statification in the end collapsed upon itself. In prerevolutionary Cuba, by contrast, even as political institutions and civil associations became distorted parodies of themselves, the contours of civil society were more defined. Capitalism, if highly uneven across the island, was deeply rooted in one sector of the economy (the sugar sector), which joined tobacco in producing a significant working class and sophisticated workers' movements. These movements, inextricably intertwined with the various struggles for independence, generated, among other things, a powerfully self-conscious nationalism if anything, heightened by the lateness of independence and the dominance of the United States. The Revolution, despite its adherence to the same ideas of modernity that Bauman discusses, further exaggerated by its deeply ingrained paternalism, has continued to use these impulses with success to rally support to its crusades. Yet, in spite of the leadership's instincts to mold and channel differences of outlook, belief, life-style, or interpretation into institutions safely under its own wing, Cuban civil society was *never* absorbed by the state in a manner parallel to Russia. Silence is not the pervading theme in contemporary Cuba; Cubans have never been silent. They openly voice their opinions in the range of formal and informal contexts. If these voices are splintered and, at moments, suppressed, nonetheless they underscore the difficulty of any project of complete statification. And these difficulties can only be compounded, or assume new forms less and less comprehensible to an aging leadership, as new generations, not directly tied to the struggles for independence and not self-consciously committed to the original project of the Revolution, come of age.

The leadership has been successful for over thirty years in disaggregating discontent, in determining the terrain on which it could coalesce in any organized manner. Yet it appears painfully clear that, to the degree the leadership continues to insist upon defining the boundaries of civil society, it *must* in the end fail. Cubans, given their nationalist heritage and the invasiveness of the presence and threat of the United States, have always been a highly political people. The Revolution has, as we have seen, passed through a series of wrenching crises, each producing and produced by an inward-turning, publicly articulated reassessment. We have argued that each of these crises, to different degrees, witnessed, an opening of the boundaries for discussion and critique and a promise of genuine popular control. Each has ended in some form of highly limited or distorted realization, the result not simply of external threats or the problems of underdevelopment, but of the internal logic of the revolutionary leadership itself. Each ended in focusing on unity as the critical issue, and in defining this unity in the narrowest of ways. Fidel Castro emerged in each as the symbol of unity and, therefore, the center of power. But given the passage of time and generations, he is a symbol who no longer has anywhere near the same hold. The critique of Fidel (evident in the increasingly bitter jokes circulating around the island) is everywhere, particularly in Havana and Santiago, the two cities that historically have been at the forefront of Cuban political activism.

The replies of the leadership to the present crisis are still unclear. The words of the 1990 Call to the Party Congress certainly promised a genuine opening. And despite the fact that Cuba is in an extreme state of emergency, this opening has been expanding and contracting in a fashion uneven enough to make the final outcome, even with all the declarations of imminent demise from Washington and Miami, not by any means completely certain. By and large Cubans, particularly of the first two postrevolutionary generations, do not want a return to the status quo ante. They remain committed to the social project of the Revolution, they watch with pain as it erodes, and they have no illusions about what Miami and Washington plan for a post-Castro era. They are well informed about the disastrous unemployment and severe problems that have been the plight of masses of Eastern Europeans and Russians. They are equally informed about the situation in Latin America and Africa: the people of the Third World, they understand, have no place in the New World Order. If the overriding question today in Cuba is one of survival, the deeper question about what must clearly be a major transition from one type of society to a very different one is the degree to which the leadership will choose to once again "make virtue out of necessity." If to some the answer to this question is foregone, they would do well to remember all the other points in the Cuban Revolution at which answers appeared equally obvious and inevitable.

Notes

Introduction

1. Karl Marx and Frederick Engels, "Manifesto of the Communist Party," in Karl Marx and Frederick Engels, *Collected Works* (New York: International Publishers, 1976), Vol. 6, page 495.

2. The phrase "actually existing socialism" is taken from Rudolf Bahro's book, *The Alternative in Eastern Europe* (London: New Left Books, 1978). Although it seems something of a misnomer, given the disappearance of a large part of the world it was coined to describe, there remains nothing to more accurately substitute for it in naming that world, even as a historical entity.

3. Ibid., page 176.

4. Fred Halliday, "The People's Republic of Yemen: The 'Cuban Path' in Arabia," in Gordon White, Robin Murray, and Christine White, editors, *Revolutionary Socialist Development in the Third World* (Brighton, Sussex: Wheatsheaf Books, 1983), page 37.

5. Mark Selden, "Socialism or 'Post-Revolutionary Society'?" in Christopher Chase-Dunn, editor, *Socialist States in the World System* (Beverly Hills, Calif.: Sage Publications, 1982), page 104.

6. See, for instance, Umberto Melotti, *Marx and the Third World* (Atlantic Highlands, N.J.: Humanities Press, 1977). Rudolf Bahro, building upon the old concept of "oriental despotism" develops this idea as his explanation for the path that Soviet society took. See Bahro, op. cit., Part I.

7. Bahro, op. cit., page 38.

8. Ibid., page 152.

9. Specifically, Marx underlines in *The Civil War in France* the actions taken by the Commune to strip the state of its powers of coercion, to destroy bureaucratic domination and control, and to insure against the possibility of the reemergence

of such domination and control. Marx celebrates what he understands to be the Commune's response to these problems: to vest the population as a whole with direct authority. Thus he points to the Commune's replacement of the standing army with a militia composed of armed populace; its merging of legislative and executive spheres of governance; its determination to elect, by universal suffrage, all officials, and to continuously monitor these officials through the mechanism of recall by the population; and its payment to elected officials of wages no more than that of the average worker. For further elaboration, see the discussion in Chapter 1.

10. Cited in Agnes Heller, "Marxist Ethics and the Future of Eastern Europe: An Interview with Agnes Heller," in *Telos,* no. 38, Winter 1978–79, page 154.

11. Rosa Luxemburg, *The Russian Revolution and Leninism or Marxism?* (Ann Arbor: University of Michigan Press, 1961), page 79.

12. See Xavier Gorostiaga, "América Latina Frente a Los Desafíos Globales," paper presented at the Latin American Sociology Conference, Havana, May 1991.

13. See, for example, Andre Gunder Frank, "Revolution in Eastern Europe: Lessons for Democratic Socialist Movements (and Socialists)," in William Tabb, editor, *The Future of Socialism* (New York: Monthly Review Press, 1990), pages 87–105.

14. Amilcar Cabral, "The Weapon of Theory," in *Revolution in Guinea* (New York: Monthly Review Press, 1969), pages 73–90.

15. Francis Fukuyama, "The End of History," *National Interest,* Summer 1983.

16. Ernesto "Che" Guevara, *Man and Socialism in Cuba* (Havana: Book Institute, 1967), page 29.

Chapter 1

1. Frederick Engels sketches the derivations of Marx's thinking in "Socialism: Utopian and Scientific," described by Marx in his preface to the French edition as an "introduction to scientific socialism." Marx and Engels, *Collected Works,* Vol. 24 (New York: International Publishers, 1976), page 339.

2. V. I. Lenin, *State and Revolution* (New York: International Publishers, 1971), page 70. Hereafter referred to as *SR*.

3. January 16, 1861, in *The Selected Correspondence of Karl Marx and Frederick Engels 1846–1895* (New York: International Publishers, 1942), page 125. Hereafter referred to as *SCME*. See also, in the same volume, Marx's letter to Engels of December 19, 1860. In this letter Marx, referring to Darwin's *Origin of the Species,* wrote, "Although it is developed in the crude English style, this is the book which contains the basis in natural history for our view" (see ibid., page 126).

4. There are numerous critiques of class reductionism in Marx's work. In this respect, see for instance, Ernesto LaClau, *Politics and Ideology in Marxist Theory* (London: Verso Books, 1979); Michele Barrett, *Women's Oppression Today* (London: New Left Books, 1980); and Samuel Bowles and Herbert Gintis, *Democracy and Capitalism* (New York: Basic Books, 1986).

5. Shlomo Avineri, in his work, *The Political and Social Thought of Karl Marx* (London: Cambridge University Press, 1968), uses this fact as further proof of his thesis that the commonly held belief in the schism between the young and the mature Marx is entirely incorrect. See in this regard pages 220–39.

6. Cited in Hal Draper, "The Death of the State in Marx and Engels," Ralph Miliband and John Saville, editors, *The Socialist Register 1970* (New York: Monthly Review Press, 1970), page 305.

7. Georg Wilhelm Friedrich Hegel, *The Philosophy of Right* (London: Oxford University Press, 1967), page 10.

8. Avineri, op. cit., page 221.

9. *SCME,* letter of February 22, 1881, page 386.

10. Marx and Engels, "The German Ideology," in Marx and Engels, *Collected Works,* op. cit., Vol. 5, page 47.

11. Eric J. Hobsbawm, "Marx, Engels, and Pre-Marxian Socialism," in Hobsbawm, editor, *The History of Marxism, Vol. 1: Marxism in Marx's Day* (Bloomington: Indiana University Press, 1982), page 1.

12. Ibid., pages 9–12.

13. Karl Marx, *The Critique of the Gotha Program* (New York: International Publishers, 1970), page 10. Hereafter referred to as *CGP*.

14. Karl Marx, "Economic and Philosophic Manuscripts of (1844)," in Marx, *Early Writings* (London: Penguin Classics, 1992), page 347.

15. *CGP,* pages 8–10.

16. See David McClellan, "Marx, Engels and Lenin on Party and State," in Leslie Holmes, editor, *The Withering Away of the State?* (Beverly Hills, Calif.: Sage Publishers, 1981), page 23.

17. Ralph Miliband, "Marx and the State," in Ralph Miliband and John Saville, editors, *The Socialist Register 1965* (New York: Monthly Review Press, 1965), page 278.

18. *MCP,* pages 486 and 505.

19. *SCME,* letter of March 5, 1852, page 57.

20. *CGP,* page 18.

21. Cited in Bertram Wolfe, *Marxism: One Hundred Years of a Doctrine* (New York: Delta, 1965), page 168.

22. See Hal Draper, "Marx and the Dictatorship of the Proletariat," *Cahiers de L'Institut de Science Économique Apliquée,* no. 129, September 1962 (Series S, no. 6, pages 5–73. An updated, extended, and more readily accessible version of Draper's work is available in his book, *The "Dictatorship of the Proletariat" From Marx to Lenin* (New York: Monthly Review Press, 1987).

23. Richard Hunt, *The Political Ideas of Marx and Engels, Vol. I: Marxism and Totalitarian Democracy 1818–1850* (Pittsburgh: University of Pittsburgh Press, 1974), pages 286–87. See also Hal Draper, "Marx and the Dictatorship of the Proletariat," op. cit., pages 6–9.

24. Hal Draper, "Marx and the Dictatorship of the Proletariat," op. cit., page 7.

25. See Hal Draper, ibid.; Miliband, op. cit., pages 278–96; Monty Johnstone, "The Paris Commune and Marx's Conception of the Dictatorship of the Proletariat," *Massachusetts Review,* Vol. 12, 1971, pages 447–62; and Bertell Ollman, "Marx's Vision of Communism," *Critique,* no. 8, Summer 1977, pages 4–42.

26. Miliband, op. cit., page 293.

27. Cited in Wolfe, op. cit., page 172.

28. Hal Draper, "Marx and the Dictatorship of the Proletariat," op. cit., pages 29–73.

29. Ibid., pages 30–36, 40.

30. *MCP,* page 495.

31. Hunt, op. cit., page 302.

32. Karl Marx, "Class Struggles in France," in Saul Padover, editor, *Karl Marx on Revolution* (New York: McGraw Hill, 1971), page 226.

33. Hunt, op. cit., page 309.

34. Cited in Monty Johnstone, "Marx, Blanqui and Majority Rule," in Ralph Miliband and John Saville, editors, *The Socialist Register 1983* (London: Merlin Press, 1983), page 303.

35. Frederick Engels, "Program of the Blanquist Commune Refugees," in Marx and Engels, *Collected Works,* Vol. 24, op. cit., page 13.

36. Hal Draper, "Marx and the Dictatorship of the Proletariat," op. cit., page 60.

37. Miliband, op. cit., page 289–90.

38. See Leo Panitch, "Liberal Democracy and Socialist Democracy: The Antinomies of C. B. Macpherson," in Ralph Miliband and John Saville, editors, *The Socialist Register 1981* (London: Merlin Press, 1981), page 157; as well as Leo Panitch's *Working Class Politics in Crisis* (London: Verso Press, 1986), pages 233–36.

39. *SCME,* letter of March 18–28, 1875, page 337.

40. For a recent example, see James Petras and Frank Fitzgerald, "Authoritarianism and Democracy in the Transition to Socialism," *Latin American Perspectives,* Vol. 15, issue 56, no. 1, Winter 1988, pages 93–111.

41. See Avineri, op. cit., pages 239–49.

42. Miliband, op. cit., passim; Monty Johnstone, "The Paris Commune and Marx's Conception of the Dictatorship of the Proletariat," op. cit., passim; and Robin Blackburn, "Marxism: Theory of Proletarian Revolution," in Robin Blackburn, editor, *Revolution and Class Struggle: A Reader in Marxist Politics* (London: Fontana 1977), pages 25–68.

43. Blackburn, op. cit., page 52.

44. Frederich Engels, "Introduction (1891)" to Karl Marx, "The Civil War in France," in Hal Draper, editor, *Karl Marx and Frederich Engels: Writings on the Paris Commune* (New York: Monthly Review Press, 1971), page 34. Hereafter referred to as *CWIF.*

45. Ibid., page 235. Hal Draper, in the more recent compilation of his investigations on this subject, seeks further proof of his conviction that Marx understood the Commune as the embodiment of the dictatorship of the proletariat in a little-known speech given by Marx in September 1871 at a banquet marking the end of a London meeting of the International, reported in an article entitled "Reds in Session" in the *New York World.* In this first gathering of the International following the fall of the Commune, Marx referred to it as "the conquest of the political power of the working classes." Its objective was the removal of any "base for class rule and oppression. . . . But before such a change could be effected, a proletarian dictature would become necessary." Richard Hunt, citing the same event, concludes that Marx here "all but calls the Paris Commune the dictatorship of the proletariat." It seems a somewhat pointless endeavor to scour Marx's words for some sort of phraseology that would commit him (or convict him, depending on one's point of view). The general and the specific interpretations Marx gives to the Commune are already quite evident. See Draper, *The "Dictatorship of the Proletariat" From Marx to Lenin,* op. cit., page 31, and Richard Hunt, op. cit., pages 308–309.

46. See Avineri, op. cit., page 242.

47. Ibid., page 247.

48. Ibid., page 200.

49. *SCME,* letter of April 6, 1871, page 307.

50. For decades there has been an ongoing controversy about a missing letter written during these two and one half weeks. No documentation exists to support its existence.

51. *SCME,* letter of May 13, 1871, page 312.

52. See Avineri, op. cit., pages 247–48.

53. Eugene Schulkind, in his "Introduction," Schulkind, editor, *The Paris Commune of 1871: The View From the Left* (New York: Grove Press, 1974), page 47.

54. *CWIF* (first draft), pages 159, 162.

55. *SCME,* pages 386–87.

56. *CWIF,* page 76.

57. *CWIF* (first draft), page 153.

58. *CWIF* (first draft), page 162.

59. *CWIF* (second draft), page 196.

60. *CWIF* (second draft), pages 196–97.

61. *CWIF* (first draft), page 152.

62. *SCME,* page 311.

63. Cited in *CWIF,* page 233.

64. *CWIF,* pages 73–74; and (second draft), pages 199–200.

65. Avineri, op. cit., pages 240–41.

66. Lenin advocates the abolition of standing armies and discusses this principle in light of the experience of the Paris Commune throughout *SR,* especially pages 36–37, 94, and 95.

67. Schulkind, editor, op. cit., page 47. For a fuller discussion of the immediate motivations of the Communards, see pages 44–46.

68. Karl Marx and Frederick Engels, "Preface to the German Edition of 1872 of the Manifesto of the Communist Party," in Robert Tucker, editor, *The Marx-Engels Reader* (New York: W. W. Norton, 1978), page 470.

69. *CWIF* (first draft), page 130.

70. See *CWIF,* pages 69–84.

71. Ibid., page 72.

72. *CWIF* (second draft), page 200.

73. *CWIF,* page 74.

74. Ibid., page 75.

75. Ibid., page 74.

76. Ibid.

77. Alec Nove, "Is There a Ruling Class in the U.S.S.R.?" *Soviet Studies,* Vol. XXXVII, no. 4, October 1975, page 621.

78. Tom Wohlforth, "The Transition to the Transition," *New Left Review,* no. 130, November–December 1981, page 79.

79. Gregor McLennan, *Marxism, Pluralism and Beyond* (Cambridge: Polity Press, 1989), page 125.

80. Eric J. Hobsbawm, "Marx, Engels and Politics," in Hobsbawm, editor, *The History of Marxism, Volume 1: Marxism in Marx's Day* (Bloomington: Indiana University Press, 1982), page 232.

81. David McClellan, op. cit., page 22.

82. Draper, "The Death of the State in Marx and Engels," op. cit., page 303.

83. Ibid., page 302n.

84. Ibid., page 281.

85. Hobsbawm, "Marx, Engels and Pre-Marxian Socialism," op. cit., pages 11–12.

86. Hal Draper, "The Death of the State in Marx and Engels," op. cit., page 282.

87. Frederick Engels, *Anti-Duhring* in Marx and Engels, *Collected Works,* op. cit., Vol. 25, page 268.

88. See Hal Draper, "The Death of the State in Marx and Engels," op. cit., page 302.

89. Ibid., page 283.

90. Ibid., page 283.

91. Cited in ibid., page 284.

92. See *MCP,* pages 505–506.

93. See E. H. Carr, *Michael Bakunin* (New York: Vintage Books, 1937), pages 417–22.

94. Hal Draper, "The Death of the State in Marx and Engels," op. cit., pages 291–92.

95. *SCME,* pages 319–20.

96. *CWIF,* Engels, "Introduction (1891)", page 34; and Frederick Engels, *The Origin of the Family, Private Property and the State* (New York: International Publishers, 1972), page 232.

97. *CGP,* page 18.

98. *MCP,* page 505.

99. *CWIF,* page 74.

100. Michael Bakunin, "Statism and Anarchy," in Sam Dolgoff, editor, *Bakunin on Anarchy* (New York: Alfred A. Knopf, 1971), page 336.

101. "After the Revolution: Marx Debates Bakunin," in Tucker, editor, op. cit., pages 544–45.

102. Christopher Pierson, *Marxist Theory and Democratic Politics* (Cambridge: Polity Press, 1986), page 82.

103. McLennan, op. cit., pages 125–26.

104. Miliband, op. cit., page 293.

Chapter 2

1. Marcel Liebman, *Leninism Under Lenin* (London: Jonathan Cape, 1975), page 193.

2. Ralph Miliband, "The State and Revolution," *Monthly Review,* Vol. 21, no. 11, April 1970, page 77.

3. Cited in Louis Althusser, *Lenin and Philosophy* (New York: Monthly Review Press, 1971), page 31.

4. James Billington, *Fire in the Minds of Men: Origins of the Revolutionary Faith* (New York: Basic Books, 1980), page 461.

5. *SR,* page 74.

6. Ibid., page 22.

7. Ibid., page 18.

8. See V. I. Lenin, *Imperialism, The Highest State of Capitalism* (New York: International Publishers, 1939).

9. *SR,* page 25.

10. Lucio Colletti, "Power and Democracy in Socialist Society," *New Left Review,* no. 56, July–August 1969, page 21.

11. *SR,* page 17.

12. *SR,* page 27.

13. Colletti, op. cit., page 20. See also Miliband, op. cit., page 78.

14. *SR,* page 30.

15. Ibid., page 31.

16. Ibid., page 69.

17. Ibid., page 73.

18. Ibid., page 73.

19. Ibid., page 53.

20. Ibid., page 37.

21. Miliband, op. cit., page 79.

22. *SR,* page 75.

23. Ibid., page 37.

24. Ibid., page 26.

25. Ibid., page 80.

26. Ibid., page 64.

27. Ibid., page 43.

28. Ibid., page 83.

29. Ibid., pages 97–98.

30. Ibid., page 83–4.

31. Ibid., page 43.

32. Ibid., page 42.

33. Miliband, op. cit., page 80.

34. Ibid., page 42.

35. Liebman points, in this regard, particularly to Lenin's essay, "Can the Bolsheviks Retain State Power?" written shortly before the October Revolution, as well as the measures and decrees of the immediate post-November period. See Liebman, op. cit., pages 191–209 and 215–22. See, in general, Lenin, *Collected Works* (Moscow: Progressive Publishers, 1964) (hereafter referred to as *CW*), Volumes 24, 25 and 26, which are littered with the language and ideas of *State and Revolution.*

36. Adam Ulam, *The Bolsheviks* (New York: Macmillan, 1965), pages 354–55.

37. See Liebman, op. cit.

38. Lenin, *CW,* op. cit., Vol. 24, page 364.

39. Robert Daniels, "The State and Revolution: A Case Study in the Genesis and Transformation of Communist Ideology," *American Slavic and East European Review,* Vol. xii, no. 1, February 1953, page 26.

40. Ibid., pages 26–29. Marian Sawer (and, after her, Stephen Cohen) sees Bukharin's articles as the basis for *State and Revolution,* or at least the pathway Lenin followed back to the sources in Marx and Engels. Her study of the notes made for the article by Lenin lead her to assert that Lenin's ideas had already coalesced by February 1917. Marian Sawer, "The Genesis of *State and Revolution,*" in Ralph Miliband and John Saville, editors, *The Socialist Register 1977* (New York:

Monthly Review Press, 1977), page 217. See also Stephen Cohen, *Bukharin and the Bolshevik Revolution* (New York: Vintage Books, 1975).

41. Daniels, op. cit., page 26.

42. Cited in N. K. Krupskaya, *Reminiscences of Lenin* (New York: International Publishers, 1975), page 335.

43. Ibid., pages 334–35. Neil Harding picks up on Krupskaya's point. Like Sawer and Cohen (and this author), he sees Bukharin's articles as the context within which Lenin began his work on *State and Revolution,* but with this major caveat: in his reading of text and events, the times had impelled Lenin to a reconsideration of the issue of the state in socialism. "Lenin's *State and Revolution,*" writes Harding, "by contrast (to the theoretically inclined Bukharin) has an emphatically practical objective. (It represents) his attempt to establish a yardstick for socialist practice." Neil Harding, *Lenin's Political Thought, Volume 2: Theory and Practice in the Socialist Revolution* (New York: St. Martin's Press, 1981), page 84.

44. *CW,* Vol. 27, page 454.

45. Liebman, op. cit., pages 198–205.

46. Marc Ferro, "Pourquoi Fevrier? Pourquoi Octobre?" cited in Liebman, op. cit., page 201.

47. Albert Rhys Williams, *Through the Russian Revolution* (New York: Boni and Liveright, 1921).

48. John Reed, *Ten Days That Shook the World* (New York: International Publishers, 1977), page 15.

49. Liebman, op. cit., page 202.

50. Marc Ferro, *The Russian Revolution of February 1917,* cited in Liebman, op. cit., page 203.

51. Ibid., page 204.

52. *CW,* Vol. 26, page 22.

53. Miliband, op. cit., page 77.

54. *SR,* page 101.

55. Gregor McLennan, *Marxism, Pluralism and Beyond* (Cambridge: Polity Press, 1989), page 113.

56. Daniels, op. cit., page 33.

57. *SR,* page 73.

58. Hal Draper, *The "Dictatorship of the Proletariat" From Marx to Lenin* (New York: Monthly Review Press, 1987), pages 80–83.

59. See Neil Harding's exhaustive and convincing treatment of Lenin's presentation of the Soviets as the Commune reincarnated in Harding, op. cit., pages 118–41.

60. V. I. Lenin, "Can the Bolsheviks Retain State Power?," *CW,* Vol. 26, page 108.

61. *SR,* page 40.

62. Ibid., page 91.

63. Ibid., page 92.

64. Ibid., page 92.

65. E. H. Carr, *The Bolshevik Revolution 1917–1923,* Volume 1 (Baltimore: Penguin Books 1966), page 253.

66. See Moshe Lewin, *Lenin's Last Struggle* (London: Pluto Press, 1975). Carr points out that Lenin's campaign against the bureaucracy was waged by both

"Lenin the administrator *and* Lenin the political thinker." See Carr, op. cit., page 252.

67. Lewin, op. cit., pages 234–35.

68. *SR,* page 92.

69. Cited in Carr, op. cit., page 252.

70. See Miliband, op. cit., pages 82–83.

71. *SR,* pages 23–24.

72. See Miliband, op. cit., page 83.

73. *CW,* Vol. 26, pages 114–5.

74. See Liebman, op. cit., pages 205–09.

75. Miliband, op. cit., pages 85–86.

76. Ibid., page 85.

77. See Norman Geras, "Classical Marxism and Proletarian Representation," *New Left Review,* no. 123, January–February 1981, pages 75–89; and Draper, op. cit.

78. Leon Trotsky, *Leon Trotsky on France,* ed. David Salner (New York: Monad Press, 1979), pages 228, 231.

79. Samuel Farber, *Before Stalinism: The Rise and Fall of Soviet Democracy* (London: Verso, 1990), page 38.

80. Ibid., page 40–1.

81. Ibid., page 44.

82. A. J. Polan, *Lenin and the End of Politics* (Berkeley: University of California Press, 1984), page 99.

83. Ibid., page 57.

84. Ibid., page 129.

85. Ibid., page 78.

86. Ibid., page 130.

87. Neil Harding, op. cit., page 91.

88. There are five direct references to *State and Revolution* as an explicit guideline in this document. See "Constitution of the Organs of Popular Power" in *Center for Cuban Studies Newsletter* (New York: Center for Cuban Studies, October–December 1975), pages 5–26.

Chapter 3

1. Rosa Luxemburg, *The Russian Revolution and Leninism or Marxism?* (Ann Arbor: University of Michigan Press, 1961), page 70.

2. Paul Bellis, *Marxism and the U.S.S.R.: The Theory of Proletarian Dictatorship and the Marxist Analysis of Soviet Society* (Atlantic Highlands, N.J.: Humanities Press, 1979), page 231.

3. Rudolf Bahro, *The Alternative in Eastern Europe* (London: New Left Books, 1978), page 38.

4. N. N. Sukhanov, *The Russian Revolution, 1917* (London: Oxford University Press, 1955), page 282.

5. Bertrand Russell, *Bolshevism: Practice and Theory* (New York: Harcourt, Brace and Howe, 1920), page 73.

6. Cited in Roy Medvedev, *On Socialist Democracy* (New York: W. W. Norton, 1977), page 134.

7. Jeffrey Hahn, "State Institutions in Transition," in Stephen White, Alex

Pravda, and Zvi Gitelman, editors, *Developments in Soviet and Post Soviet Politics* (Durham, N.C.: Duke University Press, 1992), page 91.

8. Roy Medvedev, op. cit., page 132.

9. Ibid.

10. Ibid., see pages 133–34.

11. Barrington Moore, *Soviet Politics: The Dilemma of Power* (New York: Harper and Row, 1965), page 262.

12. Roy Medvedev, *Leninism and Western Socialism* (London: Verso, 1981), page 132.

13. Bellis, op. cit., page 234.

14. Ferenc Fehér, Agnes Heller and György Márkus, *Dictatorship Over Needs: An Analysis of Soviet Societies* (Oxford: Basil Blackwell, 1983), pages 177–78.

15. Ibid., page 225.

16. Ibid., page 195.

17. See Bahro, op. cit., Part 1.

18. See Diane Koenker, "Urbanization and Deurbanization in the Russian Revolution and the Civil War," in Diane Koenker, William Rosenberg, and Ronald Suny, editors, *Party, State and Society in the Russian Civil War* (Bloomington: Indiana University Press, 1989), pages 81–104. Koenker challenges the notion that numbers were the issue in the decline of urban support for the Bolsheviks. She argues that the Bolshevik Party "made deurbanization and declassing the scapegoats for its political difficulties when the party's own policies and its unwillingness to accept changing proletarian attitudes were also to blame."

19. Cited in Marcel Liebman, *Leninism Under Lenin* (London: Jonathan Cape Press, 1975), page 230.

20. Cited in Isaac Deutscher, *The Prophet Armed* (New York: Vintage Books, 1965), page 327.

21. The phrase is Engels's. In a 1853 letter to his friend Weydemeyer that dealt with the situation in Germany, Engels wrote, with a terrible foresight: "In a backward country... which possesses an advanced party... at the first serious conflict and as soon as real danger sets in, the advanced party will come to power, and that is certainly *before* its normal time." Cited in Alfred Meyer, *Leninism* (New York: Praeger 1965), page 181.

22. Cited in Paul Avrich, *Kronstadt 1921* (New York: W. W. Norton, 1974), page 12.

23. Cited in Roy Medvedev, *Leninism and Western Socialism,* op. cit., page 127.

24. Ibid.

25. Ibid.

26. Ibid.

27. Ibid.

28. See Deutscher, op. cit., page 505.

29. Ibid., page 506.

30. Cited in ibid., page 509.

31. Roy Medvedev, *Leninism and Western Socialism,* op. cit., pages 129–31.

32. Ibid., page 130.

33. Avrich, op. cit., page 3.

34. Moore, op. cit., page 277.

35. Ibid., page 163.

36. *CW,* Vol. 33, pages 428–29.

37. Cited in Roy Medvedev, *Leninism and Western Socialism,* op. cit., page 60.

38. See, in this regard, Moshe Lewin, *Lenin's Last Struggle* (London: Pluto Press, 1975).

39. See discussion in Liebman, *Leninism Under Lenin,* op. cit., pages 318–25.

40. Leon Trotsky, *The Revolution Betrayed: What is the Soviet Union and Where is it Going?* (New York: Doubleday, Doran and Co., 1937), page 59.

41. Roy Medvedev, *Leninism and Western Socialism,* op. cit., pages 59–60.

42. István Mészáros, "Political Power and Dissent in Post Revolutionary Societies," *New Left Review,* no. 108, March–April 1978, pages 6–7.

43. Tom Wohlforth, "The Two Souls of Leninism," *Against the Current,* Vol. 1, nos. 4–5, September–October 1986, pages 37–42.

44. Luxemburg, op. cit., pages 78–79.

45. Ibid., page 70.

46. Ibid., page 62.

47. Ibid., pages 71–72.

48. Ibid., pages 78–79.

49. Perry Anderson, *Considerations on Western Marxism* (London: New Left Books 1976), page 20.

50. Roy Medvedev, *Leninism and Western Socialism,* op. cit., page 51.

51. Ibid., page 49.

52. See Roy Medvedev, *Let History Judge* (New York: Vintage Books, 1973), page 436.

Chapter 4

1. Actually, the idea that a *foco* of guerillas in the Sierra Maestra "made" the Cuban Revolution is by and large a myth, more or less dictated to Regis Debray who duly articulated it in his famous *Revolution in the Revolution*—which he himself later basically disowned. The timing of its articulation had everything to do with the project Che Guevara was in the process of undertaking in Bolivia: the story *Revolution in the Revolution* tells served as the theoretical and historical justification for Che's undertaking. Moreover—and directly related to internal Cuban politics, the fact was that the city movement—which played clearly the critical role in doing in the Batista regime—was made up of a mass of people enormously fragmented along class, but more importantly, along ideological lines. Thus, in the strategy of unity that we will trace, it made sense to lay the greatest importance upon the guerilla, even if that was stretching history a bit. (See Vania Bambirra, *La Revolución Cubana: Una Nueva Interpretación* [Santiago de Chile: Cuaderno del CESO, 1973] for an historical overview of the balance between the guerilla and the city movement.)

2. This informality was nowhere better captured than in the definition of socialism in Cuba that immediately made the rounds after Fidel declared the Revolution socialist in April of 1961. "Socialism," the line went, was "a *pachanga,*" that is, a festive dance done in rhumba style (Elizabeth Sutherland, *The Youngest Revolution* [New York: Dial Press, 1969], page 13).

3. Richard Fagen, "Continuities in Cuban Revolutionary Politics," *Monthly Review,* Vol. 23, no. 11, April 1972, page 35.

4. Cited in Ernesto Cardenal, *In Cuba* (New York: New Directions Books, 1974), page 65.

5. See Ernesto Guevara, *Man and Socialism in Cuba* (Havana: Book Institute, 1967), pages 28–29.

6. Much of what follows concerning prerevolutionary social and economic structure is taken from Robin Blackburn, "Prologue to the Cuban Revolution," *New Left Review,* no. 21, October 1963. Although Blackburn tends to caricature the Cuban bourgeoisie, like most caricatures, he communicates certain basic truths. See also, in this regard, early studies done by James O'Connor, "Cuba: Its Political Economy," in Rolando Bonachea and Nelson Valdés, editors, *Cuba in Revolution* (Garden City, N.Y.: Doubleday Anchor Books, 1972); and Dudley Seers, "The Economic and Social Background," in Dudley Seers, editor, *Cuba: The Economic and Social Revolution* (Chapel Hill: University of North Carolina Press, 1964).

7. Nelson Valdés, "Revolution and Institutionalization in Cuba," *Cuban Studies/Estudios Cubanos,* Vol. 6, nos. 1–2 January and July 1976, page 3.

8. Blackburn, op. cit., page 82.

9. Ibid., page 82.

10. For the best account of the historical and cultural dimensions of the interwoven histories of Cuba and the United States, see Louis Pérez, *Cuba and the United States: Ties of Singular Intimacy* (Athens, Georgia: University of Georgia Press, 1990). For an interpretation which challenges the view of prerevolutionary social and economic stagnation, see Jorge Domínguez, *Cuba: Order and Revolution* (Cambridge: Belknap Press, 1978), particularly Part One, Chapter 3.

11. Blackburn, op. cit., page 60.

12. Ibid., page 61.

13. Ibid.

14. Ibid.

15. Ibid., page 60.

16. International Bank for Reconstruction and Development, *Report on Cuba* (Baltimore: Johns Hopkins University Press, 1951).

17. *Time Magazine,* April 21, 1952, cited in Blackburn, op. cit., page 69.

18. Maurice Zeitlin, "Cuba: Revolution Without a Blueprint," *Transaction,* Vol. 6, no. 6, April 1969, page 40.

19. For a summary run through of the scope and dimensions of Batista's personal involvement in corruption, see O'Connor, "Cuba: Its Political Economy," op. cit., pages 70–73.

20. Blackburn, op. cit., page 72.

21. The nature and extent of the physical and economic threats generated directly by the United States that the Cuban Revolution faced in its first decade has been documented in particular for the early years of that decade, years punctuated, of course, by the collapse of economic and diplomatic relations with the United States, by the CIA-sponsored invasion at Playa Giron (or the Bay of Pigs) in 1961, and by the October Missile Crisis. Overt United States efforts to undermine the Revolution after the Missile Crisis (following the agreement between John Kennedy and Nikita Khrushchev resolving that crisis in which Kennedy promised not to invade Cuba) operated largely in the realm of economics and diplomacy, that is, in the form of a continuing economic embargo with the intention of effecting an international isolation of Cuba from Latin America and

Western Europe. Covert activities hardly disappeared after October 1962; the 1975 report of the Senate Select Committee on Political Assassination (Church Committee), which documents repeated attempts on Fidel Castro's life (to say nothing of his beard), speaks directly to one aspect of these activities. See as well, in this context, the excellent 1977 CBS documentary, "The C.I.A.'s Secret Army," which traces the continuing support given to the development and maintenance of an active anti-Castro counterrevolutionary force throughout the 1960s and into the 1970s, and the embarrassment, at least at that point, this force was beginning to represent for the Carter administration. The "secret army" soon, however, found new employment as trainers and participants in the U.S.-funded "contra" war against the Sandinistas in Nicaragua.

22. Raúl Castro, "Speech at the Closing Session of the Seminar for Delegates of People's Power in Matanzas," *Granma Weekly Review,* August 22, 1974, page 3.

23. K. S. Karol, *Guerillas in Power* (New York: Hill and Wang, 1970).

24. Ibid. See discussion in chapter V, "Hay Problemas, Hay Contradicciones," pages 405–84.

25. Maurice Zeitlin, "Inside Cuba: Workers and Revolution," *Ramparts,* March 1970, page 78.

26. Guevara, *Man and Socialism,* op. cit., page 28.

27. Karol, op. cit., page 329.

28. Ibid., page 220.

29. Ibid, page 328.

30. Ibid, page 329.

31. The field of Cubanology has always been a highly contested terrain. For discussions of the terms of these disputes, see Andrew Zimbalist, editor, *Cuban Political Economy: Controversies in Cubanology* (Boulder, Colo.: Westview Press 1988), in particular, the articles by Valdés, Fitzgerald, and Bengelsdorf. For the most recent contributions to the controversies, see Damián Fernández, editor, *Cuban Studies Since the Revolution* (Gainesville: University of Florida Press, 1992).

32. Guevara, *Man and Socialism,* op. cit., pages 28–29.

33. Note, in this context, the title of Fidel's speech to the 1975 First Congress of the Cuban Communist Party: "Unity Gave Us Victory." See *First Congress of the Communist Party of Cuba* (Moscow: Progress Publishers, 1976), pages 16–279.

34. See Ernesto Guevara, *The Diary of Che Guevara in Bolivia: November 7, 1966 to October 7, 1967,* edited by Robert Scheer (New York: Bantam Books, 1968).

35. For the most complete account of the 1954 coup in Guatemala, as orchestrated by the C.I.A., see Richard Immerman, *The C.I.A. in Guatemala* (Austin: University of Texas Press, 1982). For a more popularly written account, see Stephen Kinzer and Stephen Schlesinger, *Bitter Fruit* (New York: Doubleday, 1982).

36. See, in this regard, the public opinion survey carried out in Cuba during April and May of 1960 by Lloyd Free, the Director of The Institute for International Social Research in Princeton, New Jersey. The results of this survey are published in Lloyd Free, *Attitudes of the Cuban People Toward the Castro Regime in the Late Spring of 1960* (Princeton: Institute for International Social Research, 1960). Free's sample was drawn from residents of Havana (50 percent) and of other urban or quasi-urban areas (50 percent). Therefore, the 40 percent of the

Cuban population who lived in rural areas (and who have tended to be the most vociferous in their support of Castro) were not represented. Free identified 86 percent of his sample as supporters of the Castro regime.

37. Maurice Zeitlin, *Revolutionary Politics and the Cuban Working Class,* (Princeton: Princeton University Press, 1967), page 42.

38. Jean Paul Sartre, *Sartre on Cuba* (New York: Ballantine Books, 1960), page 85.

39. Ibid., page 86.

40. Cited in Edmundo Desnoes, "Los Cubanos," manuscript, 1972, page 192.

41. Karol, op. cit., page 170.

42. Ibid., page 139.

43. See Theodore Draper, *Castro's Revolution: Myths and Realities* (New York: Praeger, 1962), and *Castroism: Theory and Practice* (New York: Praeger, 1965).

44. *Fidel Castro Denounces Sectarianism* (Havana: Ministry of Foreign Relations, 1962).

45. Valdés, op. cit., page 3.

46. Karol, op. cit., page 171.

47. Ernesto Guevara, "Cuba: Exceptional Case or Vanguard in the Struggle Against Colonialism," in Rolando Bonachea and Nelson Valdés, editors, *Che: Selected Works of Ernesto Guevara* (Cambridge, Mass.: MIT Press, 1969), page 58.

48. Karol, op. cit., page 173.

49. Haydée Santamaría, *Haydée Habla del Moncada* (Havana: Book Institute, 1967), page 29.

50. James O'Connor, *The Origins of Socialism in Cuba* (New York: Cornell University Press, 1970), page 316.

51. Richard Fagen, "Charismatic Authority and the Leadership of Fidel Castro," in Bonachea and Valdés, editors, *Cuba in Revolution,* op. cit., page 158.

52. Karol, op. cit., page 39.

53. See the 1962 Cuban documentary film, "Historia de un Batalla," by the Cuban Film Institute (ICAIC).

54. See, for a discussion of this, Valdés, op. cit., pages 7–13.

55. See, in this regard, Theodore Draper, *Castro's Revolution: Myths and Realities,* op. cit.; Draper, *Castroism: Theory and Practice,* op. cit.; Maurice Halperin, *The Rise and Decline of Fidel Castro* (Berkeley: University of California Press, 1972); Carlos Franqui, *Family Portrait With Fidel* (New York: Random House, 1984); and most recently, Jacobo Timerman, *Cuba: A Journey* (New York: Knopf, 1990).

56. See, in this regard, Teresa Casuso, *Cuba and Castro* (New York: Random House, 1961); Edward González, *Cuba Under Castro: The Limits of Charisma* (Boston: Houghton Mifflin, 1974); and Ward Morton, *Castro as Charismatic Hero* (Occasional Publications, no. 4, Center for Latin American Studies, Lawrence: University of Kansas, 1965). Indeed, the range of studies that raise the question of Fidel and charisma is huge; it enters the work of Andres Suárez, Richard Fagen, Carmelo Mesa Lago, Lee Lockwood, among other scholars and observers of Cuban reality.

57. See, in this regard, Ramón Ruiz, *Cuba: The Making of A Revolution* (New York: Norton Books, 1970), page 169.

58. Karol, op. cit., pages 179, 181.

59. O'Connor, *The Origins of Socialism in Cuba,* op. cit., page 316.

60. Sartre, op. cit., page 122.

61. Guevara, *Man and Socialism,* op. cit., page 17.

62. Cited in Edmundo Desnoes, "Fidel Castro: Su Uso de la Palabra," in *Cuba: Transformación del Hombre* (Havana: Casa de las Americas, 1960), pages 148–49.

63. Cited in Karol, op. cit., page 29n.

64. Cited in Lee Lockwood, *Castro's Cuba, Cuba's Fidel* (New York: Vintage Books, 1969), pages 13–14.

65. Cited in Desnoes, "Fidel Castro: Su Uso de la Palabra," op. cit., pages 146–48.

66. Sartre, op. cit., pages 122–23.

67. Lockwood, op. cit., page 15.

68. Karol, op. cit., page 456.

69. Sartre, op. cit., page 123.

70. Ibid., pages 134–35.

71. Guevara, *Man and Socialism,* op. cit., page 16.

72. Ibid., pages 16–17.

73. James Petras, "Cuba, Fourteen Years of Revolutionary Government," in Clarence Thurbur, editor, *Development Administration in Latin America* (Durham, N.C.: Duke University Press, 1973), page 289.

74. Ibid.

75. Fagen, "Continuities in Cuban Revolutionary Politics," op. cit., pages 24–25.

76. Ibid., pages 31–32.

77. Ibid., page 41.

78. Ibid., page 42.

79. See Richard Fagen, *The Transformation of Political Culture in Cuba* (Stanford: Stanford University Press, 1969), pages 69–103 for an examination of the C.D.R.s as they functioned in the first decade of the revolution.

80. Ibid., page 91.

81. Robert Cantor, "New Laws for a New Society," in *Cuba Resource Center Newsletter,* Vol. III, nos. 5–6, page 12.

82. For an account of the functioning of the popular tribunals, see Jesse Berman, "The Cuban Popular Tribunals," *Columbia Law Review,* December 1969, pages 1317–54.

83. For a discussion of the Literacy Campaign, see Richard Jolly, "Education," in Seers, editor, op. cit., pages 190–219, and Fagen, *The Transformation of Political Culture in Cuba,* op. cit., pages 33–68.

84. Fagen, "Continuities in Cuban Revolutionary Politics," op. cit., page 43.

85. The best of these eyewitness accounts available in English are José Yglesias's book, *In the Fist of the Revolution* (New York: Vintage Books, 1969); Elizabeth Sutherland's *The Youngest Revolution,* op. cit.; Barry Reckord's *Does Fidel Eat More Than Your Father?* (New York: Signet Books, 1971); Ernesto Cardenal's *In Cuba,* op. cit.; and Lockwood, op. cit.

86. Fagen, "Continuities in Cuban Revolutionary Practice," op. cit., page 43.

87. Che Guevara speaks of *guerrillerismo administrativo* in "Against Bureaucratism," a 1963 article reprinted in John Gerassi, editor, *Venceremos! The Speeches and Writings of Che Guevara* (New York: Simon and Schuster, 1968), pages 220–25.

88. See Nelson Valdés, "The Cuban Revolution: Economic Organization

and Bureaucracy," *Latin American Perspectives*, Issue 20, Vol. VI, no. 1, Winter 1979, pages 19–20.

89. Cited in Karol, op. cit., page 474.

90. Cited in Karol, op. cit., page 363.

91. Carmelo Mesa Lago, *Cuba in the 1970's: Pragmatism and Institutionalization*, revised edition (Albuquerque: University of New Mexico Press, 1978), page 9.

92. González, op. cit., page 218.

93. Fidel Castro, "To Create Wealth With Social Conscience," (July 26, 1968), in Bertram Silverman, editor, *Man and Socialism in Cuba: The Great Debate* (New York: Athenaeum, 1971), page 377.

94. See Karol, op. cit., pages, 291–404.

95. Castro, "To Create Wealth With Social Conscience," in Silverman, editor, op. cit., page 377.

96. Cited in Karol, op. cit., pages 357–58.

97. For a translated selection of the key articles that comprise the "great economic debate," see Silverman, editor, op. cit., pages 31–354.

98. Ibid., pages 11–12.

99. Cited in ibid., page 5.

100. Bertram Silverman, "Economic Organization and Social Consciousness: Some Dilemmas of Cuban Socialism," in David Barkin and Nita Manitzas, editors, *Cuba: The Logic of the Revolution* (Andover: Warner Modular Publications, 1973), Reprint 262, page 1.

101. Ibid., page 20.

102. Valdés, "The Cuban Revolution: Economic Organization and Bureaucracy," op. cit., page 21.

103. The film (which won acclaim from U.S. critics when it was shown in this country almost a decade later) depicts the trials and tribulations of a young worker trying to recover the ration card that was buried by mistake with his model worker uncle.

104. Armando Hart, "La Lucha Contra el Burocratismo," in Francisco Fernández Sánchez and José Martínez, editors, *Cuba, Una Revolución en Marcha* (Paris: Ruedo Ibérico, 1967), page 174.

105. Cited in Silverman, "Some Dilemmas of Cuban Socialism," in Barkin and Manitzas, op. cit., page 13.

106. *Granma Weekly Review*, August 17, 1969.

107. Rene Dumont, *Is Cuba Socialist?* (New York: Viking Press, 1974), pages 149–50.

108. See Isaac Deutscher, *The Prophet Armed* (New York: Vintage Books, 1965), pages 491–92.

109. Karol, op. cit., page 451.

110. Ibid., page 463.

111. Lockwood, op. cit., page 352n.

112. Ibid., page 351n.

113. Isy Joshua, *Organisation et Rapports de Productions Dans Une Économie de Transition* (Paris: Sorbonne, Centre d'Études de Planification Socialiste, 1968).

114. Edmundo Desnoes, "Twenty Years in Cuba," manuscript, 1979, page 9.

115. Ibid., page 10.

116. Figure cited by officials of the Committee on Revolutionary Orientation (C.O.R.) in an interview conducted in June of 1970 in Havana.

117. Mesa Lago, op. cit., page 38.

Chapter 5

1. Fidel Castro, "Report on the Cuban Economy," in Rolando Bonachea and Nelson Valdés, editors, *Cuba in Revolution* (Garden City, N.Y.: Doubleday Anchor Books, 1972), pages 337–38.

2. Fidel Castro, in "Franco Debate Obrero Sobre Ausentismo y Trabajo Voluntario," in *Granma* (daily), September 8, 1970, page 5. We hear this critique again and again by Fidel throughout his talks and speeches during 1970 (and indeed, in every reference since then, to the 1960s experiment). For instance, he asserted during his speech to the Federation of Cuban Women in August of 1970, "We must be realists, realists." (See Fidel Castro, "Speech at the Tenth Anniversary of the Founding of the Federation of Cuban Women," *Granma Weekly Review,* August 23, 1970, page 4. Hereafter referred to as "Speech to F.M.C.") Or at the National Assembly of Popular Power in June of 1978 (see page 128 of this Chapter). It is almost as if he were constantly trying to remind himself.

3. *Granma Weekly Review,* June 27, 1971, page 1.

4. Frank Fitzgerald, "A Critique of the Sovietization of Cuba Thesis," *Science and Society,* Vol. 42, no. 1, Spring 1978, page 7.

5. Jorge Domínguez, *Cuba: Order and Revolution* (Cambridge, Mass.: Belknap Press, 1978), page 275.

6. Castro, "Report on the Cuban Economy," op. cit., page 329.

7. See Lourdes Casal, *El Caso Padilla: Literatura y Revolución en Cuba* (Miami: Ediciones Universales, 1971), for a collection of the relevant documents.

8. See Fidel Castro, "Discurso de Clausura del Primer Congreso Nacional de Educación y Cultura," April 30, 1971, reprinted in Casal, op. cit.

9. Castro, "Report on the Cuban Economy," op. cit. See, in particular, pages 329–37.

10. Cited in K. S. Karol, *Guerillas in Power* (New York: Hill and Wang, 1970), page 418.

11. Fidel Castro, "July 26th 1974 Speech in Matanzas," *Granma Weekly Review,* August 4, 1974. ·

12. *Constitución de la República de Cuba* (Havana: Department of Revolutionary Orientation) [D.O.R.], 1976), Chapter I, Article 5, page 15.

13. Castro, "Report on the Cuban Economy," op. cit., page 345.

14. Ibid., page 347.

15. Castro, "Speech to F.M.C.," op. cit.

16. Nelson Valdés, "Revolution and Institutionalization in Cuba," *Cuban Studies/Estudios Cubanos,* Vol. VI, no. 1, January 1976, page 20.

17. Castro, "Speech to F.M.C.," op. cit., page 3.

18. Ibid., page 4.

19. Fidel Castro, "Speech at the Celebration of the Tenth Anniversary of the Committees in Defense of the Revolution," *Granma Weekly Review,* September 5, 1970, page 1.

20. Castro, "Speech to F.M.C.," op. cit., page 5.

21. For a detailed description of the soviet system prior to 1987, particularly

as it functioned at the local level, see Jeffrey Hahn, *Soviet Grassroots: Citizen Participation in Local Government* (Princeton: Princeton University Press, 1988). Hahn updates his account, examining the reforms introduced during the Gorbachev era, in his article "State Institutions in Transition," in Stephen White, Alex Pravda, and Zvi Gitelman, editors, *Developments in Soviet and Post Soviet Politics* (Durham, N.C.: Duke University Press, 1992).

22. *Sobre la Constitución del Poder Popular* (Havana: 1978), pages 16 and 24.

23. Comisión Electoral Nacional, *Información Estadística del Proceso Electoral 1981* (Havana: Oficinas de la Asamblea Nacional del Poder Popular, 1982), pages 13, 14. Hereafter referred to as *Información Estadística*.

24. Ibid., page 27.

25. *Granma* (daily), March 12, 1984, page 3; and *Granma* (daily), May 24, 1984, page 2; and *Mujer y Sociedad en Cifras 1975–1988* (Havana: Editorial de la Mujer, 1990), page 91. Hereafter referred to as *Mujer en Cifras*.

26. *Mujer en Cifras,* page 91.

27. Ibid., page 92.

28. Haroldo Dilla Alfonso and Gerardo González Nuñez, *Participación y Desarrollo en los Municipios Cubanos* (Havana: CEA, 1991), page 13. A part of this study is available in English in Dilla, González, and Vincentelli, Ana, "Cuba's Local Governments: An Experience Beyond the Paradigm," *Cuban Studies/Estudios Cubanos,* vol. 22, 1992, pp. 151–70.

29. *Mujer en Cifras,* op. cit., page 91.

30. Ibid., page 90.

31. See Barbara Jancar, *Women in Communism* (Baltimore: Johns Hopkins Press, 1978).

32. Gayle McGarrity puts the figure at easily 60 percent in her recent article, "Race, Culture and Social Change in Contemporary Cuba," in Sandor Halebsky and John Kirk, editors, *Cuba in Transition* (Boulder, Colo.: Westview Press, 1992), page 197.

33. *Sobre la Constitución del Poder Popular,* op. cit., page 24.

34. Lourdes Casal, "Ethnic Composition of the Cuban Elected Popular Power Organs: A Mini-Report" (unpublished manuscript, 1979).

35. In 1976, 75.2 percent of the delegates elected to municipal assemblies were Party members, candidates for Party membership, or members of the U.J.C. (*Sobre la Constitución del Poder Popular,* op. cit., page 21). In the National Assembly, 91.7 percent of the deputies were Party members or candidates and 5.0 percent were U.J.C. members (Bard Jørgensen, "The Interrelationship Between Base and Superstructure in Cuba," *Ibero-Americana, Nordic Journal of Latin American Studies,* vol. 13, no. 1, 1983, page 39, citing figures of the 1979 Comisión Electoral Nacional of Cuba). In the 1981 elections, at the municipal level, 65.3 percent were Party members or candidates and 10.4 percent were U.J.C. members (*Información Estadística,* op. cit., page 60). The statistics have remained relatively constant in subsequent elections.

36. Dilla Alfonso and González Nuñez, op. cit., page 23.

37. Ibid., page 45.

38. Fidel Castro, "July 26th, 1974 Speech in Matanzas," in *Granma Weekly Review,* August 4, 1974.

39. Raúl Castro, "Speech at the Closing Session of the Seminar for Delegates of People's Power in Matanzas," *Granma Weekly Review,* August 22, 1974, page 4.

40. Castro, "July 26th, 1974 Speech in Matanzas," op. cit.
41. Andrew Zimbalist and Susan Eckstein, "Patterns of Cuban Development: The First Twenty-Five Years," *World Development*, Vol. 15, no. 1, January 1987, page 12.
42. See, for instance, Domínguez, op. cit., page 286. Domínguez argues that Popular Power at the base level deals only with petty secondary concerns that are handled by a form of "machine politics and ward bosses."
43. Archibald Ritter, "The Organs of People's Power and the Communist Party: The Nature of Cuban Democracy," in Sandor Halebsky and John Kirk, editors, *Cuba: Twenty-Five Years of Revolution* (New York: Praeger, 1985), page 280.
44. *Constitución de la República de Cuba,* op. cit., Chapter I, Article 4, page 14–15.
45. "Sobre los Órganos del Poder Popular," *Tesis y Resoluciones: Primer Congreso del Partido Comunista de Cuba* (Havana: D.O.R., 1976), page 184.
46. *Información Estadística,* op. cit., page 13; and *Granma* (daily), March 12, 1984, page 3.
47. See pages 122–23 in this Chapter.
48. Dilla Alfonso and González Nuñez, op. cit., page 30.
49. *Información Estadística,* op. cit., page 14.
50. Interview conducted with José Arañaburo, Secretary, Executive Committee of the National Assembly of Popular Power, in Havana Province, January 3, 1983.
51. *Granma* (daily), December 27, 1991, page 2.
52. Interview conducted with José Arañaburo in the offices of National Popular Power in the City of Havana, January 4, 1983.
53. Marta Harnecker, *Cuba: Dictatorship or Democracy?* (Westport, Conn.: Lawrence Hill, 1980), page 229.
54. Jørgensen, op. cit., pages 36–37.
55. In the workplace, the resuscitation of the trade union movement was followed with the introduction into each workplace of various mechanisms aimed at promoting a sense of collective administration, specifically Worker Production Assemblies and Management Councils, composed of representatives of both the administration and the union. And there is no question that, at the enterprise level, the sense of workers' input in actual decision making greatly increased through these mechanisms. In interviews done in 1975 by Marifeli Pérez-Stable, 55 percent of the workers felt that their input was influential and significant (See Pérez-Stable, "Whither the Cuban Working Class," in *Latin American Perspectives,* Issue 7, Vol. 11, no. 4, Spring 1975). In a survey executed the following year among 355 workers by Herrera and Rosenkranz, 80 percent replied that they felt they "always or nearly always, made a personal intervention at production assemblies and that the most important areas which came under direct discussion at these monthly assemblies were first, production plans" (cited by 95 percent of the workers interviewed) and education (cited by 57 percent). (See Antonio José Herrera and Hernan Rosenkranz in John Griffiths and Peter Griffiths, editors, *Cuba: The Second Decade* [London: Writers and Readers, 1979].) Andrew Zimbalist points out that such choices reflected "a considerably higher level of actual worker participation in Cuban enterprises than in Soviet enterprises" and the fact that Cuban workers "appear to take a greater interest in production issues" than elsewhere in the socialist world (see Andrew Zimbalist, "Cuban Economic Plan-

ning: Organization and Performance," in Halebsky and Kirk, editors, *Cuba: Twenty Five Years of Revolution,* op. cit., page 221). But, by and large, effective worker influence was limited to the plant level. There was discussion of the annual and newly introduced Five-Year Economic plans at that level and a marked effort to universalize that discussion. Castro spoke of 1.25 million workers participating in discussion of the 1975 plan in his speech in 1975 to the First Party Congress and of some 1.45 million in 1980 in his speech to the Second Party Congress. But these seemed generally educational efforts; it was only at the level of their specific enterprise plans that workers' discussions produced changes. (The Junta Central de Planificación (JUCEPLAN) in 1980 reported that workers' suggestions produced amendments in control figures for 42 percent of enterprises in 1979 and 59 percent in 1980. [Ibid.]) At the base level, workers' roles in terms of national planning remained one of reception and adjustment rather than proposal, despite a high level of discussion and base-level organization. In the workplace, then, direct participation in decision making that actually determined directions remained essentially horizontal and local. The determination of national goals, priorities, and directions remained elsewhere, at the center, with JUCEPLAN. Thus we can see, at the level of the workplace and despite the introduction of structured and direct participation by workers, the reality of tension between centralizing and decentralizing tendencies.

56. Outlined in interview with José Arañaburo, January 3, 1983.

57. Jorge Domínguez, "Revolutionary Politics: The New Demands for Orderliness," in Domínguez, editor, *Cuba: Internal and International Affairs* (Beverly Hills, Calif.: Sage Publications, 1982), pages 38–39.

58. See Asamblea Nacional del Poder Popular, *Acta: Segundo Periodo Ordinario de Sesiones: Segunda Legislatura 1–3, Julio 1982.*

59. Ibid., page 320.

60. Cited in Domínguez, "Revolutionary Politics: The New Demands for Orderliness," op. cit., page 39.

61. Asamblea Nacional del Poder Popular, *Acta: Segundo Periodo Ordinario de Sesiones: Segunda Legislatura 1–3 Julio 1982.*

62. Dilla Alfonso and González Nuñez op. cit., page 37–38.

63. Ibid., page 12.

64. Interview with Roberto Ogando, President, Special Municipality of Isle of Pines (now Isle of Youth), June 11, 1978.

65. Faustino Pérez, "Algunas Consideraciones Sobre el Funcionamiento de los Órganos Locales del Poder Popular," *Granma* (daily), June 30, 1978, pages 3–4.

66. *Granma* (daily), June 30, 1978, page 1.

67. See report of discussion in Asamblea Nacional del Poder Popular, *Acta: Primer Periodo Ordinario de Sesiones de 1978,* page 522.

68. Taken from personal tape recordings of the June 29, 1978, afternoon session of the meetings of the National Assembly of Popular Power. The translation is the author's.

69. Taken from personal tape recordings of June 29, 1978, afternoon session.

70. Taken from personal tape recordings of June 29 afternoon session.

71. The text of Fidel's intervention is taken from personal tape recordings of the June 30, 1978, morning session of the meetings of the National Assembly of Popular Power. The translation is the author's.

72. Marta Harnecker, "Lo Que el Pueblo Debe Saber: Humberto Pérez

Entrevistado por Marta Harnecker," *Bohemia,* Vol. 71, February 19, 1979, pages 58–81.

73. Ibid., page 78.

74. Ibid., pages 78–79.

75. Ibid., page 79.

76. Figures cited by Eugenio Balari, Minister of Internal Demand, in an interview in Havana, December 28, 1982.

77. Interview with José Arañaburo, in Havana, December 30, 1982.

78. The extent of the construction boom in Güira de Melena was discussed in an interview with the members of the Executive Committee of the Municipal Assembly of Güira de Melena, January 4, 1983.

79. These figures were taken from the records of the Executive Committee of the Provincial Assembly of the Province of Havana, during an interview with the members of that Committee, June 11, 1983.

80. Ibid.

81. See, in this regard, Carmen Diana Deere and Mieke Meurs, "Markets, Markets Everywhere? Understanding the Cuban Anomaly," *World Development,* Vol. 20, no. 6 (1992), pages 825–39.

82. Harnecker, op. cit., page 63.

83. Ibid.

84. Interviews conducted in Havana, June 11, 1978, and January 3, 1983.

Chapter 6

1. *New York Times* editorial, December 11, 1989, page A22.

2. George Fauriol on *NBC Nightly News,* July 27, 1989.

3. Tad Szulc on *NBC Nightly News,* July 27, 1989.

4. *All Things Considered,* National Public Radio, August 1, 1989.

5. William Safire, "Castro's Last Stand," *New York Times,* February 19, 1990, page A17; Susan Kaufman Purcell, "Is Cuba the Next Communist Domino?" *New York Times,* January 10, 1990, page A27.

6. Fidel Castro, *Granma Weekly Review,* November 12, 1989, page 4. Castro's words, in context, were as follows: "Now there are two types of socialists, two types of communists: good and bad ones, as defined by imperialism. . . . Those who do not submit to imperialism . . . they call inflexible. Long live inflexibility!"

7. *New York Times,* April 2, 1989, page A1.

8. Fidel Castro, "Speech on the 35th Anniversary of the Moncada Attack," *Granma Weekly Review,* August 7, 1988, page 5.

9. Robert W. Davies, "Gorbachev's Socialism in Historical Perspective," *New Left Review,* no. 179, January–February 1990, page 14.

10. Ibid., page 15.

11. Nathan Gardels, "The Rise of the 'Atari' Communists," *New York Times,* April 2, 1989, page F3.

12. Davies, op. cit., page 18.

13. Ibid., page 19.

14. *Granma Weekly Review,* December 14, 1986, page 13.

15. *Granma Weekly Review,* April 19, 1987, page 12.

16. Fidel Castro, "Speech at the 30th Anniversary of the C.D.R.s," *Granma Weekly Review,* October 14, 1990, page 3.

17. *Granma Weekly Review,* March 18, 1990, page 11.

18. Michael Howard, "The Gorbachev Challenge and the Defense of the West," *Survival,* Vol. 30, no. 6, November–December 1988.

19. *Granma* (daily), April 19, 1990, page 1.

20. *Granma Weekly Review,* December 17, 1989, page 3.

21. *New York Times,* May 17, 1989, page 1.

22. *Granma Weekly Review,* July 6, 1986, page 2.

23. *Granma Weekly Review,* April 19, 1987, page 11.

24. *Granma Weekly Review,* April 27, 1986, page 10.

25. Medea Benjamin, "Things Fall Apart," *NACLA Report on the Americas,* Vol. XXIV, no. 2, August 1990, page 18.

26. For published accounts, see in particular Gerardo Timossi, "Cuba: Un Agenda Diferente Para los Cambios," and Fernando Martínez Heredia, "El Socialismo Cubano: Perspectivas y Desafíos," in *Cuadernos de Nuestra América,* Vol. VII, no. 15, July–December 1990. See also Martínez Heredia, *Desafíos del Socialismo Cubano* (Havana: CEA, 1988).

27. Timossi, op. cit., page 55. As Fidel phrased it (of course, after the collapse of the Soviet Union), "One day we realized that they weren't even going to shoot a firecracker for us," Fidel Castro, "Speech to the National Assembly," *Granma International,* January 12, 1992, page 5.

28. *Granma Weekly Review,* April 8, 1990, page 10.

29. Frei Betto and Fidel Castro, *Fidel and Religion* (New York: Simon and Schuster, 1987).

30. For the Cuban account of these trials, see *Vindicación de Cuba* (Havana: Editora Política, 1989). For a journalistic examination that raises some of the critical and unanswered questions, see Julia Preston, "The Trial That Shook Cuba," in *New York Review of Books,* Vol. XXXVI, no. 19, December 7, 1989, pages 24–31. Janette Habel in her book, *Cuba: The Revolution in Peril* (London: Verso, 1991), and Andres Oppenheimer in his study, *Castro's Final Hour* (New York: Simon and Schuster, 1992), provide further interpretations of the trial and its possible meanings. See Habel, pages 177–86, and Oppenheimer, pages 15–98.

31. *Granma* (daily), March 16, 1990, page 5.

32. José Luis Rodríguez, "Los Cambios en la Política Económica y los Resultados de la Economia Cubana (1986–89)," *Cuadernos de Nuestra América,* Vol. VII, no. 15, July–December 1990, pages 69–70.

33. *Granma Weekly Review,* October 14, 1990, page 4.

34. Boris Kagarlitsky, "The Intelligentsia and Changes," in *New Left Review,* no. 164, July–August 1987, page 18. See also Moshe Lewin, *The Gorbachev Phenomenon* (Berkeley: University of California Press, 1988), page 23.

35. Ernst Mandel, *Beyond Perestroika: The Future of Gorbachev's USSR* (London: Verso, 1989), page 23.

36. *New York Times,* July 26, 1990, page A8.

37. Paul Easton, "The Rock Music Community," in Jim Riordan, editor, *Soviet Youth Culture* (Bloomington: Indiana University Press, 1989), page 50.

38. Ibid., page 49.

39. Michael Shuman, "In the East Bloc, It's Lennon, Not Lenin," *New York Times,* January 1, 1990, page A25.

40. See accounts in *New York Times,* August 19–21, 1991.

41. Mandel, op. cit., page 17.

42. Boris Kagarlitsky, " 'Glasnost,' the Soviet Press and the Red Greens," in Kagarlitsky, editor, *The Thinking Reed* (London: Verso, 1988), page 341.

43. Nancy Condee and Vladimir Padunov, "Perestroika Suicide: Not By Bred Alone," *New Left Review,* no. 189, September–October 1991, pages 82–83.

44. Boris Kagarlitsky, speaking at the University of Massachusetts, Amherst, May 5, 1991.

45. Shuman, op. cit., page 25.

46. *Granma Weekly Review,* August 13, 1989, page 1.

47. *Economist's Intelligence Unit, Country Report: Cuba,* 1991, no. 3, pages 17–18. Hereafter referred to as *E.I.U.*

48. Nelson Valdés, "Cuban Political Culture: Between Betrayal and Death," in Sandor Halebsky and John Kirk, editors, *Cuba in Transition: Crisis and Transformation in the 1990s* (Boulder, Colo.: Westview Press, 1992), page 220.

49. For a detailed discussion of the elections, see Boris Kagarlitsky, *Farewell Perestroika* (London: Verso, 1990), particularly chapter 8 "The Spring Whirlpool," pages 111–143. For a very useful series of articles which highlight the effects of *perestroika, glasnost,* and democratization on various aspects of the political system, from varying perspectives, see White, Pravda, and Gitelman, *Developments in Soviet and Post Soviet Politics,* op. cit.

50. See Bill Keller, "Two Years That Shook Baku," *New York Times,* January 29, 1990, page A8.

51. *Granma Weekly Review,* July 6, 1986, page 2.

52. *Granma Weekly Review,* October 7, 1990, page 2.

53. *Granma Weekly Review,* October 7, 1990, page 3.

54. *Granma Weekly Review,* July 23, 1989, page 12.

55. The phrase of Valery Tishkov, Director of the Institute of Ethnology and Anthropology, Moscow, cited in Ronald Grigor Suny, "Incomplete Revolution: National Movements and the Collapse of the New Soviet Empire," *New Left Review,* no. 189, September–October 1991, page 111.

56. Roy Medvedev, "Politics After the Coup," *New Left Review,* no. 189, September–October 1991, page 92.

Chapter 7

1. Comité Estatal de Estadística, *Anuario Estadístico de Cuba 1988* (Havana, 1989), page 281.

2. *E.I.U.,* no. 1, 1990, page 17.

3. Ibid.

4. Haroldo Dilla Alfonso and Gerardo González Nuñez, *Participación y Desarrollo en los Municipios Cubanos* (Havana: CEA 1991), page 13.

5. Rafael Hernández and Haroldo Dilla, "Cultura, Política y Participación Popular," *Cuadernos de Nuestra América,* Vol. VII, no. 15, July–December 1990, page 119.

6. *Bohemia,* July 6, 1990, page 7.

7. Ibid., page 5.

8. Ibid., page 6.

9. Ibid., page 6.

10. *Bohemia,* July 13, 1990, page 7.

11. Ibid., page 7.

12. Archibald Ritter, "The Organs of People's Power and the Communist Party: The Nature of Cuban Democracy," in Sandor Halebsky and John Kirk, editors, *Cuba: Twenty-Five Years of Revolution* (New York: Praeger, 1985), page 286.

13. Ibid., pages 286–87.

14. Dilla Alfonso and González Nuñez, op. cit., pages 28–29.

15. *Bohemia,* July 13, 1990, page 8.

16. Ibid., page 8.

17. See discussion in Dilla Alfonso and González Nuñez, op. cit., pages 36–38.

18. *Bohemia,* July 6, 1990, page 9.

19. *Bohemia,* July 20, 1990, page 51. See, as well, discussion in Dilla Alfonso and González Nuñes, op. cit., pages 37–38.

20. *Bohemia,* July 6, 1990, page 9.

21. Dilla Alfonso and González Nuñez, op. cit., page 25.

22. Ibid., page 25–26.

23. Ibid., page 25.

24. Ibid., page 25–26.

25. *Bohemia,* July 1990.

26. *Bohemia,* July 13, 1990, page 8.

27. Dilla Alfonso and González Nuñez, op. cit., page 48.

28. *Bohemia,* July 6, 1990, page 9.

29. *Bohemia,* July 13, 1990, page 8.

30. Ibid., page 9.

31. Ibid., page 9.

32. Dilla Alfonso and González Nuñez, op. cit., page 48.

33. E.I.U. Country Report 1990 #2.

34. Fidel Castro, "Speech to the C.D.R.s," (Granma) September 1990.

35. Interview with Gina Rey, July 11, 1991. Translation is the author's.

36. Interview with Haroldo Dilla, July 24, 1991. Translation is the author's.

Chapter 8

1. Marifeli Pérez-Stable, "Charismatic Authority, Party Politics and Popular Mobilizations: Revolution and Socialism in Cuba," in *Cuban Studies/Estudios Cubanos,* Vol. 22, 1992.

2. *Granma International,* January 12, 1992, page 3.

3. Fidel Castro, "Los Problemas de Nuestro País Solo los Puede Resolver la Revolución" (speech to the Fourth Party Congress), *Bohemia,* Vol. 83, no. 43, October 25, 1991, particularly pages 26–30.

4. Andrew Zimbalist, "Cuba 1990," in Eduardo Gamarra and James Malloy, editors, *Latin America and Caribbean Contemporary Record,* (New York: Holmes and Meier, 1990), Vol. 5.

5. *E.I.U.,* no. 3, 1993, page 10.

6. FBIS, 26 December 1991, page 2.

7. Ibid., page 3.

8. Ibid., page 3.

9. *E.I.U.,* no. 2, 1992, page 16.

10. This breakdown of special period economic programs is taken from An-

drew Zimbalist, "Teetering on the Brink: Cuba's Post-CMEA Economic and Political Crisis," *Journal of Latin American Studies,* Vol. 24, 1992, page 411.

11. For the most thorough account of the Food Program, see Carmen Diana Deere, "Cuba's National Food Program and Its Prospects for Food Security," *Agriculture and Human Values,* Vol. 10, no. 3, forthcoming, 1993.

12. Carmen Diana Deere, Ernel Gonzalez and Niurka Pérez, "The View From Below: Cuban Agriculture in the Special Period in Peacetime," manuscript, 1993.

13. *E.I.U.,* no. 3, 1990, page 17.

14. *E.I.U.,* no. 3, 1991, page 20.

15. Zimbalist, "Teetering on the Brink," op. cit., page 412.

16. Castro, speech to Fourth Party Congress, op. cit., page 38.

17. Cited in *CubaInfo,* Vol. 3, no. 15, page 5.

18. For a discussion of this, see Zimbalist, "Teetering on the Brink," op. cit., page 411.

19. *Granma* (daily), October 20, 1991, Fourth Party Congress Supplement, page 1. See also "Resoluciones del IV Congreso del Partido Comunista de Cuba," *Granma* (daily), October 23, 1991, page 3, as well as accounts of the Congress, in *Granma* (daily), October 15–19, 1991.

20. See "Amplio y Detallado Debate Sobre el Proyecto de Ley y de Reforma Constitucional," *Granma* (daily), July 11, 1992, pages 1–4. See also "Proyecto de Modificaciones a la Constitución de la República," in Hugo Azcuy, Rafael Hernandez, and Nelson Valdés, editors, *Cuba en el Mes,* University of New Mexico Latin American Studies Institute and Centro de Estudios Sobre América (Havana), October 1992.

21. Fidel Castro, "Address to the National Assembly," *Granma International,* January 12, 1992, page 2.

22. *CubaInfo,* Vol. 4, no. 3, page 5.

23. Castro, "Address to the National Assembly," op. cit., January 1992, page 2.

24. See *Granma Internacional,* November 8, 1992, page 2.

25. See Castro, "Address to the National Assembly," January 12, 1992, op. cit., page 4.

26. *Granma* (daily), July 13, 1992, page 3.

27. The changes suggested at the Party Congress are enumerated in *Granma* (daily), October 23, 1991, page 5. For the July 1992 discussion and approval of the reforms by the National Assembly, see *Granma* (daily), July 13, 1992, pages 3–5.

28. See Chapter 7 pages 160–61.

29. Castro, "Address to the National Assembly," op. cit., January 1992, page 2.

30. For the full text of Carlos Aldana's report, see *Granma International,* January 19, 1992, pages 2–6.

31. *Cuba Info,* Vol. 4, no. 8, page 7.

Conclusion

1. Zygmunt Bauman, "Living Without an Alternative," *Political Quarterly,* January–March 1991, page 40.

2. Ibid., pages 38–39.

3. Ibid., page 41.

4. Rosa Luxemburg, *The Russian Revolution and Leninism or Marxism?* (Ann Arbor: University of Michigan Press, 1972), page 69.

5. Antonio Gramsci, *Prison Notebooks* (New York: International Publishers, 1971), page 238.

Bibliography

Alier, Juan Martínez, *Cuba: Economía y Sociedad* (Paris: Ruedo Ibérico, 1973).

Althusser, Louis, *Lenin and Philosophy* (New York: Monthly Review Press, 1971).

Anderson, Perry, *Considerations on Western Marxism* (London: New Left Review Books, 1976).

——— "Trotsky's Interpretation of Stalinism," *New Left Review,* no. 139, May–June 1983, pages 49–58.

Anweiler, Oskar, *The Soviets: The Russian Workers, Peasants and Soldiers Councils 1905–1917* (New York: Pantheon, 1974).

Arato, Andrew, "Civil Society Against the State: Poland 1980–1981," *Telos,* no. 47, Spring 1981, pages 23–47.

Asamblea Nacional del Poder Popular, *Acta: Primer Periodo Ordinario de Sesiones de 1978.*

Asamblea Nacional del Poder Popular, *Acta: Segundo Periodo Ordinario de Sesiones: Segunda Legislatura 1–3 Julio 1982.*

Avineri, Shlomo, *The Political and Economic Thought of Karl Marx* (London: Cambridge University Press, 1968).

Avrich, Paul, *Kronstadt 1921* (New York: W. W. Norton, 1974).

Azicri, Max, "The Rectification Process Revisited: Cuba's Defense of Traditional Marxism," in Sandor Halebsky and John Kirk, editors, *Cuba in Transition: Crisis and Transformation in the 1990s* (Boulder, Colo.: Westview Press, 1992), pages 37–54.

Bahro, Rudolf, *The Alternative in Eastern Europe* (London: New Left Books, 1978).

Bambirra, Vania, *La Revolución Cubana: Una Nueva Interpretación* (Santiago de Chile: Cuaderno del CESO, 1973).

Bauman, Zygmunt, "Living Without An Alternative," *Political Quarterly*, January–March 1991, pages 35–44.

———, "On the Maturation of Stalinism," *Telos*, no. 47, Spring 1981, pages 48–57.

Beauvais, Jean-Pierre, "Achievements and Contradictions of the Cuban Workers' State," in Fitzroy Ambursley and Robin Cohen, editors, *Crisis in the Caribbean* (New York: Monthly Review Press, 1983).

Bellis, Paul, *Marxism and the USSR: The Theory of Proletarian Dictatorship and the Marxist Analysis of Soviet Society* (Atlantic Highlands, N.J.: Humanities Press, 1979).

Bendix, Rheinhard, "Socialism and the Theory of Bureaucracy," *Canadian Journal of Economics and Political Science*, Vol. XVI, 1950, pages 501–14.

Berman, Jesse, "The Cuban Popular Tribunals," *Columbia Law Review*, December 1969, pages 1317–54.

Bettelheim, Charles, "Dictatorship of the Proletariat, Social Class and Proletarian Ideology," *Monthly Review*, Vol. 23, no. 6, November 1971, pages 55–76.

———, "La Revolution Cubaine Sur la Voie Sovietique," *Le Monde*, December 5, 1971.

Billington, James, *Fire in the Minds of Men: Origins of the Revolutionary Faith* (New York: Basic Books, 1980).

Black, George, "Toward Victory Always, But When?" *The Nation*, October 24, 1988, pages 373–86.

Blackburn, Robin, "Marxism: Theory of Proletarian Revolution," in Blackburn, editor, *Revolution and Class Struggle: A Reader in Marxist Politics* (London: Fontana, 1977).

———, "Prologue to the Cuban Revolution," *New Left Review*, no. 21, October 1963, pages 52–91.

Bobbio, Norberto, *Democracy and Dictatorship* (Minneapolis: University of Minnesota Press, 1989).

———, *The Future of Democracy* (Minneapolis: University of Minnesota Press, 1987).

———, *Which Socialism?* (Minneapolis: University of Minnesota Press, 1987).

Bonachea, Rolando, and Nelson Valdés, editors, *Che: Selected Works of Ernesto Guevara* (Cambridge, Mass.: MIT Press, 1969).

Bowles, Samuel, and Herbert Gintis, *Democracy and Capitalism* (New York: Basic Books, 1986).

Brinton, Maurice, *The Bolsheviks and Workers' Control 1917–1921* (Montreal: Black Rose Books, 1972).

Brundenius, Claes, *Revolutionary Cuba: The Challenge of Economic Growth with Equity* (Boulder, Colo.: Westview Press, 1983).

Burawoy, Michael, *The Politics of Production* (London: Verso, 1985).

———, "Reflections on the Class Consciousness of Hungarian Workers," *Politics and Society*, Vol. 17, no. 1, March 1989, pages 1–34.

Bushnell, John, *Moscow Graffiti* (Winchester: Unwin Hyman, 1990).

Cabral, Amilcar, "The Weapon of Theory," in Cabral, *Revolution in Guinea: An African People's Struggle* (London: Stage 1, 1969).

Cardenal, Ernesto, *In Cuba* (New York: New Directions Books, 1974).

Carlo, Antonio, "The Crisis of Bureaucratic Collectivism," *Telos*, no. 43, Spring 1980, pages 3–32.

———, "The Socio-Economic Nature of the U.S.S.R.," *Telos,* no. 21, Fall 1974, pages 2–86.

———, and Umberto Melotti, "In Memory of Bruno Rizzi," *Telos,* no. 33, Fall 1977, pages 142–44.

Carr, E. H., *The Bolshevik Revolution 1917–1923,* Vols. 1–3 (Baltimore: Penguin Books, 1966).

———, "Revolution From Above," *New Left Review,* no. 46, November–December 1967, pages 17–28.

———, *Socialism in One Country,* Vols. 1 and 2 (Baltimore: Penguin Books, 1958).

Casal, Lourdes, "Cuba: On the Political Organization of Socialist Democracy," paper presented at the Latin American Studies Association Meetings, Pittsburgh, April 5–7, 1979.

———, "The Cuban National Assembly: Its First Two Years," paper presented at "Seminar on Cuba," Washington, D.C., August 13–17, 1979.

———, "Ethnic Composition of the Cuban Elected Popular Power Organs: A Mini-Report," unpublished manuscript, 1979.

———, "On Popular Power: The Organization of the Cuban State During the Period of Transition," *Latin American Perspectives,* Issue 7, Vol. II, no. 4, 1975, pages 78–88.

———, editor, *El Caso Padilla: Literatura y Revolución en Cuba* (Miami: Ediciones Universales, 1971).

———, and Marifeli Pérez-Stable, "Party and State in Post-1970 Cuba," in Leslie Holmes, editor, *The Withering Away of the State?* (Beverly Hills, Calif.: Sage Publications, 1981).

Castoriadis, Cornelius, "The Social Regime in Russia," *Telos* no. 38, Winter 1978–79, pages 32–47.

Castro, Fidel Ruz, *Fidel Castro Denounces Sectarianism* (Havana: Ministry of Foreign Relations, 1962).

———, *Fidel Castro Speaks,* Martin Kenner and James Petras, editors (New York: Grove Press, 1969).

———, *Fidel in Chile* (New York: Pathfinder Press, 1971).

———, *History Will Absolve Me* (Havana: Book Institute, 1976).

———, *Ideología Consciencia y Trabajo Político/1959–1986* (Havana: Editora Política, 1987).

———, *Por El Camino Correcto* (Havana: Editora Política, 1988).

———, "Los Problemas de Nuestra País Solo los Puede Resolver la Revolución" (Speech to the Fourth Party Congress), *Bohemia,* Vol. 83, no. 43, October 25, 1991.

———, "Report on the Cuban Economy," speech delivered on July 26, 1970, in Rolando Bonachea and Nelson Valdés, editors, *Cuba in Revolution* (Garden City, N.Y.: Doubleday Anchor Books, 1972), pages 317–56.

———, *Speeches: Volume II: Our Power Is That of the Working People* (New York: Pathfinder Press, 1983).

———, *Unity Gave Us Victory* (Moscow: Progress Publishers, 1976).

Chamberlin, William Henry, *The Russian Revolution 1917–1921* (New York: Macmillan, 1935).

Cockburn, Cynthia, "People's Power," in John Griffiths and Peter Griffiths, editors, *Cuba: The Second Decade* (London: Writers and Readers, 1979).

Codina Jiménez, Alexis, "Worker Incentives in Cuba," in *World Development,* Vol. 15, no. 1, 1987, pages 127–38.

Cohen, Stephen, "Bolshevism and Stalinism," in Robert Tucker, editor, *Stalinism: Essays in Historical Interpretation* (New York: W. W. Norton, 1977).

———, *Bukharin and the Bolshevik Revolution* (New York: Vintage Books, 1975).

Colletti, Lucio, "Power and Democracy in Socialist Society," *New Left Review,* no. 56, July–August 1969, pages 19–26.

Comisión Electoral Nacional, *Información Estadística del Proceso Electoral 1981* (Havana: Oficinas de la Asamblea Nacional del Poder Popular, 1982).

Condee, Nancy, and Vladimir Padunov, "Perestroika Suicide: Not By Bred Alone," *New Left Review,* no. 189, September–October 1991, pages 67–89.

"Constitution of the Organs of People's Power," *Center for Cuban Studies Newsletter,* October–December 1975, pages 8–26.

Coraggio, José Luis, "Revolución y Democracia en Nicaragua," *Cuadernos de Pensamiento Propio* (Managua: C.R.I.E.S., 1984), pages 5–40.

Corrigan, Philip, Harvie Ramsay, and Derek Sayer, *Socialism Construction and Marxist Theory: Bolshevism and its Critique* (London: Macmillan, 1978).

Cross, Peter, "Soviet Perestroika: The Cuban Effect," *Third World Quarterly,* Vol. 13, no. 1, 1992, pages 143–58.

Dahl, Robert, *Democracy and its Critics* (New Haven: Yale University Press, 1989).

Daniels, Robert, *Red October: The Bolshevik Revolution of 1917* (New York: Scribner, 1967).

———, "The State and Revolution: A Case Study in the Transformation of Communist Ideology," *American Slavic and Eastern European Review,* Vol. XII, no. 1, February 1953, pages 22–43.

Davies, Robert W., "Gorbachev's Socialism in Historical Perspective," *New Left Review,* no. 179, January–February 1990, pages 5–28.

Deere, Carmen Diana, "Cuba's National Food Program and Its Prospects for Food Security," *Agriculture and Human Values,* Vol. 10, no. 3, forthcoming, 1993.

———, Ernel Gonzalez, and Niurka Pérez, "The View From Below: Cuban Agriculture in the Special Period in Peacetime," manuscript, 1993.

———, and Mieke Meurs, "Markets, Markets Everywhere? Understanding the Cuban Anomaly," *World Development,* Vol. 20, no. 6 (1992), pp. 825–39.

de la Cuesta, Leonel Antonio, "The Cuban Socialist Constitution: Its Originality and Role in Institutionalization," *Cuban Studies/Estudios Cubanos,* Vol. 6, no. 2, July 1976, pages 15–30.

Departamento de Orientación Revolucionario, editors, *Tesis y Resoluciones: Primer Congreso del Partido Comunista de Cuba* (Havana, 1976).

Desnoes, Edmundo, "Fidel Castro: Su Uso de la Palabra," in *Cuba: Transformación del Hombre* (Havana: Casa de las Américas, 1966).

———, "Los Cubanos," manuscript, 1972.

———, "Twenty Years in Cuba," manuscript, 1979.

———, and Fausto Maso, editors, *La Sierra y El Llano* (Havana: Casa de las Américas, 1969).

Deutscher, Isaac, *The Prophet Armed* (New York: Vintage Books, 1965).

———, "Roots of Bureaucracy," in Ralph Miliband and John Saville, editors, *The Socialist Register 1969* (New York: Monthly Review Press, 1969), pages 9–28.

Dilla Alfonso, Haroldo, "Notas Sobre La Relación Centralización-Decentralización en la Transición Socialista Cubana," (Havana: *CEA,* no date).

————, and Gerardo González Nuñez, "Participación y Desarrollo en los Municipios Cubanos," (Havana: CEA, 1991).

Dirlik, Arif, "Postsocialism? Reflections on Socialism With Chinese Characteristics," *Bulletin of Concerned Asia Scholars,* Vol. 21, no. 1, January–March 1989, pages 33–44.

Djilas, Milovan, *The New Class* (New York: Praeger, 1957).

Domínguez, Jorge, "Cuba: Charismatic Communism," *Problems of Communism,* Vol. 34, no. 5, September–October 1985, pages 102–107.

————, "Cuba in the 1980's," *Problems of Communism,* Vol. 30, no. 2, March–April 1981, pages 49–59.

————, *Cuba: Order and Revolution* (Cambridge, Mass.: Belknap Press, 1978).

————, "Institutionalization and Civil–Military Relations in Cuba," *Cuban Studies/Estudios Cubanos,* Vol. 6, no. 1, January 1976, pages 36–66.

————, "Revolutionary Politics: The New Demands for Orderliness," in Domínguez, editor, *Cuba: Internal and International Affairs* (Beverly Hills, Calif.: Sage Publications, 1982).

————, Nelson Valdés, Edward González, and Irving Horowitz, "Comments: Forum on Institutionalization," *Cuban Studies/Estudios Cubanos,* Vol. 9, no. 2, July 1979, pages 78–90.

dos Santos, Teotonio, "Socialism: Ideal and Historical Practice," in Milos Nikolic, editor, *Socialism on the Threshold of the Twenty-First Century* (London: Verso, 1985).

Draper, Hal, "The Death of the State in Marx and Engels," Ralph Miliband and John Saville, editors, *The Socialist Register 1970* (New York: Monthly Review Press, 1970).

————, *The "Dictatorship of the Proletariat" From Marx to Lenin* (New York: Monthly Review Press, 1987).

————, *Karl Marx's Theory of Revolution: Volume I: State and Bureaucracy* (New York: Monthly Review Press, 1977).

————, "Marx and the Dictatorship of the Proletariat," *Cahiers de L'Institut de Science Économique Appliquée,* no. 129, September 1962, (Series S, no. 6), pages 5–73.

Draper, Theodore, *Castroism: Theory and Practice* (New York: Praeger, 1965).

————, *Castro's Revolution: Myths and Realities* (New York: Praeger, 1962).

Dumont, Rene, *Is Cuba Socialist?* (New York: Viking Press, 1974).

————, *Socialism and Development* (New York: Grove Press, 1970).

Easton, Paul, "The Rock Music Community" in Jim Riordan, editor, *Soviet Youth Culture* (Bloomington: Indiana University Press, 1989).

Eckstein, Susan, "Capitalist Constraints on Cuban Socialist Development," *Comparative Politics,* Vol. 12, April 1980, pages 253–274.

————, "From Communist Solidarity to Communist Solitary; The Special Period in Peacetime in Cuba," manuscript, April 1991.

————, "Why No Perestroika in Cuba?" manuscript, 1989.

Engels, Frederick, "Anti-Duhring" in Karl Marx and Frederick Engels, *Collected Works* (New York: International Publishers 1976), Vol. 25.

————, *The Origin of the Family, Private Property and the State* (New York: International Publishers, 1972).

Escudero, Roberto, "Democracia y Socialismo," paper presented at Association of Latin American Sociology Conference, Havana, May 1991.

Evans, Michael, "Karl Marx and the Concept of Political Participation," in Geraint Parry, editor, *Participation in Politics* (Manchester: Manchester University Press, 1972), pages 127–50.

Fagen, Richard, "Charismatic Authority and the Leadership of Fidel Castro," in Rolando Bonachea and Nelson Valdés, editors, *Cuba in Revolution,* (Garden City, N.Y.: Doubleday Anchor Books, 1972), pages 154–68.

———, "Continuities in Cuban Revolutionary Politics," *Monthly Review,* Vol. 23, no. 11, April 1972, pages 24–48.

———, "The Politics of Transition," in Richard Fagen, Carmen Diana Deere, and José Luis Corragio, editors, *Transition and Development* (New York: Monthly Review Press, 1986), pages 249–63.

———, *The Transformation of Political Culture in Cuba* (Stanford: Stanford University Press, 1969).

———, and Steven Sanderson, "Continuities of Revolutionary Rule and Struggle in Cuba," paper presented at Conference on Revolution and the Transformation of Social Relations in the Third World, Brooklyn College, May 7–9, 1979.

Fainsod, Merle, and Jerry Hough, *How Russia is Ruled* (Cambridge, Mass.: Harvard University Press, revised edition, 1979).

Farber, Samuel, *Before Stalinism: The Rise and Fall of Soviet Democracy* (London: Verso, 1990).

Fehér, Ferenc, Agnes Heller, and György Márkus, *Dictatorship Over Needs: An Analysis of Soviet Societies* (Oxford: Basil Blackwell, 1983).

———, and Andrew Arato, editors, *Gorbachev: The Debate* (Atlantic Highlands, N.J.: Humanities Press, 1989).

Fernández Rios, Olga, and Gaspar García Gallo, "The State and Democracy in Cuba," *Contemporary Marxism,* no. 1, Spring 1980, pages 81–88.

Fernández Sánchez, Francisco, and José Martínez, editors, *Cuba, Una Revolución en Marcha* (Paris: Ruedo Ibérico, 1967).

Ferro, Marc, *The Russian Revolution of February 1917* (London: Routledge and Kegan Paul, 1972).

Fischer, Ernst, *The Essential Marx* (New York: Herder and Herder, 1970).

———, "Sur le Probleme de la Dictature du Proletariat," *Les Temps Modernes,* November 1968, pages 895–913.

Fischer, Louis, *The Life of Lenin* (New York: Harper and Row, 1964).

Fitzgerald, Frank, "A Critique of the Sovietization of Cuba Thesis," *Science and Society,* Vol. 42, no. 1, Spring 1978, pages 1–32.

Franqui, Carlos, *Diary of the Cuban Revolution* (New York: Viking, 1980).

———, "The Soviet Model and 'Caudillismo' in Cuba," in Rossana Rossanda, editor, *Power and Opposition in Post Revolutionary Societies* (London: Ink Links, 1979), pages 207–12.

Frei Betto and Fidel Castro, *Fidel and Religion* (New York: Simon and Schuster, 1987).

Fuller, Linda, "Power at the Workplace: The Resolution of Worker-Management Conflict in Cuba," *World Development,* Vol. 15, no. 1, January 1987, pages 139–52.

———, *Work and Democracy in Socialist Cuba* (Philadelphia: Temple University Press, 1992).

Geras, Norman, "Classical Marxism and Proletarian Representation," *New Left Review,* no. 123, January–February 1981, pages 75–89.

Gerratana, Valentino, "Stalin, Lenin and Leninism," *New Left Review,* no. 103, May–June 1977, pages 59–71.

Getzler, Israel, *Martov: A Political Biography of a Russian Social Democrat* (Cambridge: At the University Press, 1967).

Gilison, Jerome, *The Soviet Image of Utopia* (Baltimore: Johns Hopkins University Press, 1975).

Gilly, Adolfo, *Inside the Cuban Revolution* (New York: Monthly Review Press, 1964).

Giovannini, Elio, "Class Struggle, East and West," in Rossana Rossanda, editor, *Power and Opposition in Post Revolutionary Societies,* (London: Ink Links, 1979), pages 133–38.

Goldfrank, Walter, "The Soviet Trajectory," in Christopher Chase-Dunn, editor, *Socialist States in the World System* (Beverly Hills, Calif.: Sage Publications, 1982).

González, Edward, *Cuba Under Castro: The Limits of Charisma* (Boston: Houghton Mifflin, 1974).

Gorky, Maxim, *Lenin* (Edinburgh: University Texts, 1967).

Gorostiaga, Xavier, "América Latina Frente a Los Desafíos Globales," paper presented at the Latin American Sociology Conference, Havana, May 1991.

Goure, Leon, and Julian Weinkle, "Cuba's New Dependency," *Problems of Communism,* no. 21, 1972, pages 68–72.

Griffiths, John, and Peter Griffiths, "Cuba: The Second Decade," in Griffiths and Griffiths, editors, *Cuba: The Second Decade,* (London: Writers and Readers, 1979), pages 1–17.

Guevara, Ernesto, *Man and Socialism in Cuba* (Havana: Book Institute, 1967).

———, *Venceremos! The Speeches and Writings of Che Guevara,* edited by John Gerassi (New York: Simon and Schuster, 1968).

———, *Che: Selected Works of Ernesto Guevara,* edited by Rolando Bonachea and Nelson Valdés (Cambridge, Mass.: MIT Press, 1969).

Gunder Frank, Andre, "Revolution in Eastern Europe: Lessons for Democratic Socialist Movements (and Socialists)," in William Tabb, editor, *The Future of Socialism* (New York: Monthly Review Press, 1990), pages 87–105.

Habel, Janette, *Cuba: The Revolution in Peril* (London: Verso, 1991).

Hahn, Jeffrey, "Power to the Soviets?" *Problems of Communism,* January–February 1989, pages 34–46.

———, *Soviet Grassroots* (Princeton: Princeton University Press, 1988).

———, "State Institutions in Transition," in Stephen White, Alex Pravda, and Zvi Gitelman, editors, *Developments in Soviet and Post Soviet Politics* (Durham, N.C.: Duke University Press, 1992).

Halperin, Maurice, *The Rise and Decline of Fidel Castro* (Berkeley: University of California Press, 1972).

Hammond, T., "Leninist Authoritarianism Before the Revolution," in Ernest Simmons, editor, *Continuity and Change in Russian and Soviet Thought* (New York: Russell and Russell, 1967), pages 144–56.

Harding, Neil, *Lenin's Political Thought, Volume 2: Theory and Practice in the Socialist Revolution* (New York: St. Martin's Press, 1981).

———, editor, *The State in Socialist Society* (New York: SUNY Press, 1981).

Harnecker, Marta, *Cuba: Dictatorship or Democracy?* (Westport, Conn.: Lawrence Hill, 1980).

——, *Cuba: Los Protagonistas de un Nuevo Poder* (Havana: Editorial de Ciencias Sociales, 1979).

——, "Lo Que El Pueblo Debe Saber: Humberto Pérez Entrevistado por Marta Harnecker," *Bohemia,* Vol. 71, February 19, 1979, pages 58–81.

Haupt, George, and Jean-Jacques Marte, *Makers of the Russian Revolution* (London: Allen and Unwin, 1974).

Hegedus, Andras, *Socialism and Bureaucracy* (London: Allison and Busby, 1976).

——, Agnes Heller, Maria Markus, and Mihaly Vajda, *The Humanisation of Socialism: Writings of the Budapest School* (London: Allison and Busby, 1976).

Heller, Agnes, "Marxist Ethics and the Future of Eastern Europe: An Interview with Agnes Heller," *Telos,* no. 38, Winter 1978–79, pages 153–74.

Hernández, Rafael, and Haroldo Dilla, "Cultura Política y Participación Popular," *Cuadernos de Nuestra América,* Vol. VII, no. 15, July–December 1990, pages 101–21.

Herrera, Antonio José, and Hernan Rosenkranz, "Political Consciousness in Cuba," in John Griffiths and Peter Griffiths, editors, *Cuba: The Second Decade* (London: Writers and Readers, 1979), pages 36–52.

Hill, John Edward Christopher, *Lenin and the Russian Revolution* (London: Hodder and Stoughton, 1949).

Hill, Ronald, Timothy Dunmore, and Karen Dawisha, "The USSR: The Revolution Reversed," in Leslie Holmes, editor, *The Withering Away of the State?* (Beverly Hills, Calif.: Sage Publications, 1981), pages 77–222.

Hinkelammert, Franz, "La Crisis del Socialismo y el Tercer Mundo," *Revista Pasos,* no. 30, July–August 1991, pages 1–6.

——, *Democracia y Totalitarismo* (San José, Costa Rica: Colección Economía-Teología, 1987).

Hirzowicz, Maria, "Is There a Ruling Class in the USSR?—A Comment," *Soviet Studies,* Vol. XXVIII, no. 2, April 1976, pages 262–73.

Hobsbawm, Eric J., "Marx, Engels and Politics," in Hobsbawm, editor, *The History of Marxism, Vol. I: Marxism in Marx's Day* (Bloomington: Indiana University Press, 1982), pages 227–64.

——, "Marx, Engels, and Pre-Marxian Socialism," in Hobsbawm, editor, *The History of Marxism, Vol. I: Marxism in Marx's Day* (Bloomington: Indiana University Press, 1982), pages 1–28.

Hodges, Donald, *The Bureaucratization of Socialism* (Amherst: University of Massachusetts Press, 1981).

Horowitz, Irving Louis, "Authenticity and Autonomy in the Cuban Experience," *Cuban Studies/Estudios Cubanos,* Vol. 6, no. 1, January 1976, pages 67–74.

——, "Cuba Libre? Social Science Writings on Revolutionary Cuba 1959–72," *Studies in Comparative International Development,* no. 10, Fall 1975.

——, "The Military Origins of the Cuban Revolution," *Armed Forces and Society,* August 1975, pages 402–18.

Hough, Jerry, "Political Participation in the Soviet Union," *Soviet Studies,* Vol. XXVIII, no. 1, January 1976, pages 3–20.

——, *Soviet Leadership in Transition* (Washington, D.C.: Brookings Institution, 1980).

Huberman, Leo, and Paul Sweezy, *Cuba: Anatomy of a Revolution* (New York: Monthly Review Press, 1960).

——, *Socialism in Cuba* (New York: Monthly Review Press, 1969).

Hunt, Alan, *Marxism and Democracy* (London: Lawrence and Wishart, 1980).

Hunt, Richard, *The Political Ideas of Marx and Engels, Vol. I: Marxism and Totalitarian Democracy 1818–1850* (Pittsburgh: University of Pittsburgh Press, 1974).

Johnstone, Monty, "Marx and Engels and the Concept of the Party," in Ralph Miliband and John Saville, editors, *The Socialist Register 1967* (New York: Monthly Review Press, 1967), pages 121–58.

———, "Marx, Blanqui and Majority Rule," in Ralph Miliband and John Saville, editors, *The Socialist Register 1983* (London: Merlin Press, 1983).

———, "The Paris Commune and Marx's Conception of the Dictatorship of the Proletariat," *Massachusetts Review,* Vol. 12, 1971, pages 447–62.

———, "Trotsky and the Debate on Socialism in One Country," *New Left Review,* no. 50, July–August 1968, pages 113–24.

Jørgensen, Bard, "The Interrelationship Between Base and Superstructure in Cuba," *Ibero-Americana, Nordic Journal of Latin American Studies,* Vol. 13, no. 1, 1983, pages 27–42.

Joshua, Isy, *Organisation et Rapports de Production Dans Une Économie de Transition* (Paris: Sorbonne, Centre d'Études de Planification Socialiste, 1968).

Kagarlitsky, Boris, *The Dialectic of Change* (London: Verso, 1990).

———, *Farewell Perestroika* (London: Verso, 1990).

———, *The Thinking Reed* (London: Verso, 1988).

Kapcia, Antoni, "Martí, Marxism and Morality: The Evolution of an Ideology of Revolution," in Richard Gillespie, editor, *Cuba After Thirty Years* (London: Frank Cass, 1990), pages 161–83.

Karl, Terry, "Work Incentives in Cuba," *Latin American Perspectives,* Issue 7, Supplement 1975, Vol. II, no. 4, pages 21–41.

Karol, K. S., "Gorbachev and the Dynamics of Change," in Ralph Miliband, Leo Panitch, and John Saville, editors, *The Socialist Register 1988* (London: Merlin Press, 1988), pages 12–36.

———, *Guerillas in Power* (New York: Hill and Wang, 1970).

———, "How to Change Things for Good? What is to be Done? With Whom?" in Rossana Rossanda, editor, *Power and Opposition in Post Revolutionary Societies,* (London: Ink Links, 1979), pages 138–49.

Keane, John, *Democracy and Civil Society* (London: Verso, 1988).

———, editor, *Civil Society and the State* (London: Verso, 1988).

Keep, John, *The Russian Revolution: A Study in Mass Mobilization* (New York: W. W. Norton, 1976).

Klein, L. B., "The Socialist Constitution of Cuba," in Irving Louis Horowitz, editor, *Cuban Communism,* fifth edition, (New Brunswick, N.J.: Transaction Books 1984) pages 452–74.

Kolakowski, Leszek, "Marxist Roots of Stalinism," in Robert Tucker, editor, *Stalinism: Essays in Historical Interpretation* (New York: W. W. Norton, 1977), pages 283–98.

Kollontai, Alexandra, "The Workers' Opposition in Russia," in *Selected Writings of Alexandra Kollontai* (Westport, Conn.: Lawrence Hill, 1977).

Korsch, Karl, *Three Essays on Marxism* (New York: Monthly Review Press, 1972).

Krupskaya, N. K., *Reminiscences of Lenin* (New York: International Publishers, 1975).

Kuron, Jacek, "Not to Lure the Wolves Out of the Woods: An Interview with Jacek Kuron," *Telos,* no. 47, Spring 1981, pages 93–97.

LaClau, Ernesto, *Politics and Ideology in Marxist Theory* (London: Verso Books, 1979).

Landau, Saul, "Socialist Democracy in Cuba: An Interview with Fidel Castro," *Socialist Revolution,* Vol. 1, no. 2, March–April 1970, pages 126–43.

Lane, David, *The End of Inequality: Stratification Under State Socialism* (Baltimore: Penguin Books, 1977).

———, "The Structure of Soviet Socialism: Recent Western Theoretical Approaches," *The Insurgent Sociologist,* Vol. XII, nos. 1–2, Winter–Spring 1984, pages 101–12.

Lenin, V. I., *Collected Works* (Moscow: Progress Publishers, 1966).

———, *Imperialism, The Highest Stage of Capitalism* (New York: International Publishers, 1939).

———, *State and Revolution* (New York: International Publishers, 1971).

LeoGrande, William, "Civil-Military Relations in Cuba," in Irving Louis Horowitz, editor, *Cuban Communism,* fifth edition, (New Brunswick, N.J.: Transaction Books, 1984), pages 655–77.

———, "The Communist Party of Cuba Since the First Congress," manuscript, 1979.

———, "Continuity and Change in the Cuban Political Elite," *Cuban Studies/ Estudios Cubanos,* Vol. 8, no. 2, July 1978, pages 1–32.

———, "Cuba's Maturing Revolution," *Problems of Communism,* no. 27, May–June 1978.

———, "The Development of the Party System in Cuba," *Latin American Monograph Series* (Erie: Northwest Pennsylvania Institute for Latin American Studies, 1978).

———, "Mass Political Participation in Socialist Cuba," in Booth and Seligson, editors, *Political Participation in Latin America, Volume 1: Citizen and State* (New York: Holmes and Meier), pages 114–28.

———, "The Theory and Practice of Socialist Democracy in Cuba: Mechanisms of Elite Accountability," *Studies in Comparative Communism,* Vol. XII, no. 1, Spring 1979, pages 39–62.

———, "Two Decades of Socialism in Cuba," *Latin American Research Review,* Vol. 16, 1981, pages 187–206.

Lewin, Moshe, *The Gorbachev Phenomenon* (Berkeley: University of California Press, 1988).

———, *Lenin's Last Struggle* (London: Pluto Press, 1975).

Lichtheim, George, *Marxism: An Historical and Critical Study* (New York: Praeger, 1961).

Liebman, Marcel, *Leninism Under Lenin* (London: Jonathan Cape, 1975).

———, *The Russian Revolution* (New York: Vintage Books, 1972).

Liss, Sheldon, *Roots of Revolution: Radical Thought in Cuba* (Nebraska: University of Nebraska Press, 1987).

Llina Quintana, editor, *Asamblea Nacional del Poder Popular* (Havana: Editorial Orbe, 1981).

Lockwood, Lee, *Castro's Cuba, Cuba's Fidel* (New York: Vintage Books, 1969).

———, "Has the Cuban Revolution Failed?" *New York Review of Books,* Vol. XV, no. 2, September 24, 1970.

Lowy, Michel, "Mass Organization, Party, and State: Democracy in the Transition to Socialism," in Richard Fagen, Carmen Diana Deere, and José Luis Coraggio, editors, *Transition and Development,* (New York: Monthly Review Press, 1986), pages 264–79.

———, *The Marxism of Che Guevara* (New York: Monthly Review Press, 1973).

Lukács, Georg, *Lenin: A Study on the Unity of His Thought* (Cambridge, Mass.: MIT Press, 1971).

———, "The Twin Crises," *New Left Review,* no. 60, March–April 1970, pages 36–48.

Lutjens, Sheryl, "Democracy and Socialist Cuba," in Sandor Halebsky and John Kirk, editors, *Cuba in Transition: Crisis and Transformation in the 1990s* (Boulder, Colo.: Westview Press, 1992), pages 55–76.

Luxemburg, Rosa, *The Russian Revolution and Leninism or Marxism?* (Ann Arbor: University of Michigan Press, 1961).

MacEwan, Arthur, "Incentives, Equality and Power in Revolutionary Cuba," *Socialist Revolution,* no. 23, 1975.

———, *Revolution and Economic Development in Cuba* (New York: St. Martin's Press, 1981).

Macpherson, C. B., *The Real World of Democracy* (New York: Oxford University Press, 1978).

Magri, Lucio, "L'Etat et la Revolution Aujourd'hui," *Les Temps Modernes,* nos. 266–67, August–September 1968, pages 388–430.

Mandel, Ernst, *Beyond Perestroika: The Future of Gorbachev's USSR* (London: Verso, 1989).

———, "Liebman and Leninism," in Ralph Miliband and John Saville, editors, *The Socialist Register 1975* (London: Merlin Press, 1975), pages 95–113.

———, "On the Nature of the Soviet State," *New Left Review,* no. 108, March–April 1978, pages 23–46.

———, *Revolutionary Marxism Today* (London: New Left Books, 1979).

———, "Why the Soviet Bureaucracy is Not a New Ruling Class," *Monthly Review,* Vol. 31, no. 3, July–August 1979, pages 63–76.

Mankiewicz, Frank, and Kirby Jones, *With Fidel* (New York: Ballantine Books, 1975).

Marcuse, Herbert, *Soviet Marxism* (New York: Columbia University Press, 1958).

Martínez Heredia, Fernando, *Che, el Socialismo y el Communismo* (Havana: Casa de las Américas, 1989).

———, "Cuba: Problemas de la Liberación, la Democracia, el Socialismo," paper presented at the Latin American Sociology Conference, Havana, May 1991.

———, *Desafíos del Socialismo Cubano* (Havana: CEA, 1988).

———, "El Socialismo Cubano: Perspectivas y Desafíos," in *Cuadernos de Nuestra América,* Vol. VII, no. 15, July–December 1990.

Martov, J., *The State and the Social Revolution* (New York: International Review, 1938).

Karl Marx, "Class Struggles in France 1848–1850," in Saul Padover, editor, *Karl Marx on Revolution* (New York: McGraw Hill, 1971), pages 154–242.

———, *Critique of the Gotha Program* (New York: International Publishers, 1970).

———, and Frederick Engels, *Collected Works* (New York: International Publishers, 1976).

———, and Frederick Engels, *The Selected Correspondence of Karl Marx and Frederick Engels 1846–1895,* edited by V. Adoratsky (New York: International Publishers, 1942)

————, and Frederich Engels, *Writings on the Paris Commune,* edited by Hal Draper (New York: Monthly Review Press, 1971)

Matthews, Herbert, *Fidel Castro* (New York: Simon and Schuster, 1969).

Mattick, Paul, *Anti Bolshevik Communism* (London: Merlin Press, 1978).

McClellan, David, *Karl Marx: His Life and Thought* (New York: Harper, 1973).

————, "Marx, Engels and Lenin on Party and State," in Leslie Holmes, editor, *The Withering Away of the State?* (Beverly Hills, Calif.: Sage Publications, 1981), pages 7–32.

————, *Marxism After Marx* (Boston: Houghton Mifflin, 1979).

McLennan, Gregor, *Marxism, Pluralism and Beyond* (Cambridge: Polity Press, 1989).

Medvedev, Roy, *Leninism and Western Socialism* (London: Verso, 1981).

————, *Let History Judge* (New York: Vintage Books, 1973).

————, "New Pages From the Political Biography of Stalin," in Robert Tucker, editor, *Stalinism: Essays in Historical Interpretation* (New York: W. W. Norton, 1977), pages 199–238.

————, *The October Revolution* (New York: Columbia University Press, 1979).

————, *On Socialist Democracy* (New York: W. W. Norton, 1977).

————, *On Soviet Dissent* (New York: Columbia University Press, 1980).

————, "Politics After the Coup," *New Left Review,* no. 189, September–October 1991, pages 91–109.

Medvedev, Zhores, "Soviet Power Today," *New Left Review,* no. 179, January–February 1990, pages 65–80.

Meiksins Wood, Ellen, "Capitalism and Human Emancipation," *New Left Review,* no. 167, January–February 1988, pages 1–20.

————, "Liberal Democracy and Capitalist Hegemony: A Reply to Leo Panitch on the Task of Socialist Political Theory," in Ralph Miliband and John Saville, editors, *The Socialist Register 1981* (New York, Monthly Review Press, 1981), pages 169–84.

Melotti, Umberto, *Marx and the Third World* (Atlantic Highlands, N.J.: Humanities Press, 1977).

————, "Socialism and Bureaucratic Collectivism in Developing Countries," *Telos,* no. 43, Spring 1980, pages 174–81.

Mesa Lago, Carmelo, *Cuba in the 1970's: Pragmatism and Institutionalization,* revised edition (Albuquerque: University of New Mexico Press, 1978).

Mészáros, István, "Marx's 'Social Revolution' and the Division of Labour," *Radical Philosophy,* no. 44, Autumn 1986, pages 14–23.

————, *Marx's Theory of Alienation* (London: Merlin Press, 1970).

————, "Political Power and Dissent in Post Revolutionary Societies," *New Left Review,* no. 108, March–April 1978, pages 3–22.

Meyer, Alfred, *Leninism* (New York: Praeger, 1965).

Miliband, Ralph, "A Commentary on Rudolf Bahro's Alternative," in Miliband, editor, *Class Power and State Power* (London: Verso, 1983), pages 203–214.

————, "Marx and the State," in Ralph Miliband and John Saville, editors, *The Socialist Register 1965* (New York: Monthly Review Press, 1965), pages 278–96.

————, *Marxism and Politics* (Oxford: Oxford University Press, 1977).

————, "The State and Revolution," *Monthly Review,* Vol. 21, no. 11, April 1970, pages 77–90.

———, "What Comes After Communist Regimes?" in Miliband and Leo Panitch, editors, *The Socialist Register 1991,* (London: Merlin Press, 1991), pages 375–89.

Moore, Barrington, *Soviet Politics: The Dilemma of Power* (New York: Harper and Row, 1965).

Mottin, Marie-France, *Cuba Quand Même* (Paris: Éditions du Seuil, 1980).

Mujer y Sociedad en Cifras, 1975–1988 (Havana: Editorial de la Mujer, 1990).

Nikolic, Milos, editor, *Socialism on the Threshold of the Twenty-First Century* (London: Verso, 1985).

Nove, Alec, *An Economic History of the USSR* (New York: Penguin Books, 1976).

———, *The Economics of Feasible Socialism* (London: Allen and Unwin, 1983).

———, "Is There a Ruling Class in the USSR?" *Soviet Studies,* Vol. XXXVII, no. 4, October 1975.

Nuñez Soto, Orlando, "Ideology and Revolutionary Politics in Transitional Societies," in Richard Fagen, Carmen Diana Deere, and José Luis Coraggio, editors, *Transition and Development,* (New York: Monthly Review Press, 1986), pages 231–48.

O'Connor, James, "Cuba: Its Political Economy," in Rolando Bonachea and Nelson Valdés, editors, *Cuba in Revolution,* (Garden City, N.Y.: Doubleday Anchor Books, 1972), pages 52–81.

———, *The Origins of Socialism in Cuba* (New York: Cornell University Press, 1970).

Ollman, Bertell, "Marx's Vision of Communism," *Critique,* no. 8, Summer 1977, pages 4–42.

Oppenheimer, Andres, *Castro's Final Hour* (New York: Simon and Schuster, 1992).

Organos de Poder Popular: Documentos Rectores Para la Experiencia de Matanzas (Havana: Book Institute, 1974).

Panitch, Leo, "Liberal Democracy and Socialist Democracy: The Antinomies of C. B. Macpherson," in Ralph Miliband and John Saville, editors, *The Socialist Register 1981* (London: Merlin Press, 1981), pages 144–68.

———, "The State and the Future of Socialism," *Capital and Class,* no. 11, Summer 1980, pages 121–37.

———, *Working Class Politics in Crisis* (London: Verso, 1986).

———, and Sam Gindin, "Perestroika and the Proletariat," in Ralph Miliband and Leo Panitch, editors, *The Socialist Register 1991,* pages 28–66.

Parry, Geraint, "The Idea of Political Participation," in Parry, editor, *Participation in Politics* (Manchester: Manchester University Press, 1972), pages 3–38.

Pérez, Louis, *Cuba and the United States: Ties of Singular Intimacy* (Athens, Ga.: University of Georgia Press, 1990).

Pérez-Stable, Marifeli, "Charismatic Authority, Party Politics and Popular Mobilizations: Revolution and Socialism in Cuba," *Cuban Studies/Estudios Cubanos,* Vol. 22, 1992.

———, *The Cuban Revolution: Origins, Course, and Legacy* (New York: Oxford University Press, 1993).

———, "Institutionalization and Workers' Response," *Cuban Studies/Estudios Cubanos,* Vol. 6, no. 2, July 1976, pages 31–54.

———, "Whither the Cuban Working Class," *Latin American Perspectives,* Issue 7, Vol. II, no. 4, Spring 1975, pages 60–77.

Pethybridge, Roger, *The Social Prelude to Stalinism* (London: Macmillan, 1974).

Petras, James, "Class and Politics on the Periphery and the Transition to Socialism," *Review of Radical Political Economy,* Vol. 8, no. 2, Summer 1976.

———, "Cuba, Fourteen Years of Revolutionary Government," in Clarence Thurber, editor, *Development Administration in Latin America* (Durham, N.C.: Duke University Press, 1973).

———, "Has the Cuban Revolution Failed?" *Science and Society,* Vol. XXXVI, no. 1, Spring 1972, pages 86–90.

———, and Frank Fitzgerald, "Authoritarianism and Democracy in the Transition to Socialism," *Latin American Perspectives,* Issue 56, Vol. 15, no. 1, Winter 1988, pages 93–111.

———, and Michael Morley, "Cuban Socialism: Rectification and the New Model of Accumulation," in Sandor Halebsky and John Kirk, editors, *Cuba in Transition* (Boulder, Colo.: Westview Press, 1992), pages 15–36.

Pierre-Charles, Gerard, *Genesis de la Revolución Cubana* (Mexico City: Siglo XXI, 1976).

Pierson, Christopher, *Marxist Theory and Democratic Politics* (Cambridge: Polity Press, 1986).

Poder Popular: Reglamento de la Asamblea Nacional y Normas Reglamentarias de las Asambleas Provinciales y Municipales (Havana: Editorial de Ciencias Sociales, 1982).

Polan, A. J., *Lenin and the End of Politics* (Berkeley: University of California Press, 1984).

Post, Ken, and Phil Wright, *Socialism and Underdevelopment* (London: Routledge, 1989).

Poulantzas, Nicos, *State, Power, Socialism* (London: New Left Books, 1978).

Preston, Julia, "The Trial That Shook Cuba," *New York Review of Books,* December 7, 1989, Vol. XXXVI, no. 19, pages 24–31.

Prieto González, Alfredo, and Haroldo Dilla Alfonso, "Para Una Reflexión Sobre la Democracia en Cuba," in *El Caribe Contemporaneo* (Mexico City, 1988), pages 36–52.

Rabkin, Rhoda Pearl, "Cuban Political Structure: Vanguard Party and the Masses," in Sandor Halebsky and John Kirk, editors, *Cuba: Twenty-Five Years of Revolution* (New York: Praeger, 1985), pages 251–69.

———, *Cuban Politics: The Revolutionary Experiment* (New York: Praeger, 1991).

———, "Cuban Socialism: Ideological Responses to the Era of Socialist Crisis," *Cuban Studies/Estudios Cubanos,* Vol 22, 1992.

———, "Implications of the Gorbachev Era for Cuban Socialism," *Studies in Comparative Communism,* Vol. XXIII, no. 1, Spring 1990, pages 23–46.

Radosh, Ronald, editor, *The New Cuba: Paradoxes and Potentials* (New York: William Morrow and Company, 1976).

Raptis, Michel, *Socialism, Democracy and Self Management* (London: Allison and Busby, 1980).

Reckord, Barry, *Does Fidel Eat More Than Your Father?* (New York: Signet Books, 1971).

Reed, John, *Ten Days That Shook The World* (New York: International Publishers, 1967).

Riordan, Jim, editor, *Soviet Youth Culture* (Bloomington: Indiana University Press, 1989).

Ritter, Archibald, "The Authenticity of Participatory Democracy in Cuba," in

Ritter and David Pollock, editors, *Latin American Prospects for the 1980s* (New York: Praeger, 1983), pages 182–213.

———, "The Organs of People's Power and the Communist Party: The Nature of Cuban Democracy," in Sandor Halebsky and John Kirk, editors, *Cuba: Twenty-Five Years of Revolution* (New York: Praeger, 1985), pages 270–90.

Rossanda, Rossana, "Power and Opposition in Post-Revolutionary Societies," in Rossana Rossanda, editor, *Power and Opposition in Post Revolutionary Societies,* (London: Ink Links, 1979), pages 3–20.

Rubel, Maximilian, *Karl Marx: Essai de Biographie Intellectuelle* (Paris: Rivière, 1957).

———, "Marx's Concept of Democracy," *Democracy,* Vol. 3, no. 4, Fall 1983, pages 94–105.

———, "Notes on Marx's Concept of Democracy," *New Politics,* Winter 1962, pages 78–90.

Sanderson, J., "Marx and Engels on the State," *Western Political Quarterly,* Vol. XVI, no. 4, December 1963, pages 946–55.

Santamaría, Haydée, *Haydée Habla del Moncada* (Havana: Book Institute, 1967).

Sartre, Jean-Paul, *Sartre on Cuba* (New York: Ballantine Books, 1961).

———, "Socialism in One Country," *New Left Review,* no. 100, November 1976–January 1977, pages 143–64.

Saul, John, "The Role of Ideology in the Transition to Socialism," in Richard Fagen, Carmen Diana Deere, and José Luis Coraggio, editors, *Transition and Development,* (New York: Monthly Review Press, 1986), pages 212–30.

Sawer, Marian, "The Genesis of *State and Revolution,*" in Ralph Miliband and John Saville, editors, *The Socialist Register 1977* (New York: Monthly Review Press, 1977), pages 209–28.

———, "Theories of the 'New Class' From Bakunin to Kuron and Modzelewski: The Morphology of Permanent Protest," paper presented at APSA, August 26–28, 1976.

Schulkind, Eugene, editor, *The Paris Commune of 1871: The View From the Left* (New York: Grove Press, 1974).

Seers, Dudley, editor, *Cuba: The Economic and Social Revolution* (Chapel Hill: University of North Carolina Press, 1964).

Selden, Mark, "Socialism or 'Post Revolutionary Society'," in Christopher Chase-Dunn, editor, *Socialist States in the World System* (Beverly Hills, Calif.: Sage Publications, 1982).

Serge, Victor, *Year One of the Russian Revolution* (Chicago: Holt, Rhinehart and Winston, 1972).

Silverman, Bertram, "Economic Organization and Social Conscience: Some Dilemmas of Cuban Socialism," in David Barkin and Nita Manitzas, editors, *Cuba: The Logic of the Revolution* (Andover: Warner Modular Publications, 1973), Reprint 262, pages 1–28.

———, editor, *Man and Socialism in Cuba: The Great Debate* (New York: Athenaeum, 1971).

Sirianni, Carmen, "Production and Power in a Classless Society: A Critical Analysis of the Utopian Dimensions of Marxist Theory," *Socialist Review,* no. 59, September–October 1981, pages 33–82.

———, *Workers Control and Socialist Democracy: The Soviet Experience* (London: Verso, 1982).

Slater, David, "Socialism, Democracy and the Territorial Imperative," manuscript, 1985.

——, "State and Territory in Post-Revolutionary Cuba: Some Critical Reflections on the Development of Spatial Policy" (Amsterdam, CEDLA, no date).

Sobre la Constitucón del Poder Popular (Havana: 1978).

Suny, Ronald Grigor, *The Baku Commune 1917–1918* (Princeton: Princeton University Press, 1972).

——, "Incomplete Revolution: National Movements and the Collapse of the Soviet Empire," *New Left Review,* no. 189, September–October 1991, pages 111–25.

Sutherland, Elizabeth, *The Youngest Revolution* (New York: Dial Press, 1969).

Sweezy, Paul, "The Nature of Soviet Society: Parts I and II," *Monthly Review,* Vol. 26, no. 6, November 1974, pages 1–16, and no. 8, January 1975, pages 1–15.

Tesis y Resoluciones: Primer Congreso de Partido Communista de Cuba (Havana: D.O.R., 1976).

Therborn, Goran, *What Does The Ruling Class Do When It Rules?* (London: New Left Books, 1978).

Thomas, Clive, "The Non-Capitalist Path as Theory and Practice of Decolonization and Socialist Transformation," *Latin American Perspectives,* no. 17, Spring 1977, pages 10–28.

——, *The Rise of the Authoritarian State in Peripheral Societies* (New York: Monthly Review Press, 1984).

Timerman, Jacobo, *Cuba: A Journey* (New York: Knopf, 1990).

Timossi, Gerardo, "Cuba: Un Agenda Diferente Para Los Cambios," *Cuadernos de Nuestra América,* Vol. VII, no. 15, July–December 1990.

Trotsky, Leon, *The Revolution Betrayed: What is the Soviet Union and Where is it Going?* (New York: Doubleday, Doran and Co., 1937).

Tucker, Robert, *Philosophy and Myth in Karl Marx* (London: Cambridge University Press, 1961).

——, "Stalinism as Revolution From Above," in Tucker, editor, *Stalinism: Essays in Historical Interpretation* (New York: W. W. Norton, 1977), pages 77–110.

Vajda, Mihaly, *The State and Socialism* (London: Allison and Busby, 1981).

Valdés, Nelson, "Cuban Political Culture: Between Betrayal and Death," in Sandor Halebsky and John Kirk, editors, *Cuba in Transition: Crisis and Transformation in the 1990s* (Boulder, Colo.: Westview Press, 1992), pages 207–28.

——, "The Cuban Revolution: Economic Organization and Bureaucracy," *Latin American Perspectives,* Issue 20, Vol. VI, no. 1, Winter 1979, pages 13–37.

——, "Revolution and Institutionalization in Cuba," *Cuban Studies/Estudios Cubanos,* Vol. 6, nos. 1–2, January and July 1976, pages 1–38.

Valier, Jacques, "Cuba 1968–1971: le Développement des Déformations Bureaucratiques et des Difficultés Économiques," *Critiques et l'Économie Politique,* no. 6, 1972.

Vellinga, M. L., "The Military Dynamics of the Cuban Revolutionary Process," *Comparative Politics,* no. 8, pages 245–71.

Vindicación de Cuba (Havana: Editora Política, 1989).

Walker, Martin, *The Waking Giant: Gorbachev's Russia* (New York: Pantheon, 1986).

White, Gordon, Robin Murray, and Christine White, editors, *Revolutionary Socialist Development in the Third World* (Brighton, Sussex: Wheatsheaf Books, 1983).

White, Stephen, *Gorbachev in Power* (Cambridge: Cambridge University Press, 1990).

——, Alex Pravda, and Zvi Gitelman, editors, *Developments in Soviet and Post Soviet Politics* (Durham, N.C.: Duke University Press, 1992).

Williams, Albert Rhys, *Through the Russian Revolution* (New York: Boni and Liveright, 1921).

Wohlforth, Tom, "The Transition to the Transition," *New Left Review,* no. 130, November–December 1981, pages 67–81.

——, "The Two Souls of Leninism," *Against the Current,* Vol. 1, nos. 4–5, September–October 1986, pages 37–42.

Wolfe, Bertram, *Marxism: One Hundred Years of a Doctrine* (New York: Delta, 1965).

Wolter, Ulf, editor, *Rudolf Bahro: Critical Responses* (White Plains, N.Y.: M. E. Sharpe, 1980).

Yglesias, José, *In the Fist of the Revolution* (New York: Vintage Books, 1969).

Zaslavskaya, Tatyana, *The Second Socialist Revolution* (Bloomington: Indiana University Press, 1990).

Zeitlin, Maurice, "Cuba: Revolution Without a Blueprint," *Transaction,* Vol. 6, no. 6, April 1969, pages 38–42.

——, "Inside Cuba: Workers and Revolution," *Ramparts,* March 1970.

——, *Revolutionary Politics and the Cuban Working Class* (Princeton: Princeton University Press, 1967).

Zimbalist, Andrew, "Cuban Economic Planning: Organization and Performance," in Sandor Halebsky and John Kirk, editors, *Cuba: Twenty-Five Years of Revolution* (New York: Praeger, 1985).

——, "Cuban Industrial Growth, 1965–84," *World Development,* Vol. 15, no. 1, January 1987, pages 83–94.

——, "Teetering on the Brink: Cuba's Post-CMEA Economic and Political Crisis," *Journal of Latin American Studies.*

——, editor, *Cuban Political Economy: Controversies in Cubanology* (Boulder, Colo.: Westview Press, 1988).

——, and Claes Brundenius, *The Cuban Economy: Measurement and Analysis of Socialist Performance* (Baltimore: Johns Hopkins University Press, 1989).

——, and Susan Eckstein, "Patterns of Cuban Development: The First Twenty-Five Years," *World Development,* Vol. 15, no. 1, January 1987, pages 5–22.

Index